INDONESIA &I

Soegih Arto

TIMES BOOKS INTERNATIONAL
Singapore • Kuala Lumpur

This book is published by
Times Books International,
an imprint of Times Editions Pte Ltd
Times Centre
1 New Industrial Road
Singapore 1953

Times Subang
Lot 46, Subang Hi-Tech Industrial Park
Batu Tiga
40000 Shah Alam
Selangor Darul Ehsan
Malaysia

Printed by Press Ace Pte Ltd, Singapore

ISBN 981 204 507 4

Contents

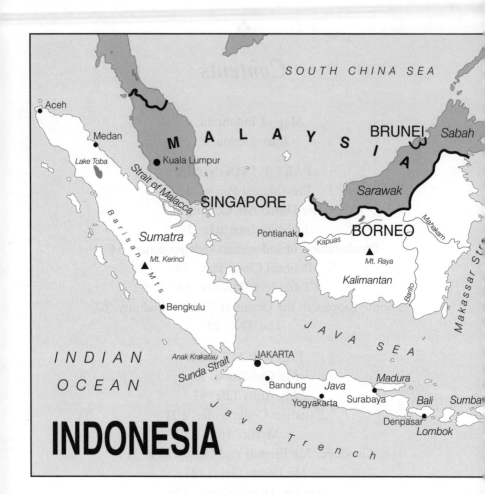

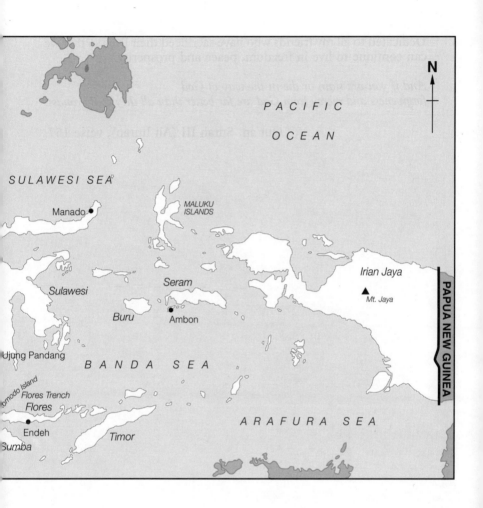

N

PACIFIC

OCEAN

SULAWESI SEA

Manado

MALUKU
ISLANDS

Seram

Irian Jaya

Sulawesi

Mt. Jaya

Buru

Ambon

Ujung Pandang

BANDA SEA

PAPUA NEW GUINEA

Komodo Island

Flores Trench

Flores

ARAFURA SEA

Endeh

Sumba

Timor

Dedicated to all my friends who have sacrificed their lives so that we can continue to live in freedom, peace and prosperity.

And if you are slain or die in the way of God
forgiveness and mercy from God are far better than all they could amass.

Qur'an, Surah III (Ali Imran), verse 157.

Introduction

Oh my Lord! Expand me my breast, ease my task for me, and remove impediments from my speech, so that they may understand what I say.

Qur'an, Surah XX (Ta-Ha), verses 25–28.

Hello, I am Soegih Arto, an Indonesian general. One among so many, and unknown to people outside my small circle. This might sound strange to you. How can a general be unknown? There are lots of reasons for this strange phenomenon. I do want to be famous – a daredevil on the battlefield and a wily, shrewd politician in matters of state. But to be an unknown general is not unusual. Before 1965, President Soeharto was also unknown, but then God destined him to play a major role in the affairs of Indonesia. He had the ability and opportunity, so now he is a famous man.

Richard Pyle wrote the following about 6 foot 3 inches 230 pound General H. N. Schwarzkopf: "Just six months earlier, an obscure military officer, running an equally obscure headquarters on the west coast of Florida, he would have seemed an unlikely candidate for instant world fame. And look what he is now."

Both of them stepped out of obscurity and became famous, because they had the opportunity and the ability. Chance and ability must go together. opportunity alone, without ability, will get you nowhere; the same applies to ability alone. No man has ever become famous without both.

To be honest, I have tried very hard to be popular with the press, with politicians, and with people generally. But it seems I am not built of material interesting enough for the media. In Indonesia we

7

have a saying, that when a dog bites a man, then that is not news, but if a man bites a dog, then that is news. Several times I have bitten dogs, so to say, but nobody cares or pays attention so I am still a nobody, while other people bask in the limelight by doing nothing, not even biting dogs. I envy them. Yes I do. To see my name splashed on the front pages of newspapers and magazines, to see my handsome face on the television screen, would be quite exciting.

But don't think that being unknown is without advantages. It has plenty. I can go to places where no VIP goes, such as the flee market or a roadside foodstall – I can come and go as I please. I am the master of my own time.

But my ego is not happy. This is one of the reasons why I am trying to reach you through this book. I am going to be right in the centre of all those stories, playing the leading role. Paper is patient, it accepts without protest everything you write. But I am an honest man and I assure you that everything written here, good or bad, is the truth and nothing but the truth, so help me ALLAH, Almighty, the Merciful.

But since I am only human, and have a limited memory capacity, I may have forgotten some episodes. I have written this book entirely on my own, without any professional help, and without a ghostwriter. There was nobody I could turn to, there was nobody who wanted to write my biography for reasons I fully understand. Firstly, I am not famous and dashing enough to be HOT, and thus from the commercial point of view not profitable. Nevertheless I want people to know that I have not spent my life idly. I have given a large part of my life to the struggle for independence, and I especially want my children and grandchildren to know about this. They must not get the impression that I have lived selfishly.

I am not a hero, and I am like so many people who tremble with fear at the sound of gunfire. I am not an orator who can inspire with great and mighty words. I am like so many millions who prefer to listen. I am not a brilliant politician who can convince even the strongest opponents, but am one of the voiceless masses. So in conclusion I am an average man with an average IQ, like many others who have wholeheartedly contributed and sacrificed their time, wealth and life for their country, asking nothing in return. We are happy because Indonesia becomes strong and prosperous. To us, the voiceless ones, goes the honour of our victory.

Now you know what motivated me to write this book, although I have no writing experience. The important question I had to ask myself was, will there be any readers? Sometimes I dream that I am a famous writer and my book, which is going to be serious, romantic, witty and humorous, becomes a bestseller. People are fighting to get hold of a copy of my book. It is reprinted again and again and later translated into several languages. I see my book on the shelves of all the famous bookstores and in every household from Alaska to Mozambique, read by both Eskimos and Hottentots.

Alas it was only a dream, but nevertheless nice.

Please help me make this dream come true; buy and read my book. Do not borrow my book from your friends or neighbours, and do not let other people borrow from you.

Thank you for your patience and understanding.

PART I: INDONESIA

Pre-colonial Period

According to history books, Indonesia was once a well-known and powerful country whose trade extended as far as southern India. V. Leur, in his book, *Indonesian Trade and Society*, mentions that in the southern part of India trade was dominated by Indonesia. The Indonesians of that period were very good sailors, and the prowess of Malayan seamanship propagated the Malay family of languages as far as Madagascar to the west and the Philippines to the east. That is what Professor Toynbee, the famous English scholar and historian, says. The name 'Indonesia' was introduced by Adolf Bastian, curator of the Ethnographic Museum in Berlin, in 1884.

Indonesia was situated on the main trade route between China and India, and historically the influence of both these cultures has been considerable. An ancient brass Buddha statue unearthed in southern Sulawesi is proof of the influence of Indian culture. Similar statues were found in Jember in eastern Java, and in Bukit Siguntang in south Sumatra and Kutai in east Kalimantan. Several documents were also discovered written in the Pallava script of southern India. Extensive trade between China and India led to the Malay Archipelago being included in this trade. Melaka, on the west coast of the Malay Peninsula became a trade centre, where Indonesians brought their commodities (cloves and pepper) to be sold to the Indians and Chinese. So Indonesia was situated on the international trade route of ancient times.

Commercial traffic between China and India began as early as the third century A.D. Java became well-known to the Indians. These foreigners paid little attention to the outer islands, especially those in the east. Kutai, in Borneo, was reported only in the sixth century, while the Javanese kingdoms were known from the fifth century. This was because Kalimantan was not on the trade route.

At this time, Indonesia was primarily an agrarian country, except for those people on the coast who were engaged in fishing and trade. Buddhist priests travelled from China to India to study Buddhism and usually stayed en route in Indonesia, gathering information on the people and religion. At that time, the sea route was the safest method of travelling from China to India. This is how Buddhism and Hinduism were first introduced into the Malay Archipelago. Indian influence was exerted through these two religions, of which there is plenty of evidences: the names of kings, temples, and scripts like Pallava and Sanskrit can be found everywhere. Contact with China was mainly commercial rather than cultural.

The powerful kingdom of Srivijaya occupied the western part of Indonesia from the 7th to 14th century, as well as part of the Malay Peninsula and the southern Philippines. Palembang in Sumatra was the centre of this kingdom. Gradually this kingdom disintegrated and ultimately, in 1275, Palembang was overwhelmed by the Singhasari kingdom of eastern Java.

The last of the great Hindu Javanese kingdoms was that of Majapahit, established in 1292 and lasting for about a century. Majapahit managed to rule much of the Malay Archipelago and South-East Asia. If Shrivijaya had concentrated on trade, Majapahit, however, was more of an agrarian state.

The most famous man in Majapahit's history was the prime minister of King Hayam Wuruk (1350–1389), Gajah Mada. The name 'Gajah Mada' is now used by one of the oldest and prestigious universities of Indonesia situated in Yogyakarta. Gajah Mada tried to unite the whole archipelago. His famous vow to unite the archipelago was called the vow of *Palapa*. The name 'Palapa' is now used for our national satellite, which in a sense unites the whole country through communication.

Majapahit conducted an aggressive foreign policy. Treaties were signed, called *mitreka satata*, with Anam, Cambodia, Campa, Sailan, and Ayodyapura (Burma), indicating their mutual friendship and cooperation. Diplomatic relations with China were initiated. Territories not willing to recognise the supremacy of Majapahit were subjugated. Gajah Mada died in 1364 and King Hayam Wuruk in 1389. With them the power and glory vanished. Hayam Wuruk was succeeded by weak monarchs, and ultimately Majapahit was swamped in the early 16th century by Adipat Unus, the Muslim king of Demak.

King Jayabaya of Kediri (1135–1160), or to name him fully, His Majesty King Sang Mapanji Jayabaya Sri Dharmaishwara Madus Sudana Warthanindita, was said to have the ability to predict the future. Jayabaya predicted that small yellow people would come to Indonesia and stay for three and a half years, which is exactly what happened with the Japanese occupation of the 1940s. Jayabaya also predicted that in the year 1877 (Javanese calendar) or 1945 in the international calendar a just king would arrive in Indonesia. That was the year Indonesia proclaimed its independence. Believe it or not, strange but true. During the difficult years of the Japanese occupation this prophecy became a source of strength for all Indonesians, since we knew their time would end. Even during the Dutch colonial period, Indonesian politicians quoted Jayabaya's prophecies in the parliament and warned the Dutch that their time was running out, and that they had better adopt a more realistic policy towards Indonesia.

Jayabaya also ordered the translation of the Indian classics, the *Ramayana* and *Mahabharata*, into Indonesian, but had the tales adjusted to be set in Indonesia rather than India.

Jayabaya was succeeded by another king with an even longer name – Sri Maharaja Rakai Sirikan Sri Sarweswara Janar Dhanawatara Wijayagrajasana Singhanadaniwarwirya Parakrama Digjayottunggadewanama!

The Dutch Are Coming

Spices are a very sought after commodity for both flavouring and preserving food and because of this the Europeans began their adventure to the East in search of spices. First came the Portuguese, followed by the Spaniards. Other Europeans, such as the Dutch, began to take an interest in what were then called the "spice islands," and the first Dutchman to land in the region was Cornelis de Houtman at Bantam in western Java in 1596.

The four ships of Cornelis de Houtman formed the advance guard of the great armadas to come. Their reception by the natives cannot be termed friendly. The Dutch were attacked several times. To the Portuguese, who came earlier, the arrival of the Dutch was felt as both a shock and a threat, because of the competition in trade. For the Indonesians, however, this situation was advantageous. The competition between the Dutch and the Portuguese, as well as between the various Dutch traders, doubled the price of the spices from which the Indonesians profited greatly.

The Dutch became increasingly involved in Indonesian politics. The first contracts between the Indonesians and Dutch were of great political significance, since they laid the basis for the future political development of the whole archipelago. In March 1602 the Vereenigde Oost-Indische Compagnie (VOC), or United East-India Company, was established and received from the Dutch government the monopoly rights for all trade in eastern Asia. Besides this, the charter gave full power to the VOC to act on behalf of the government of the Netherlands.

The VOC had a board of directors consisting of 17 members, called *De heeren seventien*, or the 17 gentlemen. Several years later Pieter Both was appointed by the Dutch as the first governor-general (1609–1614) of the region. The company sent many ships to the East. In the first three years, 38 heavily armed ships arrived in the archipelago. These ships were obviously not meant for commercial use only. The conquest of the Portuguese fortress in Ambon became the Dutch's first territorial possession. Monopoly of trade was included in a treaty the Dutch signed with the natives of Ambon.

In the beginning the presence of Europeans, who mostly concentrated their efforts in commerce, brought little political change to the archipelago. Native kings and princes continued to reign, and enjoyed great profits through trade with the Europeans. The British East India Company, established in 1600, followed the Dutch into the region and tried to gain a major trading foothold.

Profits were considered unsatisfactory and the directors of the VOC issued orders to the governor-general to secure the monopoly of the spice trade by all means, if necessary by force, and to reduce production in order to raise prices in Europe. A young Dutchman by the name of Coen started to play an important role and later was appointed governor-general in 1618.

Jan Pieterszoon Coen introduced a political programme based on two premises. Firstly, that commerce was vital for the welfare of the Netherlands, and secondly, that the Netherlands had a legal right to continue to monopolize the trade. To guarantee the interests of the company he proposed building Dutch settlements and secure possessions of vital areas. A powerful fleet was urgently needed to drive the Spaniards and Portuguese out of their strongholds. He acted with enormous brutality to secure authority for the Dutch. What happened in Banda is a good example of his ruthlessness. This act of cruelty, in which he practically exterminated the Banda people, shocked even the Dutch. A Dutch chronicler of the time wrote: "We should realize that the Bandaneze fought for their freedom, in exactly the same way as we have in Holland." Coen was reprimanded.

Coen was twice appointed as governor-general, first in 1618 at the age of 31, and again in 1627. The Dutch considered him a statesman of great vision. He died in 1629 of cholera.

After some decades the VOC effectively controlled all the important sea lanes, though their territorial possessions were actually very limited. Although they had the power to expand their land territories, they tried in the beginning to avoid quarrels with the local kings and princes.

The VOC was dissolved on the 31st of December 1799 and from then on the whole archipelago came under the jurisdiction of the Dutch government. The Dutch government dissolved the VOC because of widespread corruption and mismanagement, which was causing considerable financial loss. This change of hands did not affect the political and economic situation of the Indonesians.

But the French Revolution brought a fresh wind in Holland and a liberal group who advocated improvement in the conditions of the Indonesians. Holland became part of France under Napoleon, and with the permission of the Emperor, Herman William Daendels became governor-general from 1808 until 1811. According to our history books, Daendels was the man who built the 1,000 kilometre long trans-Java road in one year. Several Dutch scholars doubt this; because of the conditions of the time and the tools available, it would have been impossible to build a road averaging three kilometres per day.

At that time the British and French were at war in Europe and the British, under Lord Minto, captured Java from the French in 1811. As a consequence of the defeat of Napoleon in 1813, Indonesia changed hands and Lord Minto, the governor-general of the British East India Company, appointed Sir Thomas Stamford Raffles as governor of Java, assisted by an advisory council. His main task was to improve the financial condition of the country. The total defeat of the French in 1815 resulted in a treaty being signed between Britain and King William V of Holland, in which it was agreed that Holland would regain its colonial possessions in exchange for the Cape of Good Hope in South Africa and Ceylon.

Following the debilitating Napoleonic Wars, the Dutch government was faced with a very precarious economic situation. To overcome this situation the new governor-general, Van Den Bosch, invented the *Cultuur Stelsel* (Culture System), whereby the people of the archipelago were forced to plant at least 20% of their land with products the government could sell in European markets. In reality the people had to use much more than 20% for the benefit of this *Cultuur Stelsel*. Because of this forced agricultural policy the Netherlands became very wealthy, while the Indonesians became poorer and poorer. The Indonesians practically saved Holland from bankruptcy but gained nothing in return.

Some circles in Holland began to feel guilty and said that Holland had a moral debt that should be repaid. Hence the ethical policy recommended by Nieuwenhuis and Theodor Conradt van Deventer. The Dutch community responded to this appeal. Concrete steps were taken in the fields of local government, education and healthcare, and the Indonesian people gained political representation through the establishment of the Volksraad or parliament, with very limited powers and responsibilities.

Dutch supremacy in Indonesia was accomplished in part because of the assistance of petty local rulers. They quarrelled among each other and usually one party asked the help of the Dutch, with a promise of ample compensation. By playing one ruler against the other, the Dutch gained either territory or an additional lucrative trading contract. The governor-general became more and more powerful, while the power of the local rulers steadily diminished.

Dutch success might give the impression that the Indonesians were passive and did nothing whatsoever to halt Dutch influence. On the contrary, several attempts were made to resist the Dutch. But due to the superiority of the Dutch army's armaments and experience, these attempts ended in dismal failure. Another factor to consider was that resistance was sporadic, localised and uncoordinated.

In 1628 and 1629, Sultan Agung Anyokrokusumo (1591–1645), king of Mataram, tried in vain to expel the Dutch from Batavia. It was a fight of spears and daggers against rifles and canons. He attacked the Dutch from the sea. It failed. In 1629 the Sultan tried again, now with a bigger army, reinforced with cavalry and an army of elephants. They succeeded in occupying Batavia, but not for long, because the Dutch attacked the food storage and set it alight. Sultan Agung had to retreat due to lack of supplies. This resulted in the Dutch becoming masters of Mataram.

Another example of the Javanese spirit of defiance was the Java War of 1825–1830, under the inspired leadership of Prince Diponegoro, son of Sultan Hamengkubuwono III. The response to his call to resist the Dutch was tremendous. Members of the aristocracy, spiritual leaders and peasants joined in the fight. This was a difficult time for the Dutch so they decided to use deceitful tactics. In 1830, they invited the Prince to come to Magelang for peace talks. The Dutch guaranteed the Prince a safe return if the talks failed. Instead he was arrested and exiled to Manado. He died in Ujung Pandang in 1855.

In Kalimantan the name Pangeran Antasari (1809–1862) is well known for his uncompromising stand against the Dutch. Although from a noble family, he was brought up outside the palace. He gained a large following of anti-Dutch fanatics. In April 1859, the Banjar war broke out. This war lasted for more than 14 years.

Sumatra was also the scene of much fighting. The Dutch had to fight Tenku Cik Di Tiro, an Achinese leader. At their first attempt to conquer Aceh in 1873, they met stiff resistance and the Dutch commander was killed in action. Cik Di Tiro conquered several Dutch strongholds. However, the Dutch, through a traitorous subordinate, poisoned Di Tiro to death in 1891.

South of Aceh, in the land of the Bataks, was a leader called Patuan Bosar Ompu Pulo Batu, better known as Si Singamangaraja XII. Using guerrilla tactics, the Bataks inflicted heavy losses on the Dutch. Several times the Dutch tried to win over Si Singamangaraja but always in vain. Even with a bounty of 2,000 guilders on his head no one betrayed the great leader. After 30 years of continuous fighting Si Singamangaraja died.

These are random examples of battles fought against the Dutch in the archipelago. In fact the 17th, 18th and 19th centuries was full of local, uncoordinated and unsuccessful attempts to repel the Dutch.

The Early 20th Century

Unlike the previous centuries, which had been marked by many violent clashes with the Dutch, the early 20th century was relatively calm. The Dutch were masters of the whole archipelago and lawfully recognized as such. The Indonesians, realizing the futility of armed struggle, switched to political opposition. The archipelago was one political unit under the colonial masters, the Dutch. Communications and transportation improved. This enable the Indonesians to communicate with each other from various parts of the archipelago and offered the possibility of them forming a united front.

A major stumbling block for the Indonesian independence movement was that the people of the archipelago did not see themselves as Indonesians but as being Achinese, Sumatran, Javanese, Balinese, Bugis, Ambonese, etc. Notions of Indonesian nationhood had yet to be born. The Dutch tried very hard to maintain feelings of difference in language, culture and background. This Indonesian weakness became their strength. Our people's ethnic loyalties became the Dutch's main weapon for maintaining their hold over the archipelago. *Divide et impera.*

As the people became more educated and increased contacts with the outside world, their horizons became wider. The 20th of May 1908 was later proclaimed by the Indonesian government as the beginning of "national reawakening," taken from the date of the birth of the first Indonesian nationalist organization, Budi Utomo. In the beginning this group's activities were limited to education and politics was not yet on the agenda. Actually, this was the right step to take. The people had to have some sort of education before they could be asked to think about politics. Ideology, isms, and political freedom were things which were far from their minds. The stomach was still more important than the brains. But gradually people realised that to guarantee a full stomach they must use their brains. Seen in this light education became important.

One outstanding man, Ki Hajar Dewantoro, founded the chain of Taman Siswa schools. Dewantoro consistently refused all help from the Dutch in this project, fearing that their help would be accompanied by interference and control.

Another famous politician who made education a priority was Dr. Soetomo, with his 'general study club.' They established schools, engaged in social work among the illiterate masses, and founded cooperatives. According to Dr. Soetomo, non-cooperation should not be made a principle of the freedom struggle, but only a tactic in achieving the objectives. In January 1931 the study club became a political party called Persatuan Bangsa Indonesia, or Indonesian Peoples Union, and membership was restricted strictly to Indonesians. Other organizations followed. In 1911 the Islamic Trade Association was formed by Haji Samanhudi in Surakarta. There was also the Partai Nasional Indonesia (PNI). Other parties or organizations came into existence, some based on religion, some on ethnic origin, but their activities were still very limited.

The first association that began to propagate Marxist ideology was the Indische Social Demokratische Vereniging (ISDV) or Indies Social Democratic Association. The ISDV was established on the 9th of May 1914 in Surabaya. They advertised their cause through their daily broadsheet, called *Het Vrije Woord*, or The Free Word. Six years later, in 1920, the ISDV officially changed their name to the Indonesian Communist Party, and in December 1920 joined the Russian led Communist International (Comintern). In 1926 they incited their first rebellion, a very poor performance. In November 1926, prominent leaders were arrested and that was the end of the show. The Communists called this the "white terror."

The Dutch secret police had eyes and ears everywhere. They attended all meetings and gatherings so the central government got reports regularly and accurately. Even the movements of ants were reported, said the people jokingly. For all political meetings there were strict police regulations, the police had access to all public meetings and were given the power to interrupt speakers and dissolve gatherings, if these meetings developed into a rally for anti-government sentiments. Sometimes political parties were disbanded.

The Volksraad

To show that the Dutch understood that times had changed and that they should modernise institutions in Indonesia and introduce more democracy, they established the Volksraad or Peoples Council, which was officially opened by the governor-general on the 18th of May 1918.

The whole thing was just for show, because this council did not have the power or legislative rights of a normal parliament. The queen of Holland appointed the chairman, who had to be a Dutchman; plus there were 46 other members, of whom only 20 were Indonesians. However, although only a showcase, the Volksraad became an arena of practical political training for Indonesians.

Another milestone in the move toward Indonesian national identity was the *Sumpah Pemuda* or Youth Pledge on the 28th of October 1928. The Youth Congress proclaimed that Indonesia was one nation, had one fatherland, and spoke one language. For the first time *Indonesia Raya*, composed by Wage Rudolf Supratman, was played. This song later became the Indonesian national anthem. The Dutch reacted mildly, saying that *Indonesia Raya* was just a club song and nothing more. Members of the government services were instructed to ignore the whole thing.

Indonesian leaders were far from being a homogenous group. They come from different backgrounds, some were university graduates, even from universities in Holland, France or Switzerland. Some had barely tasted any formal education. Very few came from the nobility.

When you think of Indonesian leaders, then one man stands out: Soekarno, the first president of the Republic of Indonesia, and a man who considered himself a great lover. He loved his country, his people, women, art, and above all, himself. He was born at sunrise on 6th of June 1901, and the Javanese people believe that children born at dawn are predestined to become great leaders. He was born at the dawn of a new day and a new century. He was arrested several times by the Dutch government, but this did not dampen his spirits. He continued fighting the Dutch, not with weapons, but through

Ambonese soldiers of the Dutch-sponsored KNIL, early 20th century.

politics. He was a great orator and a nation builder in *optima forma*. Of course he was not the only one to lead Indonesia to independence; people like Dr. Hatta, H. Agus Salim, Sutan Syahrir, Adam Malik, B. M. Diah and many others are also firmly engraved in the hearts and minds of Indonesians.

After World War I the situation in Holland became worse, especially with the coming of an economic crisis in 1921. The Dutch, to save themselves, became increasingly politically cruel and the Indonesians suffered. Several rebellions occurred, and the Indonesian political parties proclaimed non-cooperation with the Dutch. The number of Indonesian members in the Volksraad was cut, differences of opinion between the governor-general and the Volksraad were referred to the Crown to decide, and the budget was controlled by the Dutch parliament.

The political atmosphere intensified. To overcome this situation Soetardjo, a leading Indonesian member of the Volksraad, tabled a motion where he proposed a meeting between Indonesians and Dutch to talk about changes in Indonesia, so that after 10 years Indonesia would gain self-government. The Dutch flatly rejected this motion, which worsened already critical relations. In 1936, Indonesians demanded the establishment of an Indonesian parliament. This request fell on deaf ears.

Japanese Interlude

Very little was known about the Japanese people during the Dutch period. We knew them through their shops that were everywhere in Indonesia, but we did not suspect that some of them were active military officers spying for the Japanese government. From this it can be concluded that the Japanese had been preparing for the Pacific War for quite some time. We knew of Japanese products, most of them of inferior quality but very competitively priced. After the Depression of 1930 Japan began to flood Indonesia with its goods. The great Japanese victory over the Russians in 1905 opened our eyes, and created doubts about European superiority and Asian inferiority. During the Japanese occupation this was frequently mentioned, mostly, of course, by the Japanese, as proof that Asians, especially the Japanese, were not inferior to the Europeans.

In 1939 World War II began. The Germans swept over Europe in record time and made the term *blitzkrieg* popular. Holland was overrun and the Dutch royal family fled. The majority of Indonesians did not moan or cry, because they felt this had little or nothing to do with them. In Indonesia nothing dramatic happened, the war was not directly felt, except that the Dutch were becoming more nervous. The Koninklijke Nederlands Indise Leger (Royal Netherlands East-Indies Army) or KNIL was strengthened, Dutch civilians were called for military duty, and Indonesians were asked to join in several civil defence activities. In December 1941 and without any formal declaration of war, Japan attacked the Americans at Pearl Harbour, and suddenly the war had come to Asia.

On the 24th of July 1941, Japan sent an ultimatum to French Indo-China requesting permission to use Cam Ranh Bay, Saigon and all French airfields in the region. The French Vichy government gave their consent and from that time on, Japanese war material flooded into Indo-China. The Dutch considered this as a threat to the security of the Dutch East Indies, and they seriously started to increase their fighting power. They ordered from America US$ 200 million worth of war materials. But most of this was not delivered in time to help the Dutch. Allied help was negligible, the Dutch said it was too little and too late. Even Van Mook's visit to America to plead for help was unsuccessful.

The KNIL was never trained to fight a war. Their task was to maintain domestic law and order. They numbered only about 350,000 men with an additional 25,000 militia. Equipment was in a sad state, and not fit to face a superior and well-trained army like the Japanese. But everyone pretended that they were the best equipped army in South-East Asia.

Despite the existence of a united Allied front (ABCD front or American-British-Chinese-Dutch) the Japanese Imperial Army moved south with a speed we thought impossible. The Philippines, Malaya and Singapore soon fell prey to the swiftly advancing Japanese, leaving them knocking on Indonesia's door.

The Japanese 16th Army was transported by the Southern Fleet Command under Vice Admiral Kondo Nobutake. Part of the Allied navy was formed into one striking force under the command of Dutch Rear-Admiral Karel Doorman. On the 26th of February 1942, they left for their first mission, which turned out to be their last. The Japanese never met any serious resistance from the allied fleet, and easily dealt with the task force under Rear-Admiral Doorman, who went down with his flagship. From the very beginning the Japanese had air superiority. The conquest of the Dutch East Indies was a piece of cake.

Opposing the Japanese in western Java were three Dutch Infantry regiments, three Australian battalions supported by two armoured companies, and one cadet company of the Dutch Royal Military Academy and students of the Reserve Officers Corps. The Japanese had three infantry regiments, one cavalry regiment, supported by artillery, engineers, and transportation units. Beside this the Japanese still had a reserve force consisting of a detachment from the 38th Division and two more infantry battalions. It was clear that the

Japanese had superiority in numbers and more importantly they were more experienced and their morale was very high from their recent victories.

Indonesia was subjugated by the Japanese 16th Army under Lieutenant-General Imamura Hitoshi. They landed at Banten and conquered western Java, making Batavia (now called Jakarta) their headquarters. The Japanese met with no significant or serious resistance, and in one short week the war in the whole of the former Dutch colony was over. The other Japanese divisions were spread out over southern Sumatra, western Kalimantan, and eastern Java. Down went the Dutch red, white and blue flag and up went the Rising Sun.

The Indonesians wondered how this was possible. We were told that the KNIL was the best equipped army in South-East Asia. This turned out to be empty propaganda. And worse still the KNIL proved to be an army with no fighting spirit, no guts, and most of all, no motivation. Most Indonesian soldiers in the KNIL asked themselves why and for whom were they fighting and according to unconfirmed stories, these Indonesians had civilian clothes packed in their knapsacks, so that they could easily escape and hide among the population if the situation became difficult.

The Indonesians were confused. Did the Dutch lose a war or just a battle, because the war seemed far from over. Was there the possibility of the Dutch returning, or was Japan our new master? It looked that way, at least for the time being. The Indonesians felt like some thing handed from one owner to another, from a seller to a buyer, or in this case from the loser to the winner.

However, when the Japanese army marched through Bandung, hundreds of people lined the streets and shouted enthusiastically, "Banzaai! Banzaai!" without knowing what it meant. Most of the Indonesians shouted like happy children, only because of the change, and cheered the change rather than the victorious Japanese. The Japanese were greeted as liberators by some and with scepticism by others.

As the war against the Dutch was ending, Tokyo radio played *Indonesia Raya*, the song considered by Indonesians as their national anthem. Japanese planes dropped pamphlets with pictures of Japanese soldiers and Indonesians waving their respective flags together. This was felt as a good sign that the Japanese were going to be different after all, because, they said, they came as our elder brothers to free their younger brothers from European oppression.

This honeymoon period was fake and did not last very long. On the 20th of March 1942, the military government issued a ban on public gatherings and the flying of the red and white Indonesian flag. The friendly mask fell and the real and cruel face of the Japanese was exposed.

The Japanese needed the occupied countries to support their war efforts and in this scenario Indonesia performed a very important function. We had the minerals they needed, we had a vast territory and a big population, which could supply food and the necessary labour force. We had enough oil reserves to keep their war machine functioning.

The Japanese wanted to forge the Indonesians into a cohesive unit capable of contributing to their war effort. The Japanese tried to use religion as a unifying factor and as the majority of Indonesians are Muslims, they created the MASYUMI (Majelis Syuro Muslimin Indonesia), through which they hoped to be able to exploit the Indonesians. The next step was to get recognised Indonesian leaders to work for them, while giving the impression that all this was for the good of Indonesia.

The "quartet," consisting of Soekarno, Dr. Hatta, Ki Hajar Dewantoro, and Kyai Haji Mas Mansur, was formed. Under the leadership of this quartet, an organisation called PUTERA (PUsat TEnaga RAkyat, or Centre of People's Power) was established, in March 1943. 'Putera' can also mean son. Perhaps the Japs hoped that the Indonesians would become their loyal children.

The Indonesians used this as an opportunity to prepare for independence. Soekarno in particular, with his oratory gifts, could reach the masses through open air meetings, and through the radio which was available in the villages. Perhaps the Japs sensed that this step was not sound because the quartet "misused" the facilities offered to them. They decided to create something else to curtail the activities of the quartet, and in January 1944 they created the *Jawa Hokokai*, which freely translated means "an association of dedicated Javanese." Here, Japanese officers were given a bigger role to play.

As the war situation became worse, the Japanese had to offer more than just slogans and the formation of non-political organisations if they wanted to maintain good relations with the Indonesians. In September 1944 P.M. Koiso promised that Indonesia would be given independence sometime in the future. When that would be they did not dare to promise.

However, there were two great gifts from the Japanese that proved to be of strategic importance in our forging an Indonesian nation. Of course the Japanese did not act out of consideration for Indonesia but circumstances forced them to take these steps and the Indonesians made the best out of it.

Gift no. 1: Making the Indonesian language official and banning Dutch and English.

Gift no. 2: Giving military training to some Indonesians.

Let us unpack gift no.1.

Under the Dutch, the Dutch language was the official medium of instruction, from elementary school up to university. All of the educated people spoke Dutch fluently, and if you wanted to climb up the social ladder you had to master Dutch. At high school, English, French and German were compulsory besides Dutch. By making Indonesian the official language, the Japanese returned to us our national tongue. This meant that all school texts had to be translated into Indonesian. We also had to learn Japanese, but not as extensively as we had had to learn Dutch, and it was useful as a means of communicating with our temporary bosses.

Let us now unpack gift no. 2.

Firstly, the Japs created the *Seinendan* or youth units and *Keibodan* or police auxiliary forces. At the end of the war their numbers totalled around one million. Other units like the *Suishintai*, or the pioneer army, was created in November 1944, the *Jibakutai*, or the suicide army, in December 1944, followed by the birth of the student units, the *Gakutotai*. The youngsters enthusiastically participated because military training and uniforms always attracts youth. These youngsters got tough physical and military training and learned the value of discipline and how to endure hardships. One day the Indonesians hoped these youths would fight for Indonesian independence.

An experience which haunted the Indonesian leaders was the creation of *Romusha*, established with their forced consent. This hard-labour force was used by the Japanese for construction and other manual labour. The regulations said that it was a voluntary organisation, but in fact it was the opposite; people in these units were treated cruelly and were sent to Thailand and even as far as Burma. Many died while working for the Japanese. This was a black page in our history.

Another very big advantage in our preparation for independence was the existence of two other organisations in the military field. One was the *Heiho*, an auxiliary force consisting of Indonesians attached to Japanese anti-aircraft and transportation units. This meant that regular Japanese units could be used for front line operations. *Heiho* was never an independent Indonesian organization and there were no Indonesian officers in command. They were integrated in and formed a part of the Japanese army.

Another military organization created by the Japanese was the PETA (Pembela Tanah Air), or home guard. These units consisted of 100% Indonesian soldiers under Indonesian officers, and so were quite different from the *Heiho* men.

The PETA was formed into battalions consisting of four companies of three platoons each, with each platoon having four squads. Officers were given ranks indicating their positions. All in all the PETA had only five ranks, i.e., *gyuhei* (soldiers), *bundanchoo* (NCOs), *syoodanchoo* (platoon commanders), *chudanchoo* (company commanders) and *daidanchoo* (battalion commanders).

The Japs placed a Japanese observer, usually with the rank of captain, to assist the Indonesian battalion commander, acting as an adviser, especially in matters of training. These were purely infantry units, armed with rifles, light machine-guns, and some mortars.

At the end of the war we had around 66 battalions in Java and three in Bali. These battalions were independent and had no relation or coordination with one another. This was one of the reasons why the uprising of the PETA in Blitar, eastern Java, against the Japanese died an infant death, because there was no support from other battalions. However, PETA formed the nucleus of the Indonesian armed forces to be.

Pembala Tanah Air, the Home Guard

It might be interesting to know how these PETA battalions came into being. Why did the Japanese allow the formation of these troops? There were a total of 66 battalions in existence. If we add to this the 40,000 or so *Heihos*, then this was really quite a force. They could pose a military danger to the Japanese occupational forces. It is very difficult to believe that the Japanese loved Indonesia so much that they created these military units for unselfish reasons. They obviously did it because it was to their advantage. Let us look briefly at the war situation at that time.

A chain of island groups nearly 2,000 miles long stretches southward across the Pacific from Japan to the Marianas and Caroline Islands. Many of these islands were fortified and had good military airfields. Behind this shield lay Formosa, the Philippines and China. This shield protected the Japanese supply line going to their more advanced positions in New Guinea and the Pacific.

America, who suffered heavy naval losses in the peace time attack on Pearl Harbour, rebuilt its Pacific fleet in record time. Starting with three carriers in the autumn of 1942, they had 50 a year later and almost 100 at the end of the war.

After careful preparations and long discussions on what course of action to take, General MacArthur and Admiral Nimitz began their two-pronged attack with the intermediate goal being the Philippines. In Indonesia, MacArthur planned to attack Halmahera in the northern Moluccas, but he discovered that the Japanese garrison was about 30,000 strong. He changed his plan and instead landed with his 28,000 men on the neighbouring island of Morotai, which was defended by only 500 Japanese. It was a picnic and no shots were fired. The next target was Talaud, then Minadao and ultimately Leyte. American navy planes from Admiral Halsey's fleet supported the operation and in a relatively short time shot down 173 Japanese planes, destroyed 300 or more planes on the ground, while the Americans themselves lost only 8 planes and 10 men.

A shock for the Imperial forces was the fall of Saipan, only 1,300 miles from Tokyo. General Tojo's government was dismissed because of this defeat. Now the American heavy bombers had a first class base to attack the Japanese mainland.

In the Straits of Melaka, a strong flotilla of submarines from the Allied Eastern Fleet under Admiral Somerville caused considerable damage to Japanese merchant ships. In April 1944 Sabang was attacked and in May, Surabaya. Oil supplies from Indonesia became very precarious and the supply line to Burma was completely severed. In October 1944 a Japanese fleet under Admiral Kurita was seen off the coast of Kalimantan. American submarines attacked and sunk two heavy cruisers, one of which was Kurita's flagship. On the 24th of October 1944, one day after the subs had sank the two cruisers, Admiral Halsey's planes attacked and sunk the giant battleship *Musashi*.

So far the Japanese army in Indonesia was not much involved in the fighting, but they felt that they had to be prepared for the worse. In Indonesia the Japanese had not enough troops, and could not expect reinforcements, while most of the occupation forces were already too old for active duty. It was from their precarious position in Indonesia that the Japanese conceived the idea of an Indonesian home guard. The Japanese wanted to give the impression that the Indonesians were part of the war effort and were responsible for defending their territory. So this idea must appear as if it came from the Indonesians themselves and not something created by the desperate Japanese. General Inada conceived the idea. After getting the official nod, Inada informed the 16th, 25th and 29th armies and the garrison of Kalimantan of his decision and asked them to begin preparations to create an indigenous army. This began in September 1943.

The army selected Gatot Mangkupradja, an Indonesian close to the Japanese, to act as the petitioner. The petition was handed over on the 7th of September 1943. On the 3rd of October 1943, the military government issued the order to create an indigenous army to defend Java, so the Pembala Tanah Air, or PETA, was born. Actually it was not very important whose idea the home guard originally was. The fact was it served both the Japanese and the Indonesians.

During the Dutch time, no Indonesian could get a position of responsibility in the army. We weren't considered good enough. But during the Japanese period, positions that were usually reserved for the Dutch fell into Indonesian hands. This was a change well received by the Indonesians. Although still limited, this gave the Indonesians the necessary experience for holding high offices, and it proved that we were capable. During the Dutch time, we simply were not given the chance to prove our worth.

On the 17th of July, 1945 British Prime Minister Churchill received a coded message, which said "Babies satisfactorily born." This message meant that the atomic bomb experiment in the Mexican desert was a success. After a detailed study of the bomb and its capabilities, everyone realised that this could be a speedy end to World War II. Previously, the Allies had planned a massive assault upon Japan, preceded by heavy air and naval bombing. The Allies contemplated the fiery resistance they would meet, having to fight for literally every yard of territory. The Allies had experienced Japanese fanaticism and their fight-to-the-death spirit when capturing the Japanese islands of Iwo Jima and Okinawa. To bring Japan to its knees the Allies could well lose more than one million lives.

In the months preceding the dropping of the atom bomb, heavy bombing was conducted from the air and the sea. By July the Japanese fleet had virtually ceased to exist. On 26th of July an ultimatum for unconditional surrender was published, but rejected by Japan. On the 6th of August 1945 the bomber *Enola Gay* dropped an atom bomb on Hiroshima, followed by the bombing of Nagasaki by the bomber *Grande Artiste* on the 9th of August. Each atom bomb equalled the power of 20,000 tonnes of TNT. The Japanese surrendered on 14th of August and the formal surrender was signed on 2nd of September 1945 aboard the US battleship *Missouri*.

But what about Indonesia? Were we to celebrate end of the war, or did this mean that the Dutch, members of the Allied forces, would return to reclaim their former colony? Indonesian's fate was hanging in the air. This was as good a time as any for us to decide what our fate would be.

Proclamation of Indonesian Independence

Verily never will God change the condition
of a people until they change it themselves

Qur'an, Surah XIII (Ar-Ra'd), verse 11.

Writing about the anxious moments preceding the Proclamation of Independence is a very difficult task, especially when you want to be factual and avoid trying to explain who were the most responsible people in this great event, and to whom should go the honour. I prefer to say that independence came because the circumstances were ripe for the fruit to be harvested. We all had a share in nursing the tree of independence. The war situation, the deteriorating economic situation, the sympathetic attitude of some high-ranking Japanese officers, and many other factors contributed to making the proclamation possible. All Indonesian people shared in this and deserve the praise.

The desire to become independent was not something new, not something born during the Japanese time, but had existed in the hearts and minds of Indonesians since the Dutch colonial period. Japan encouraged this idea for reasons earlier mentioned. The older politicians accepted Japanese promises with scepticism, but were prepared to wait and see. The Indonesian youth were not as patient as the older politicians. From several sources they gathered information telling them that the Japanese were losing the war. They wanted action, they wanted freedom, *merdeka*, and they wanted it now. To hell with the Japanese military power. The youth was prepared and ready to fight. They wanted to proclaim Indonesian independence – take it with their own hands rather than have it given by the Japanese. From early May 1945, members of the youth organizations held meetings and in June 1945, several prominent youth leaders under the chairmanship of B.M. Diah decided that they wanted freedom there and then.

On 7th of August 1945 General Terauchi's headquarters in Saigon announced that an all-Indonesian committee would be created to make preparations for the transfer of authority from the Japanese to the Indonesians. This committee was called the Panitia Persiapan Kemerdekaan Indonesia (Indonesian Independence Preparatory Committee) or PPKI, and chaired by Soekarno.

On the 8th of August Soekarno, Hatta and Radjiman were called to the Japanese headquarters, and on the 11th they were promised that independence would be granted on 24th of August. But this gift was not welcome by the youth organisations and the underground resistance. They were determined to wrest unconditional independence from the Japs, even if this meant bloodshed. This was considered a better way than receiving a gift from a dying power, better than a gift presented out of selfish considerations. The wording of the draft proclamation prepared by the underground and others, was strongly anti-Japanese. Copies were sent to all parts of Java.

Soekarno, the recognised leader, tried to avoid bloodshed, because the Japanese army was still intact, and certainly the *pemuda* (youth) were no match for these seasoned war veterans. It was a moral dilemma for Bung Karno, because in his heart of hearts he was in full accord with the *pemudas*. But Soekarno was not 100% convinced of the capability of the *pemudas*. This was a difficult time for our leaders. It was not that they lacked courage, because Soekarno had shown lots of courage in confronting the Dutch at a time when the Dutch were still in full control. *Merdeka* was now within reach, and he did not want to jeopardise this through miscalculation. You must keep a cool head and a burning spirit.

But the other groups became impatient and at around 4 a.m. on 14th of August 1945, they "kidnapped" Soekarno and Hatta and brought them to the PETA garrison in Rengasdengklok, on the outskirts of Jakarta. Here an understanding was reached and Indonesian *merdeka* was proclaimed on the 17th of August.

The text of the proclamation was short and simple.

We, the people of Indonesia, hereby declare the independence of Indonesia. Matters concerning the transfer of power and other considerations will be executed in an orderly manner and in the shortest possible time.

On behalf of the Indonesian people,

(signed) SOEKARNO and HATTA.

Indonesia was free at last but not free of problems. The real struggle had just begun, we had just won the first round, and there were still many rounds to follow. The next real test of strength came on the 19th of September, when Indonesians held a mass meeting under the noses of the Japanese. It was important for us to gauge what attitude the Japanese forces would take when confronted with mass demonstrations supporting independence, while strict orders had arrived from the Allied Command to maintain a status quo, pending the arrival of the Allied forces. Secondly, it was vital to find out how enthusiastic the people were in supporting independence, and whether they were willing to fight for freedom. Lastly, it was important to find out how popular Soekarno and Hatta were with the masses.

In spite of the presence of fully armed Japanese soldiers reinforced by tanks, people kept arriving from all over Jakarta. Ikada Square became an ocean of enthusiastic people, young and old. The only thing the Japanese forces could do was watch. At around three o'clock in the afternoon Bung Karno and Bung Hatta, or better still the President and Vice-President, arrived and were welcomed by a spontaneous cry of hail Bung Karno, hail Bung Hatta. Calmly Bung Karno ascended the podium, looked to the left and right as was his custom, waved his hands as a response to the greetings and asked the people to be silent.

The President's speech lasted three minutes, the shortest ever in his life. He asked, "Do you have confidence in the government?"

A thunderous "Yes!" was the answer.

"We will continue to defend our proclamation. Nothing will be withdrawn. I know you came here to see your President and to hear his orders. Well, if you still have faith and confidence in your President, follow his first command. Go home quietly. Leave this gathering now, orderly and peacefully."

We found the answer to all our questions and that was a boost for our spirits.

Bruce Jenkins from Cambridge, Massachusetts wrote: "Power flows not from the barrel of a gun, but from the courageous actions of the people." How true.

The Dutch, 1945 to 1950

However, we still had to fight the Dutch, who stubbornly tried to cling to their old colonial empire. The Dutch had a saying, "Indie verloren, rampsoed geboren," which means, roughly, "When the Indies are lost disaster is born." This is because Indonesia is a very rich territory, rich in spices, rich in minerals, rich in raw materials, and able to provide copious cheap labour. The Dutch were more dependent on Indonesia than other European colonial powers were on their overseas colonies. The Dutch became a rich nation precisely by exploiting this immense wealth.

Times, however, changed. World War II ended with the complete victory of the Allies. All over the world, colonised peoples started to demand their share of a place in the sun, and the Indonesians were no exceptions. The Allies, especially the British and Americans, were faced with a dilemma in their attitude toward Indonesia; on the one hand they recognized that political changes were unavoidable and bound to occur, but on the other hand, the Dutch colonial masters were their allies during the war and hence they felt partially bound to support them. Whatever the position of the Allies, the Indonesians wanted freedom. They were determined to fight the Dutch or any other power that stood in the way of independence.

Political Chess Play

> *To those against whom war is made*
> *permission is given to fight*
> *because they are wronged*
> *and verily God is most powerful*
> *for their aid.*

Qur'an, Surah XXII (Al Hajj), verse 39.

All in all five political games were played:
Game one: In De Hoge Veluwe, Holland. Result: disappointment.
Game two: In Linggardjati, western Java. Result: war.
Game three: On the US ship Renville. Result: another war.
Game four: Jakarta, Roem-Royen. Result: wry smiles.
Game five: The Hague, Holland. Result: victory for Indonesia.

After the Japanese surrender, the Dutch returned to Indonesia. However, President Soekarno, Dr. Hatta and other political leaders were experienced and wily politicians. They knew the Dutch inside out. They knew how treacherous the Dutch could be. But to show the world that Indonesia was a sincere peace-loving nation, they agreed to talk. They thought that there was no harm in talking. The President said that as long as our national goals could be achieved by peaceful means, we must follow this direction and avoid war.

The people, especially the young and the freedom fighters, sensed intuitively that they could not trust the Dutch, and that talks were a waste of time and energy. For them, fight was the right attitude and the right course to take. But as obedient and responsible citizens who had just proclaimed their independence and had elected a lawful government, they had to go along with their leaders.

The Dutch were not interested in a solution involving abandoning their colony. Governor-General De Jong (1931–1936) had said: "We have ruled here for 300 years, using the whip and the club, and we shall still be doing it in another 300 years." The Dutch agreed to talk only because they needed time to build up their armed strength. Once they felt that they were strong enough, they could do what they liked. They thought that they could rely on the support of their World War II allies, especially the British.

De Hoge Veluwe

In February 1946, Van Mook conveyed to Indonesian PM Syahrir his plan to create an Indonesian commonwealth, which would become part of the Kingdom of the Netherlands. This would be, according to Van Mook, only a temporary arrangement. Later, the members of this commonwealth could decide for themselves a more permanent structure, based on voluntary cooperation. Meanwhile, the British had appointed Sir Archibald Clark Kerr, a senior diplomat, to act as chairman of the Dutch-Indonesia negotiations.

Syahrir submitted a counter proposal: firstly, that the Netherlands should officially recognize the Republic of Indonesia, with jurisdiction over the whole area of the former Dutch East Indies. Secondly, Holland and Indonesia should create a federation. These proposals clearly contradicted those of Van Mook.

After intensive talks between Syahrir and Van Mook, the following points were agreed: firstly, that the draft agreement would take the form of an international agreement with a preamble; and secondly, that the Dutch would extend de facto recognition to Sumatra and Java. Van Mook also explained that those proposals came from him without any consultation with his government. Both sides then decided to go to Holland for further talks. The Indonesian delegation consisted of Mr. Soewandi, Mr. Sudarsono and Mr. Pringgodigdo. They arrived in April 1946. The talks were scheduled for the 23rd and 24th of April.

The meeting in De Hoge Veluwe was a complete failure. The Indonesian delegation was treated like a delegation from a colony and not from a free and sovereign country. The Dutch refused to sign any agreement, because this would imply that Indonesia and Holland were on equal terms. The main outcome was that the Indonesians were more then ever convinced that the Dutch were not going to change their colonial policy.

The situation became worse, but on the 2nd of May there seemed to be a silver lining in the dark sky. The new prime minister, Dr. Beel, proposed to recognise Indonesia as part of the United States of Indonesia and accord a de facto recognition to Java and Sumatra as constituting Indonesia, minus the occupied territories. This proved to be a delaying tactic only, because the Dutch were still sending more and more troops to Indonesia.

Meanwhile the domestic political sky darkened, and on the 27th of June extreme groups kidnapped Syahrir. He was released several days later. However, this was not the end of domestic trouble. On the 3rd of July, General Soedarsono staged a coup, but thank God it failed.

Divide et impera continued as Dutch policy. Starting on the 16th of July, Van Mook convened a meeting in Malino, where the formation of other states was discussed. Talks continued, Dutch military operations continued. The Indonesians fought back. Talks and fighting, fighting and talks, became the fashion. To prevent a complete deterioration of the situation, ceasefire talks were held, which ended in failure on the 29th of September. In spite of the failure of ceasefire talks, preparation for political talks continued. The British, who had moved into Indonesia following the Japanese surrender, planned to leave at the end of 1946. But they would not leave until the situation was fully under control.

Linggardjati Talks

New talks began in an atmosphere of suspicion. The involvement of other countries as umpires made the reaching of some sort of agreement possible. On the 7th of October 1946 tripartite talks started and a week later an agreement was reached on a ceasefire. They agreed to continue talks in Linggardjati, a small town in western Java.

Dutch violations of the ceasefire agreement continued and intensified. The Dutch entered the Linggardjati talks with all kinds of cunning plans in their mind. The atmosphere remained tense, and the Dutch did not cooperate in trying to achieve a peaceful situation.

However, an agreement, initiated on the 15th of November, was formally signed on the 25th of March 1947 under rather sad circumstances, because several days before the signing, Dutch troops attacked Mojokerto in eastern Java. This was more or less a repetition of what happened on the 16th of November 1946, one day after the signing of the first Linggardjati agreement, when Dutch troops had attacked Bogor.

Linggardjati was a very difficult meeting and the Dutch were not very keen to reach an agreement. What they wanted was time to reinforce their armed forces so that they could negotiate from a position of strength. They thought that military strength alone would bring the Republic to its knees. They did not pay enough attention to the international political situation and the international sympathy Indonesia had won.

However, something substantial was achieved:
1. The Dutch government would give a de facto recognition to an Indonesia consisting of Java, Madura and Sumatra.
2. Holland and Indonesia would establish a United States of Indonesia no later than the 1st of January 1949.
3. Holland and the United States of Indonesia would form a union under the Crown of Holland.

The signing of the Linggardjati agreement created political problems because both nations were not happy with the results. The interpretation of Linggardjati became a source of conflict between Indonesia and Holland. Two Dutch brigades were already positioned in Sumatra, two divisions totalling five brigades in western Java, one brigade in Semarang, and two in Surabaya. Their total strength was around 100,000 men.

The situation in the Republic developed into a full-fledged crisis because all political parties rejected Syahrir's attempts to compromise and the Syahrir cabinet fell on the 26th of June 1947. On the 13th of June 1947, the Dutch sent a message to the Republic that had to be answered within a fortnight. It looked like an ultimatum. The Dutch knew that the Republic would reject the contents of the note.

The prepared answer made various concessions to the Dutch, but the Indonesians stood firm on one issue, and that was the existence of a common police force having authority over all Indonesia. The issue of a common police force formed the biggest stumbling block, but Indonesia stood firm. This was the excuse the Dutch had been looking for.

With all their troops in position the Dutch felt that the right time to act had come. The Dutch wanted to avoid the impression that they were launching a military campaign, so they called their operation a "police action." But what's in a name? For the Dutch it was important to be in charge of the economically important areas. The whole show started with a speech from Dutch prime minister Dr. Beel, where he stated that the Dutch were not bound by the agreement any more. Dutch troops began their operations on the 21st of July. Valiantly the Indonesian fought back. The Dutch aggression shocked the whole world and became a subject for the United Nations Security Council.

On the 1st of August a ceasefire order was issued by the UN Security Council, and a committee was formed consisting of three countries to mediate between the warring parties and find a peaceful solution to the conflict. Indonesia selected Australia, while the Netherlands preferred Belgium; both countries then elected the United States as the chairman of the committee. These talks took place on board the US ship Renville.

Renville Talks

From the outset the meeting did not go well. The Dutch wanted a complete ceasefire before they were prepared to embark on political talks. Indonesia, on the other hand, wanted to tackle political problems first, because this was considered the basis for the settlement of the whole conflict. The Dutch said peace and order should be the foundation of freedom, while Indonesia wanted freedom first as a basis for peace and order.

From the very beginning the Dutch belittled the importance of the meeting. They wanted to show the world that the Republic did not represent the whole of Indonesia, and was in fact a minority. While the Indonesian delegation was formed at ministerial level the Dutch delegation was headed by a nobody, an Indonesian called Abdulkadir; the rest of the delegation were members of Van Mook's staff. Kleffens, the Netherlands' representative at the United Nations, said: "Before long the world will realise that the Republic is not a government of peace and good intentions. It is supported by cruel and uncivilised criminals and robbers, who succeeded in imposing their will on the Indonesian people only because of Japanese help. The Indonesian government easily gives promises but is never prepared to keep them."

If Linggardjati was a war of interpretations, Renville developed into a war of accusations. Both parties accused the other party of violations. But in the end the Republic retreated and accepted almost all the Dutch proposals, with the hope that with the acceptance of the agreement Indonesia's favourable image as a peace-loving nation would be maintained.

The Renville agreement was signed on the 17th of January 1948. Indonesian army units had to be evacuated to Republican areas in central Java. This was the end of one drama but also the beginning of another tragedy. The Dutch repeatedly accused the Indonesians of violations but continued themselves to take political steps and violate the Renville agreement.

On the 9th of November 1947, the Dutch had created the Committee of Federal Indonesia, with the following programme:

1. Create a provisional government in preparation for the formation of a free and sovereign United States of Indonesia.
2. Take steps about the position of the armed forces.
3. Make changes to the Dutch constitution.

On the 13th of January 1948 this committee became the Interim Council of Federal Indonesia. In March 1948, the Dutch increased the authority of this council and the name became the Interim Government of Federal Indonesia.

The Republic officially protested at these steps taken by the Dutch, but the Dutch answered that Indonesia should recognise the sovereignty of the Dutch on trade. The Republic complied. The Dutch next demanded control of the Republic's foreign relations, to which the latter complied. Following this the Dutch became bolder and demanded the Tentara Nasional Indonesia (TNI), or Indonesian army, be disbanded. General Soedirman, the Indonesian commander in chief, stood firm. He said that if the government agreed to this, the TNI would take the responsibility of continuing the revolution on its own. The Republic stood firm.

Van Mook was very disappointed and wrote: "We are sure that the next talks will end in failure. The United Nations close their eyes to the fact that the Indonesian government has no power and no sense of responsibility."

The Indonesian leaders sensed that another crisis was coming, but they prepared to stand firm or lose everything so far gained.

Roem-Royen Agreement

In early December 1948, the United Nations Security Council received a very pessimistic report from the United Nations Commission on Indonesia (UNCI), stating that all efforts to bring the warring parties together had failed and the situation was rapidly deteriorating. People expected the Dutch to launch another military operation.

According to the Dutch, there was a great political and ideological gap between the Republic and other "states" in the archipelago created by the Dutch. The Dutch were convinced most Indonesians wanted a federation formed under their auspices. On the 18th of December 1948, the Dutch decided that due to all these differences it was impossible to continue talks.

War started and the Dutch were very sure that within two weeks the Republic would cease to exist. They occupied Yogyakarta on the 20th of December 1948, and what happened next with our government is well-known. The Dutch succeeded in conquering certain areas, but failed to subjugate the hearts and minds of the Indonesians.

Although there were no official reactions from foreign governments, all influential newspapers in Britain, France and the United States condemned the Dutch action. Merle Cochran, an American member of the UNCI, reported to the Security Council that he was very disappointed at the attitude of the Dutch government, who had ignored both the UNCI and international opinion. The Dutch had not given enough time to the Republic to consider the Dutch proposals on the Interim Federal Government. Although Dutch representative Royen tried to defend the Dutch actions, most members of the Security Council criticised the Dutch and asked for an end to all hostilities and the release of the imprisoned president, vice-president and others.

Negotiations to begin talks were suggested in March 1949, but Soekarno and the Sultan of Yogyakarta refused to talk until the Security Council's resolution had been carried out first, i.e., the cessation of hostilities, the release of all political detainees and the return of the government to Yogyakarta.

On the other hand, the Dutch wanted to avoid the involvement of the Security Council and considered Indonesia a domestic problem. Soekarno, sensing that he now had the world behind him, stood firm. He demanded to be returned to Yogyakarta first, as a preliminary to a meeting. The Dutch puppet states smelled defeat and realised that the Republic was a power they had underestimated. Slowly they began converting to the Republic's viewpoint.

After some political bargaining both sides agreed to begin negotiations under the auspices of the UNCI. The Dutch appointed

Van Royen, their representative in the United Nations, as chief delegate. His Indonesian counterpart was Mohammed Roem, a political prisoner in Bangka.

The first meeting started on the 4th of April 1949 in Hotel Des Indes under the chairmanship of Merle Cochran. The Indonesians were rather sceptical that talking was the right course of action when Indonesia was in a position of strength. Even the commander in chief, General Soedirman, had his doubts and was not fully convinced. On the 1st of May 1949 he issued an order to the army in which he stated that all units had to maintain their discipline and loyalty. The talks, he said, were the responsibility of the government. "Have confidence that freedom gained on the piles of thousands of our dead patriots cannot be taken away by any human force. Continue fighting. I will continue to lead you and God will protect our fight."

On the 7th of May an accord was reached, which became known as the Roem-Royen Agreement. The following points were agreed by both parties. Firstly, the Dutch would restore the Republic and its leaders to Yogyakarta. Secondly, the Republic would issue a ceasefire order to all fighting units, and thirdly, both parties agreed to have a round table conference to discuss the unconditional transfer.

Not everybody was happy. Dr. Beel, representative of the Dutch crown, tendered his resignation and was replaced by Lovink. For the Dutch warmongers, this agreement was a slap in the face. A Dutch general resigned and another, General Spoor, died under very mysterious circumstances. All efforts to eliminate the Republic and the TNI had ended in complete failure.

But it was not all smiles and laughter in the Republican camp. Suspicion, scepticism and pessimism was overwhelming. Only the figure of the Sultan of Yogyakarta, who became the central point of hope and confidence, prevented emotional eruptions and the disintegration of our movement. His steadfast, uncompromising stand and refusal to meet any Dutch official during the occupation had won the admiration of the people. Thanks to him, everything went as planned.

On the 6th of July 1949, President Soekarno and Vice-President Hatta arrived in Yogyakarta on board an American plane, welcomed by thousands of happy people, who lined the streets from the airport to the palace. They shouted, "Merdeka! Merdeka!" and many cried openly.

Syafruddin Prawiranegara, prime minister of the provisional government, arrived in the capital and handed his mandate back to the President. On the 13th of July, Hatta's cabinet accepted the Roem-Royen Agreement and held its first meeting.

As a follow up to the Roem-Royen Agreement a conference was held in Holland, from the 23rd of August to the 2nd of November 1949. The Indonesian delegation was led by Vice-President Hatta. President Soekarno was elected as the first president of the United States of Indonesia and officially sworn in on the 17th of December 1949, and the Dutch recognised Indonesian independence 10 days later on the 27th of December.

Turbulent Weather

*That He might justify truth, and prove falsehood false
distasteful though it be to those in guilt.*

Qur'an, Surah VIII (Al Anfal), verse 8.

When the war was over and the Dutch recognized our independence,
we thought a period of peace and stability would follow so that we
could start developing our country. Alas this was far from the truth.
Our infant Republic, without money or experience and a poorly
equipped army, was faced with enormous problems. Problems of
gigantic proportions, politically, economically, as well as militarily
and what not. When we proclaimed our independence on the 17th
of August 1945 the biggest asset we had was our never-say-die
spirit. Our slogan was *merdeka atau mati* – freedom or death.

We had fought many battles. Freedom fighters, strangers to
discipline and organization, armed with bamboo spears, machetes,
knives, iron bars, old rifles from World War I and sometimes stones
and catapults, facing an experienced well organized Dutch or British
army. Our superiority lay in our spirit and motivation and the iron
determination to achieve independence.

Even after the war against the Dutch was officially over, the
armed forces continued to play an important role, politically as well
as militarily, a role inherited from the time since the proclamation of
independence. Foreigners found it difficult to understand the
composed and obedient attitude of the Indonesian armed forces, a
powerful organization in a developing country still groping for
national stability and identity. They compared Indonesia with the
situation in Africa and South America, where military coups were

the order of the day. Our army, the TNI, adored and admired by the people, never attempted to seize power and rule the country. It stayed loyal throughout to the government and to the constitution. We do not deny that we played an important role, but that was because we were asked to do so, not because we were power hungry. When ever the people needed us we were ready to respond. We are true servants of the people and we intend to stay that way.

The Indonesian armed forces had to stay close to and maintain close relationships with the government. In a democratic and republican set up, the government represents the people, and the armed forces are born from within the people, work for the people, and are ready to sacrifice everything for the welfare of the people. The armed forces actions are directed towards the protection of the interests of the people, and not of the armed forces. We are and will remain their humble servants. That is why the armed forces has to stay close to the power centre.

The armed forces are the only cohesive and well managed organization dedicated to the welfare of the country, living and thinking along the lines stipulated in the constitution and the state philosophy of *Pancasila*. We are a military organisation, and yet we are also by law recognised as a social force. This privilege has to be used sparingly, and only when it is necessary to uphold democratic values in the context of the role as stabiliser, and when staying aloof will harm the people's interest. Everything the armed forces did was legal according to the constitution.

The Communists

In early 1946 the young Republic encountered the first Communist-inspired revolt. Not a revolt by orthodox Communists, but by another leftist group, the National Communists under Tan Malakka. Tan Malakka Sutan Ibrahim Gelar Datuk was born in Sumatra in 1896. He was a teacher by profession and gained his degree in Holland. After the successful Russian Revolution of 1917 he joined the Communist ranks and became very active and ambitious. He was arrested by the Dutch, but later at his request he was allowed to go to Holland, where he met Dr. Hatta for the first time. At that time the Dutch allowed Indonesians whose presence in Indonesia was politically undesirable, to go to Holland and lead a normal free life, out of harms way. Politicians like Ki Hajar Dewantoro, Cipto Mangunkususumo, Tan Malakka, and Dutchmen like Sneevliet and Douwes Dekker belonged to this category.

Tan Malakka returned to Indonesia during the Japanese occupation, but stayed underground and worked in the gold mines in Banten. One week after independence was proclaimed he emerged and began his political activities. He had a number of political admirers. It seemed that even Bung Karno admired Tan Malakka. Soekarno's political testament illustrates Tan Malakka's ambition. In one of his meetings with Soekarno, Tan Malakka proposed that he should be appointed as the political heir to the President. He pointed out that the situation at that time, around October 1945, was very uncertain, and that the possibility of Soekarno being assassinated was very high. The revolution could not stop just because Soekarno was dead, so an heir should be appointed who would continue to lead the revolution. Tan Malakka volunteered himself for this position.

Soekarno agreed and wrote the testament requested by Tan Malakka, but instead of naming Tan Malakka as the sole heir, Soekarno appointed four people, representing the various political streams at that time. Soekarno named Sutan Syahrir (representing the left of centre), Soekiman (Islamic parties), Wongsonegoro (nationalist parties), and Tan Malakka (leftist groups). Tan Malakka was, of course, disappointed and according to some unconfirmed reports he drafted a new will, where he was named the sole heir. The whereabouts of this now remains a mystery.

With the blessing of the President, Tan Malakka, chairman of the Partai Rakyat Indonesia (PRI), organized the Fighting Front or Persatuan Perjuangan on the 6th of January 1946. Within a very short time he had succeeded in uniting more than 140 organizations into a Fighting Front. Tan Malakka felt very strong and confident. On the 15th of January 1946, he presented Syahrir, the prime minister, with a six point program, which he called "minimum" demands, hoping that they would be rejected.

The six points were:

1. Negotiations on the basis of 100% independence of the Republic.
2. Composition of the government in conformity with the people's wishes.
3. Composition of the armed forces in conformity with the people's wishes.
4. Disarmament of all Japanese forces.
5. Repatriation of European POWs.
6. Confiscate and exploit the enemy's industries.

Contrary to Tan Malakka's expectations, these minimum demands were accepted by Syahrir, which meant he had no reason to topple Syahrir.

Then Tan Malakka demanded immediate implementation of his demands. Syahrir refused and abruptly resigned on the 28th of February 1946. President Soekarno, however, asked Syahrir to form a new cabinet, which he did, and implemented the following programme:

1. Talks with the Dutch, assuming that they recognized Indonesian independence.
2. Prepare the population politically, militarily, economically and socially to defend the Republic.
3. Give democratic shape to the central and provincial government.
4. Improve distribution of goods and clothing.
5. Industry and estates must comply to article 33 of the constitution.

Tan Malakka, who expected to be appointed to form the next cabinet, was disappointed and planned a coup. His plan was thwarted and he was arrested on the 17th of March, together with Yamin and Chaerul Saleh. When, on the 25th of June, the government announced the transfer of the police force from the ministry of domestic affairs to the prime minister's office, Tan Malakka's followers interpreted this as a move to liquidate his forces. General

Soedarsono, a sympathiser, started the ball rolling by setting Tan Malakka free, on the 27th of June 1946.

Syahrir and three others were abducted. This kidnapping was deplored by the President. Later an army patrol discovered and freed Syahrir, who was unharmed. On the 3rd of July Tan Malakka sent generals Soedarsono and Yamin to the palace to demand the resignation of Syahrir. Soedarsono was arrested and Tan Malakka's coup crumbled.

Tan Malakka, Soedarsono, Yamin, Subardjo, Iwa, Sukarni and Adam Malik were arrested, only to be released in the wake of the Madiun coup in 1948. Later some of these people became very important national leaders, and occupied positions in the cabinet.

Another front was opened by the Partai Komunis Indonesia (Communist Party of Indonesia) or PKI, in Madiun, eastern Java, on the 19th of September 1948. They proclaimed the Soviet Republic of Indonesia under Muso, who returned to Indonesia in August 1948 from a self-imposed exile in Russia. This Soviet Republic formed a new government, changed the national flag to a red communist flag and replaced the national anthem, *Indonesia Raya*, with the "International."

The first stage of the coup was a complete success. Captured by the Communists, Radio Madiun broadcasted: "The hour of revolution has come. Madiun has risen. The revolution has begun. Workers and peasants have formed a new government. Arms will not be laid down until all of Indonesia is liberated."

President Soekarno reacted instantly and made his now famous speech to the people, which was very clear and to the point: "Muso and his Communist Party staged a coup, seized power and established a Soviet government. Muso's Communist Party is attempting to seize our beloved Republic. Anyone arresting Muso serves the Republic and anyone joining him is a traitor. I call on you to make a choice – follow Muso and his Communist Party, which will bring bankruptcy to Indonesia, or follow Soekarno and Hatta, who with God's help, will lead our Republic to independence."

It did not take long for the people to rally behind the government. In an effort to crush the revolt the government began arresting

Communists on a massive scale. Communists arrested included Tan Ling Djie, Alimin, Abdul Madjid, Sakirman and Siauw Giok Tjan. Suripno and Aidit eluded capture. Amir and ten other leaders were sentenced to death and executed on the 19th of December 1948. Practically the whole leadership was eliminated, except some minor younger members, among who was Djafar Nawi Aidit, destined to play a prominent role in the Communist organization, and also to meet a tragic death by bullet.

Muso was killed only three months after his return from almost 20 years of exile. The Communist revolt, generated from within, was met and defeated from within, without any foreign intervention. On 20th of September 1948, the Dutch foreign minister, D.U. Stikker, offered the Republic assistance in suppressing the rebellion. Hatta responded immediately and said: "The Madiun revolt is an internal problem and we will use our own methods to suppress it." The Dutch offer was not sincere. In Indonesia we say, this help was treacherous like a snake with two heads. According to General Wolf, Dutch air force chief of staff at that time, and right hand man of General Spoor, they were planning to attack and finish off the Republic while the situation was still chaotic. The Dutch army's strength was at its peak.

So why did this Communist revolt fail?

George McTurnan Kahin wrote: "The western-educated Communist leaders clearly failed to understand the strength and character of Indonesian nationalism and in particular the loyalty of the population."

This was the second rebellion of the PKI, who were established on the 23rd of May 1920. The first one had occurred in 1926, during the Dutch colonial period, and failed. This second rebellion was crushed by the government on the 7th of December 1948.

After the Dutch officially recognized the sovereignty of the Republic, the PKI switched tactics. Firstly, they rewrote the history of the Madiun affair. The official party history stated: "It was said that in Madiun the Communists staged a coup and established a Soviet state. This was a lie. This empty accusation from the government was followed by military actions, so there was nothing else we could do except defend ourselves."

The next step they took was changing their tactics. On this Professor Donald Hindley wrote: "From 1951, then, the Aidit leadership directed much of the party's propaganda and activities to building a favourable image of the PKI as a nationalist anti-colonial party, as a party sympathetic to religion, as a party opposed to the use of violence in the pursuit of political objectives and as a resolute defender of democracy." The first task of the Aidit's leadership was to disprove the accusations that the Madiun rebellion had been an anti-nationalist insurrection. The PKI published an account of Madiun which set the lines for a new patriotic interpretation. It denied that a rival government had been formed at Madiun, that the national flag had been lowered, and the national anthem banned. How shameless were their lies.

After the Communist rebellion was crushed, the tolerant Indonesians made one big political mistake, which was to let the PKI continue to exist. The Republic emerged intact from the Communist rebellion. Following the abortive coup, one communist emerged as the undisputed leader – Tan Malakka.

He planned to avenge his previous defeats. But his actions caught the government's attention and Hatta was in no mood for half-hearted steps. The government's attentions alerted Tan Malakka and he decided to hurry with his plans. The crisis in the Republic deepened with the Dutch plan to eliminate the Republic by starting a new war on the 19th of December 1948. Communist leaders responsible for the Madiun coup were executed that day. Tan Malakka continued to fight and claimed that he was able to lead the revolution. But his efforts failed and he was arrested and later executed on the 16th of April 1949.

Dr. Sukiman was well-known for his strong anti-Communist stand and he was determined to use every opportunity to crush his foe. During his tenure as Prime Minister (April 1951 to February 1952) another anti-Communist raid was conducted in August 1951. This raid happened because of labour unrest and other disturbances. Strikes occurred in spite of the anti-strike military regulation of 13th of February.

In June the cabinet's position was undermined by Minister of Justice Yamin's actions, who released 900 detainees, including former Tan Malakka followers, without consulting the cabinet. Yamin had to resign. On the 1st of August a grenade was thrown at a fair in Bogor, injuring many people. On the 5th of August an armed gang carrying communist symbols attacked a police post in Tanjung Priok. Rumours went round that another Madiun affair was in the offing. On the 16th of August mass arrests were carried out, and the government explained that captured documents showed that a coup d'etat had been planned.

Members of parliament, among whom were Abdullah Aidit, father of D.N. Aidit, were arrested. Many PKI leaders were arrested, but Aidit, Nyoto, Lukman and Alimin, were not on the list. By the end of August the government had arrested more than 2,000 politicians, among whom were Pardede, Sakirman, and Tjugito. President Soekarno, in a speech on the 17th of August, said that the government was determined to destroy all armed bands, whether of left or right, whatever their political hue or colour.

Darul Islam, 1948 to 1962

Darul Islam, Muslim fanatics, wanted to create an Islamic country, called Negara Islam Indonesia, or the Indonesian Islamic State. This state was proclaimed in western Java on the 7th of August 1949. Darul Islam literally means house of Islam, or Islamic family. Theoretically they could easily gain the sympathy of the people, because the majority of the population embraced Islam.

But Darul Islam's rigid concept of an Islamic state was unacceptable to the population, who wanted a *Pancasila* state. *Pancasila* represents the five principles of the Republic: belief in one God; humanity; unity; democracy; and social justice. Another factor which turned the people against the Islamic fundamentalists was their terrorism.

The seeds of Darul Islam were sowed as early as 1945, but for the time being all the leaders agreed to recognise the 1945

Constitution and the state philosophy of *Pancasila*, with the hope that later on, when the Dutch were defeated, they could change the Indonesian Republic into an Islamic state, according to their beliefs. In the beginning, the growth of Darul Islam was rather slow because all Indonesians concentrated on defeating the common enemy, the Dutch.

They became more active after the signing of the Renville agreement, in which it was stipulated that the Indonesian Army had to vacate the pockets of resistance and evacuate to central Java. The whole Siliwangi Division, except my battalion, was evacuated to central Java. This created a kind of power vacuum in western Java which the Darul Islam took the opportunity to exploit.

Their supreme leader was an experienced Muslim scholar, S.M. Kartosuwiryo, who was well-known for his non-cooperative attitude toward the Dutch. He was captured in 1962 and later sentenced to death. This marked the end of Darul Islam in Java.

In southern Sulawesi another branch under Kahar Muzakar continued to fight. In 1961 a preliminary understanding to end the rebellion was reached with the government, but later broke down. In a mopping up operation on the 3rd of February 1965, Kahar Muzakar was surrounded and in an attempt to flee was shot dead. His most trusted military adviser, Dee Gerungan, a Christian (and a graduate from the Dutch Staff College and my senior), was captured on the 19th of July 1965 and later sentenced to death.

Darul Islam's activities lasted for about 15 years.

Republik Maluku Selatan (Republic of South Moluccas)

On 25th of April 1950, a man called Manusama and his cronies proclaimed the so called Republic of the South Moluccas. Manusama said that the Moluccas was one integrated area and capable of looking after itself. He claimed that the Indonesian Republic was a Japanese creation. He also gained the support of the Dutch.

Manusama and Soumokil played a decisive role in the birth of this Republic and tried very hard to gain recognition and arms from

Holland, America and Australia. Many Ambonese believed that they would gain both international recognition followed by a supply of arms.

On the 14th of July 1950 a task force under the command of Colonel Kawilarang landed at Lala, Buru Island. The whole operation ended when Ambon, the capital of the Moluccas, was captured on 11th of November 1950.

The leaders and their rebel units fled to Seram, and during the following 12 years, continued their flight, first to Irian Jaya and eventually to Holland. Manusama managed to escape to Holland and created a government in exile, while Soumokil was arrested in 1962 and sentenced to death in 1966.

Angkatan Perang Ratu Adil (APRA), 1950

This was a short-lived rebellion, led by the notorious Captain Westerling, son of a Dutch father and Turkish mother. In South Sulawesi (formerly called Celebes), he was responsible for the slaughter of 40,000 innocent civilians, an action to which the Dutch kept their eyes conveniently closed.

Westerling was commander of the green berets, a battalion supposedly consisting mostly of Timorese. They were supposed to be elite troops of the KNIL, the Royal Netherlands East Indies Army. His army was, however, composed of non-Timorese soldiers. They succeeded in making a surprise attack on the Siliwangi divisional headquarters and killed some officers. They had very big plans that never came to fruition and the rebellion died an infant death.

The second phase of the rebellion was to capture Jakarta. Here they acted in close coordination with Sultan Hamid. Westerling planned to attack the cabinet meeting and kidnap or kill the ministers. Defence Minister Sultan Hamengku Buwono IX was a special target. However, on the 22nd of February 1950 the whole plan failed and Westerling left Indonesia in a Dutch military plane. The APRA uprising lasted for a few days and was the shortest rebellion ever in the history of modern Indonesia.

The Republic suspected officials of the puppet state, Pasundan, having a hand in this rebellion. On the 25th of January 1950, some high-ranking Pasundan officials were arrested and on the 30th the head of the state of Pasundan, R.A.A. Wiranatakusumah, officially resigned. Parliament passed a vote of no confidence, and proposed that the state transfer it's powers to the United States of Indonesia. The central government appointed Sewaka as it's governor.

This political incident created a snowball effect that engulfed the other puppet states. In the following months others followed in relinquishing their power to the central government. On the 19th of May an agreement was reached between all the states to implement in the shortest possible time the formation of a unitary state based on the proclamation of 17th of August 1945.

Army Rebellions

These uprisings differ from the previous ones, because the perpetrators were active TNI military officers using military units under their command. It is worthwhile to note that the opposing armies came from the same source, had the same military tradition, used the same doctrines, had gone through the same military exercises, and had fought side by side against the Dutch oppressors.

The reason they rebelled was because they felt that politically the central government was leaning more and more towards Communism and economically the regions outside Java were being neglected and not treated fairly, especially since most of the foreign exchange was earned by the regions and not Java.

The rebellions gained some sympathy abroad, especially from the United States, who saw the rebels as fighting Communism in Indonesia. Through the CIA America supported the rebels. A clear report of America's clandestine involvement in foreign countries' internal affairs, including Indonesia, can be read in ex-CIA top official Victor Machetti's book, *The CIA.*

Our intelligence people reported that the United States was supporting the rebels of the Sulawesi Revolutionary Air Force with one B-29 bomber and about 40 mercenaries. An American pilot, Allan Lawrence Pope, was shot down and captured documents proved beyond doubt the involvement of the United States in Indonesian internal affairs. The American government also tried to interfere in Sumatra, with the pretext that they wanted to protect their citizens working in the rubber plantations. The Americans had a Marine battalion ready for action in Singapore. The Christian Science Monitor wrote in November 1977: "A major effort was made in 1958 to organize a revolution in Indonesia against President Soekarno. It was an ignominious failure."

An Indonesian rebel captain confessed that one night before troop landings, America has dropped a substantial amount of weapons, such as M-20 rifles, heavy machine-guns and Browning machine-guns, complete with plenty of ammunition. But the surprise early arrival of government troops prevented the rebels from using the dropped supplies. The supplies fell into the hands of government forces, and were later displayed for the whole population to see. The situation caused acute embarrassment in the American press, but in an editorial in May 1958 the *New York Times* denounced Indonesian allegations about American aid to the rebels, stating that America would not deviate from a correct neutrality. But slowly the truth came out and embarrassment grew into a growing cynicism and doubts about the credibility of the American government.

For some time in 1956 dark clouds had been gathering in the political sky and the central figure was a colonel named Zulkifli Lubis, deputy army chief of staff, and a close relative of the army chief of staff, General Nasution.

As a prologue to the main performance, several incidents occurred in Java itself. In November 1956, troops moved to Jakarta and tried to press the state leadership to change the corrupt government and the incompetent army leadership. Intelligence circles reported that there would be drastic action taken by the red berets during a ceremony at the Staff and Command College in Bandung, where Soekarno and the army chief of staff were among the guests. Thank God, the attempt was foiled and the commander of the elite red berets was arrested.

All these incidents were part of a greater conspiracy. What started as an innocent reunion of ex members of the Banteng Division in November 1956 grew into a full-fledged rebellion in December. This reunion, with the apparent aim of improving the welfare of ex Banteng members, had the blessing of the army leadership and was held in Jakarta.

The first rebellious act was Lieutenant-Colonel Husein's decision to take over the governorship from the legal Javanese governor, Ruslan Mulyoharjo. This happened on the 20th of December 1956, the same day the existence of the Dewan Banteng (Bull Council) was announced. All this happened in western Sumatra.

Trouble upon trouble was faced by the government, problem after problem emerged. But the greatest shock at that time was the announcement of the resignation of Dr. Hatta as vice-president, effective from the 1st of December 1956. He was the champion of the anti-Communist forces and of the outer regions. A man of cool and realistic temperament and indeed strongly anti-Communist. Dr. Hatta resigned because he felt he had ceased to be effective. It was a pity he did this at such a crucial time, but the breach with Bung Karno was irreparable.

In Medan, northern Sumatra, Colonel Simbolon convened a meeting of commanders and staff members on the 4th of December 1956. They wanted a change of state leadership and army command. The officers decided to separate themselves from the central government. This vow was taken with dimmed lights and after a toast the glasses were thrown against the wall. Not a very original idea I would say, and smells like an imitation of a Western horror film. At this meeting, army officers from outside Sumatra, especially from Java, were excluded. On the 22nd of December 1956 they proclaimed the birth of the Dewan Gajah (Elephant Council) and severed relations with the central government. Unlike in central Sumatra, there was no civilian take-over of power because the governor happened to be a Sumatran.

As well as this, a conference of government agencies in southern Sumatra was held on the 18th and 19th of December 1956. The result was a "development charter" and a vote of no confidence against the Javanese Governor Winarno. Winarno submitted his resignation on the 27th of December 1956. Establishing councils became the fashion, so here we witnessed the birth of Dewan Garuda (Eagle Council). Sumatra was becoming like a zoo.

Let us look at what happened in the eastern part of Indonesia. On the 3rd of March 1957, the *Permesta* (meaning universal struggle) charter was announced by the Seventh Territorial Army. It did not attack the central government head-on like Dewan Banteng and Dewan Gajah. The essence of the *Permesta* charter was a demand for fair distribution of foreign earnings and a greater autonomy.

Had this action any connection with what had happened in Sumatra? I would say it had, because in an interview in Jakarta on the 9th of March 1971, Sumual said that he had had informal talks with Simbolon and Husein, during a Sekolah dan Staf Komando (Army Command and Staff School) reunion in Bandung in November 1956. *Permesta* stated specifically that theirs was not a separatist movement and they had no intention of violating the principle of "unity in diversity" and the 1945 proclamation.

But the subsequent steps taken contradicted this. Sumual went in search of weapons and tried to woo foreign countries to recognise their movement. The three leaders – Sumual, Husein and Barlian – signed an anti-Communist declaration on the 8th of September 1957.

Kalimantan decided to follow the example of the other territories and proclaimed the birth of Dewan Lambungmangkurat, but without any clear aims. With the birth of all those councils, the cabinet decided to resign, which they did on the 4th of March 1957. A new cabinet called the working cabinet, under Prime Minister Juanda, was sworn in on the 9th of April 1957.

After the National Conference for Reconciliation failed to reconcile the various parties, the outer regions and their councils became bolder and on the 10th of February 1958 Dewan Banteng issued an ultimatum to the central government calling for it to resign within five days. The government flatly refused. Dewan Banteng announced the formation of the Pemerintah Revolusioner Republic Indonesia (Revolutionary Government of the Republic of

Indonesia) or PRRI on the 15th of February 1958.

On the 17th of February Colonel Somba of northern Sulawesi extended his unconditional support for the action taken by Dewan Banteng and at the same time announced that he was severing relations with the government in Jakarta.

On the 16th of March 1958, Major Boyke Nainggolan from Medan voiced his support for the PRRI by announcing what he called *Operasi Sabang Merauke*, supported by one battalion under Major Henry Siregar. All non-Sumatran officers were arrested. Boyke failed in his attempt and on the 17th of March 1958 left Medan in a hurry after hearing that the central government was going to drop paratroopers to restore law and order. The whole movement collapsed on the 27th of April 1958.

The central government thought enough is enough and secretly prepared to take military action against the rebels. Troops from the largest army divisions and the Jakarta garrison command remained solidly behind the government.

Operasi Tegas (Operation Firm) under the command of Colonel Kaharudin Nasution, *Operasi 17 Agustus* (Operation 17th of August) under the command of Colonel Yani, and *Operasi Insaf* (Operation Conscious) under the command of Colonel Yonosewoyo, were carefully planned against southern and western Sumatra and northern Sulawesi. The rebels were no match for the combined operations of the armed forces and police and had to surrender.

Due to so many setbacks and the mass surrender of rebel forces, the PRRI tried to consolidate and reorganize their political and military apparatus. Another disappointment for the rebels was the decision of the Americans to allow shipment of enormous quantities of military equipment to the legal government in Jakarta. The American government was convinced that the army was as anti-Communist as the rebels and that a prolonged fight would weaken their strength. The Americans had switched allegiance.

The rebels proclaimed the Republik Persatuan Indonesia on the 8th of February 1960 and were soon joined by the Darul Islam rebels in Aceh under Daud Beureueh. Daud Beureueh preferred to use the name of Republik Islam Aceh. Opinion in the *Permesta* camp was divided; Sumual decided to join, while Somba and Hawilarang declined. Hawilarang argued that *Permesta* only wanted a change of government and not a change in the structure of the Republic they had proclaimed on the 17th of August.

On the 4th of April 1961 Somba and his troops surrendered officially in a ceremony witnessed by the military area commander and on the 14th of April Kawilarang officially rejoined the TNI. In August 1961 PRRI troops from Sumatra reported back to General Gatot Subroto. The whole affair officially ended on the 20th of October 1961 when the nominal boss of PRRI, H.N. Sumual, submitted in writing that he surrendered unconditionally.

In 1961 Soekarno issued decree no. 332, welcoming back all dissidents, and the later presidential decree no. 449 included former rebels of the Darul Islam, Republic of South Moluccas, and others. At last we had peace, only to be disturbed again in 1965 by the Communists.

The Communists Try Again

In 1965, on the 30th of September to be exact, the Communists tried for the third time to seize power using the elite palace guards, the Cakrabirawa regiment, as their spearhead. Under the command of Lt-Col. Untung, and with a sympathetic nod from the People's Republic of China, the PKI tried their luck again, and failed again. This became known as the G30 S/PKI, short for Gerakan (operation) on the 30th of September by the PKI.

This was a very different situation from that of 1948. At that time the President and the armed forces formed one strong front against the Communists, which could not be said in 1965. One day after hearing of the rebellion in Madiun, the President reacted and condemned the action. This did not happen in 1965. In fact President Soekarno never condemned the coup.

Why did the President take such a different attitude? That is a very interesting question. Was the President involved in the coup? That again is very interesting.

After their defeat in 1948, the PKI slowly but surely gained in strength and in Asia their numbers grew to a total second only to the Chinese Communist Party. Their influence was felt in every sphere of life, politically, socially and economically. A Jakarta-Peking axis flourished, and confrontation between the OLDEFOS (Old Established Forces) and the NEFOS (New Emerging Forces) intensified. To strengthen the position of the PKI, China proposed the formation of a "fifth force," besides the existing four services of the armed forces in Indonesia. The fifth force would be the armed labourers and peasants. The armed forces rejected this.

When it became clear that in October 1965 the Communists were again attempting a coup, Major General Soeharto, commander of the Army Strategic Reserve, acted quickly, resolutely and with great confidence. Again the Communists failed, but only after causing considerable loss of lives and material. But Allah was on our side. How could it be otherwise, because we were fighting the unbelievers.

In my heart of hearts I believed and I was convinced that this coup was God-sent, to end the role of the Communists in Indonesia, so that Indonesia could start developing both socially and economically, something for so long neglected. Mysterious are the ways of Allah.

In the end we fulfilled to them Our promise, and We saved them and those whom We pleased, but We destroyed those, who transgressed beyond the bounds

Qur'an, Surah XXI, verse 9.

Actually the G 30 S/PKI did not come as a complete surprise, because the non-Communist political parties already sensed that something was going to happen. At the end of 1963 and the beginning of 1964 the political climate steadily intensified, due to the behaviour of the Communist Party, more or less sponsored by the President.

Through separate channels the religious parties, Nahdatul Ulama (Islamic), Partai Kristen Indonesia (Protestant), and the Catholic Party had regular contacts with General Yani, the army chief of staff. Secret inter-party meetings were regularly held. To this group also belonged Mr. Hardi, ex prime minister and leader of a faction of the Partai Nasional Indonesia (Nationalist Party) or PNI.

The burning topic was the coming confrontation between the army and the Communists, which would most likely start in Jakarta, as the political centre of the country. This conclusion was reached after noticing that all previous rebellions that had started outside Jakarta had failed. But the talks did not result in a consensus of what to do and how to do it. So they decided to ask General Yani's advice. Yani proposed to approach General Nasution because he was the most senior armed forces leader, and ask him to act immediately before things got out of hand. Confrontation between the army and the Communists would surely come. It was only a matter of time. Yani told the representatives of the parties to assure Nasution that whatever he decided, the army would back him up 100%, on condition that the President not be harmed or dislodged from his position.

However, General Nasution refused to act, even with the assurance that no harm would come to Soekarno personally and as president. Had he agreed to act, a national tragedy could have been averted.

Fortunately, in 1965 we did not make the same mistake as in 1948, when we had quelled the Communist rebellion in Madiun, afterwards letting the Communists continue their political life. This time we learned from our previous bitter experience. General Soeharto, using the 11th of March mandate from the President, decided to ban the Communist Party, and declared the PKI an illegal organization in Indonesia. So the PKI was legally dead. Now we had to try to kill this party in reality, which of course was more difficult than just declaring them dead on paper. But at least they could not reappear again as a lawful and legal organization. This 11th of March mandate from President Soekarno, popularly known as SUPERSEMAR (SU from surat = letter, PER from perintah = order, SE from sebelas = eleven, and MAR from Maret = March) changed the whole political, social and economic situation.

It so happens that *Semar* was a very famous character in our *wayang* or shadow play. *Semar* was supposed to be a *Dewa* (God) sent to the world in the disguise of a servant to fight evil. *Semar* was endowed with great powers. If *Semar* is powerful, how much more powerful must be *Supersemar!* This is how we viewed it, believe it or not.

Because of SUPERSEMAR Indonesian life became more pragmatic and more realistic. The most urgent problem was the economy, which was in a shambles. Previously, political matters had been our primary concern. Now we switched to economic matters. We felt that when people had enough to eat and had proper housing, Communism would have little chance to gain influence.

The students, through their *Tritura* or three demands, correctly analysed the problem. Their demands were:

1. Dissolve the 100 ministers cabinet.
2. Fight inflation.
3. Ban Communism.

A 25 year development plan was created, divided into five five-year plans or what we called REPELITA (RE from rencana = plan, PE from pembangunan = development, LI from lima = five, and TA from tahun = years).

Some Ripples in the Ocean of Political Stability

The Communist coup of 1965 brought far-reaching changes in Indonesian politics and society, and the country enjoyed a period of stability and prosperity. At last we were able to enjoy the fruits of our independence struggle. In this chapter I would like to mention some of the more minor disturbances since independence.

17th of October Affair

On the 17th of October 1952, disturbances in Jakarta climaxed with the demonstration of some 30,000 people, backed by army officers with tanks and artillery. So why did this demonstration come about?

In 1949, following the recognition of the Republic, the army leadership planned to create a small efficient army led by well trained officers. This idea created suspicions amongst the ex-PETA officers, because they were afraid that they would be dismissed due to lack of education and training, compared to the new up and coming military technocrats. This group further resented the use of a Dutch Military Mission to organise staff training, because many of the Dutch officers in this mission had fought against the Republic in the struggle for independence.

The vocal leader of the field officers was Colonel Bambang Supeno, a close confidant of the President. In fact the president took the side of the field officers. The opposition parties in parliament also supported the cause of the field officers.

This was felt by the technocrats to be an unwarranted and intolerable interference in army matters by the government. There was a growing hostility towards parliament because in the army's eyes parliament had failed completely in its political tasks. The only thing they seemed to be good at was overthrowing cabinets. In the seven years since proclamation (1945–1952), Indonesia had had twelve different cabinets, the majority of which were brought down by Parliament. This was considered as evidence of the incompetence and selfishness of the members, who were putting their own well-being above the interests of the nation.

Lack of funds was also a matter of dissatisfaction, while the army needed new equipment badly. The Indonesian armed forces were allocated only 19% of the national budget, while neighbouring countries at that time spent about 50% of their national budgets on the armed forces.

On the 17th of October about 30,000 people gathered to occupy Parliament for a short period and then proceeded to the palace.

As already explained, the army supported this demonstration with tanks and artillery, but with very clear instructions not to open fire. The demonstration was intended only as a show of force. Demonstrators shouted slogans calling for the parliament to be dissolved.

Representatives of the demonstrators were later received by the President. After explaining their aims, Soekarno asked them whether they wanted him to become a dictator? The answer was NO. The President then said that he could not dissolve Parliament, but he promised that he would hold elections very soon. The President asked the people to disperse peacefully, which they did. After that he received a delegation from the army, lead by General Nasution, who appointed Lieutenant-Colonel Sutoko as spokesman. This meeting was attended by Vice-President Hatta, the Prime Minister, the Minister of Defence, the acting Speaker of Parliament, and General Simatupang.

Sutoko handed the President a document signed by all officers present calling for the dissolution of Parliament. Sutoko pointed out that Parliament was responsible for ministerial instability, giving no time to the government to plan and implement policies. Furthermore, it was not democratic, since the members had not been elected.

The meeting was tense but otherwise friendly. The officers denied that this was a coup attempt, Sutoko emphasized that this was a visit by the children to their beloved father. The officers had no plans to go beyond this petition. They honestly believed that their grievances were correct and just, and there was no other alternative for the government but to agree. However, the President continued to create an anti Nasution atmosphere in the army, using Colonel Bambang Supeno to do the dirty work. But ultimately the President bowed to the real pressure from the army and Bambang Supeno was dismissed.

This was not the end of the 17th October affair. The aftermath took a long time to settle. But one clear outcome of this affair was that the parliament began to seriously consider holding a general election. The composition of the parliament at that time was not considered democratic, because two-thirds of the members had continued from the previous state's federal parliament, and had not been elected.

After the demonstrations the government began to seriously think of holding elections, and on 21st of October 1952, four days after the demonstrations, the government decided to hold elections as soon as possible. On 25th of November 1952 the government submitted to Parliament the draft election law, and on 4th of April 1953 Parliament ratified this draft as the first election law of the Republic.

Senior army officers felt that the existing antagonism within the army should end. A conference attended by about 270 officers was held in Yogyakarta from the 17th to 25th of February 1955. A document produced by this conference was considered to contain the guiding principles of army attitudes. This document, called the "charter of unity" or more popularly known as Piagam Yogyakarta, was ceremoniously signed by the army chief Bambang Sugeng, in the presence of the President and Vice-President and other prominent politicians.

Bambang Sugeng soon realised that he could not cope with the existing problems and handed in his resignation. The officers reminded the government that the appointment of the new army chief should be based on seniority. But the government ignored this consensus and appointed Bambang Utoyo, a junior officer, as the next army chief. This appointment was boycotted by the army and a humiliated government had to resign.

Malari

Another case I would like to mention is the so called *Malari* (an abbreviation from Lima Belas Januari, meaning 15th of January). Indonesians are very clever at creating abbreviations and acronyms, which easily stay in the minds of the common people. One of our political ripples, which almost became a big wave, was the *Malari* incident.

Several months before, in August 1973, various discussions were organised by students and economists to review our strategy for national development, foreign financial aid and the distribution of economic wealth. All kinds of bodies and committees sprang into life, such as The Young Generation of Oppositionists, The Committee Against Luxury, The Committee of National Pride, and the Generation of Debt Payers.

Sporadic and uncoordinated demonstrations took place, at first small, though gradually some of these demonstrations showed signs of growing into anarchy. The climax of this wave of popular feeling happened on the day that the Japanese prime minister, Kakue Tanaka, landed in Jakarta for an official state visit on 14th of January 1974.

The timing was planned in such a way as to appear as a protest against Japanese economic domination. Most cars damaged were Japanese cars. The worst day of rioting was the 15th of January.

After the government had succeeded in controlling the situation and had assessed the damage done in Jakarta on that day, it was discovered that 11 people had been killed, 177 seriously injured, 120 slightly injured, and 775 arrested, plus 807 cars were wrecked, 187 motorcycles destroyed, several buildings damaged, and about 160 kilos of gold stolen from goldsmiths.

These violent demonstrations shocked the international financial world, and many countries started to doubt the wisdom of investing in Indonesia. Coordinated and well planned explanations were organised by the government, and ministers visited foreign countries to assure future investors that the situation was under control and that the government would protect all foreign investments.

The Sawito Affair

The so-called Sawito Affair involved a subversive movement planning to replace the state leadership of Soeharto and hand over the presidency to Dr. Hatta, ex vice-president, and one of the original leaders of the Republic. The leader was a Mr. Sawito, a government official in the ministry of agriculture.

Sawito, assisted by Mr. Singgih and Mr. Soedjono, cleverly organised meetings, which in the beginning were harmless, but later developed into political discussions. Several important persons attended these meetings, because the invitations clearly stated it was a get-together, or dinner, and even once to celebrate the 72nd birthday of Dr. Hatta. Hence important people were unwittingly trapped into attending these meetings – Dr. Hatta, Mr. Hamka, an outstanding Muslim scholar, T.B. Simatupang, ex chief of staff of the armed forces, Cardinal Yustinus Darmoyuwono, a well-known Catholic leader, and Ishak Juwarsa, an army general.

Discussion revolved around topics such as deterioration in the Republic and widespread corruption. The meeting came to the conclusion that Soeharto should step down and Dr. Hatta replace him for the time being. Sawito, who had mystical leanings, said that following meditations, he saw a blue light in the sky moving from the east which entered his body. According to Sawito this was a clear indication that Sawito was destined to be leader of Indonesia.

Several documents were issued by this movement, including *Towards a Just Indonesia, Appeal to Pardon Soekarno,* and *The Road to Safety.* This last documents was created on the 17th of July 1976 and Sawito managed to get signatures from very important persons from all walks of life – Christian leaders, Catholic leaders, prominent

Muslims and last but not least from Dr. Hatta himself. Sawito planned ultimately to proclaim himself as leader of Indonesia.

Sawito was arrested on 14th of September 1976 and sentenced to eight years imprisonment. Following his disappearance from the political arena, the movement died a natural death. Intelligence organizations tried to discover whether there was a connection between Sawito and the Soviets, because around that time a Soviet espionage network had been unearthed, headed by an Indonesian naval officer, Commander J.B. Soesdaryanto. But we could not prove that there was a connection.

The TNI

No story about Indonesia would be complete without mentioning the TNI, for the simple reason that its contribution to the life and shape of the Republic has been decisive. The TNI's role as a military, political and social force is unique. TNI is an abbreviation of Tentara Nasional Indonesia, or Indonesian National Army.

The Indonesian armed forces consist of four services: the army, navy, air force and police, under one commander, the armed forces commander in chief, who is usually an officer from the army. The oldest service is the police, who are a legacy from the Dutch colonial time. When independence was proclaimed, the government deliberately omitted the creation of an army. The government did not want to give the impression that the new Republic was aggressive, hostile and militaristic. But in the opinion of most people, an army is a necessary attribute of a sovereign country and does not necessarily express a hostile attitude.

On the 18th of August 1945 the Japanese army disbanded the PETA and *Heiho*, collected all the weapons, and sent the soldiers home. A golden chance to have a moderately equipped army, right from the very beginning, was missed. The feelings of the people, however, were different. They were more realistic. They wanted an army, they wanted action, they wanted to be able to fight and defend their new country, if and when the time came. They did not understand diplomacy or its uses. Pressure from the people was very strong and becoming stronger every day.

Politically oriented youth leaders like Sukarni, Adam Malik and Chaerul Saleh, handed a draft presidential decree proclaiming the formation of the army. The government rejected this. These disappointed youth leaders formed an action committee and were later joined by other youth organizations. Soon youth organizations sprang up all over the country, like mushrooms in the rainy season. They all supported the action committee. The government had to give in, they had no choice, and so on the 23rd of August a people's security body was created. For the moment this was as far as the government dared to go. They created just a body, not an army.

Our leaders, realising their weakness in terms of armed units, tried to follow a very cautious path, the path of deliberation and diplomacy. They tried to avoid a bloodbath. But the people had other ideas. They thought that the only right path to follow was to fight, so that our enemy would realise that Indonesians were strong and determined to sacrifice everything for their freedom. Fight now and talk later. This was the basic difference in attitude between a cautious government and an impetuous populace caught up in revolutionary fervour.

Fighting units sprang into existence. Everybody wanted to take part in defending their country's freedom. Nobody wanted to remain a spectator. For outsiders the great numbers of fighting units, each and every one independent and not under government control, looked like chaos. For us it was a heartwarming situation, a spontaneous expression of the free spirit of our people.

Fighting units were created by political parties, by ethnic groups, religious organizations or sometimes by individuals who wanted to become famous and to satisfy their own ego. We had the Pesindo, the Hisbullah, and the Sabilillah, all affiliated to political parties. We had the Kris Minahasa, the PIM from the Moluccas, the PI from northern Sumatra, plus many ethnic organizations. Even women formed their own units like LASWI. We still had the Lasykar Rakyat, BPRI, DPPR, Barisan Banteng, Lasykar Tani, Lasykar Buruh, Lasykar Merah, Lasykar Jakarta Raya, Lasykar PRD, GPII, and many more.

Indonesia is a country of great natural beauty, with many breathtaking panoramas, plush green vegetation, and an enormous variety of beautiful fauna – a serene and heavenly atmosphere. Suddenly because of the Proclamation of Independence, these soft-spoken, hospitable and peaceful Indonesians changed overnight into resolute uncompromising fighters. These freedom fighters had never had any military training, knew nothing about tactics or strategy, and were strangers to discipline and organization. No uniforms, every man wore what he liked – colourful shirts, with red and white headbands. And of course a samurai-like sword at their hips, as a token of some sort of authority. Amulets would be hung around their necks, to prevent them from getting killed by bullets. They believed that these amulets made them invulnerable and invisible to their enemies. You may laugh at them, but this was taken very seriously. What they lacked in weapons they compensated for with confidence and high spirits. These teenage freedom fighters would drive around in open trucks shouting, "Merdeka! Merdeka!" meaning freedom, freedom, showing the non-combatants their readiness to fight.

Slowly pressure mounted and ultimately the government realised the urgent need of having an army. On the 6th of October 1945, Soekarno issued a decree creating the Tentara Keamanan Rakyat (TKR), or Peoples Security Army. This became the birth date of the armed forces. The membership of the non-governmental fighting forces grew steadily in numbers and in strength. In some places these armed units were better armed than the official government's army.

Here lies the superiority of the Indonesian leaders, who were able to cope with an unique, difficult, and uncertain situation. Here we had two men, Soekarno and Hatta, the duumvirate, with no strong official army to back them, facing a great number of armed freedom fighters, with little discipline and no clear organization, sometimes demanding things against their policy. And yet they had the courage to say NO. This was a show of real moral courage.

On the 12th of November 1945 the TKR convened it's first grand meeting, attended by most of the army divisional commanders. The agenda was to improve the organization and elect the commander in chief and minister of security, just like any other organization electing it's chairman. What a unique situation for an army. The commander in chief was elected by the rank and file, and not appointed by the government. Where in the world would you find a situation like this? Colonel Soedirman was elected commander in chief of the army. His Highness the Sultan of Yogyakarta, Hamengku Buwono

IX, was elected minister of security. Prime Minister Sutan Syahrir was not very happy, because he felt this to be an infringement on the prerogative rights of a head of government to appoint his own ministers. Syahrir wanted Amir Syarifuddin, a politician with a large following, to become the minister of security. Syahrir needed his political support badly.

Soekarno was in a dilemma. He wanted to satisfy everybody. And so on the 18th of December 1945 he appointed Colonel Soedirman as the commander in chief with the rank of general, confirming the election. But he agreed to drop the Sultan and instead appointed Amir Syarifuddin as minister of security. This department changed its name to the Department of Defence on the 1st of January 1946.

Gradually the government improved the organization of the army and on 25th of January 1946 changed the name of the army from TKR to TRI, or Tentara Republik Indonesia (Indonesian Republican Army). The name indicated clearly their status and responsibility. The government also managed to bring under the army umbrella the various fighting units formed after the declaration of independence. The TRI plus these freedom fighters then became the Tentara Nasional Indonesia (Indonesian National Army), or TNI.

Dual Function of the Army

Foreigners find it hard to understand the wider function of our army, but it is a role that has naturally developed from the very beginning of the independence movement.

Members of the army took care of logistics, transportation, fair distribution of food and clothing, functioned as village heads, took over teaching when there was lack of teachers, etc., etc. In short, members of the army were here, there and everywhere. They were involved in everything. This actually was not surprising, because in the beginning army members came from all walks of life. They were not professional soldiers but ordinary people.

The army was active in every field of national life, ideological, political, economical and socio-cultural. It is difficult to approach the dual function of the army from the viewpoint of Western industrialised nations, where the armed forces play a strictly military role within the life of the country. From the very beginning it must be emphasized that the dual function was not a creation of the armed forces to justify their role, but was a natural historical growth, starting from the early days of our war of independence. It was clearly a product of the Indonesian political culture. Being the product of the Indonesian political culture, this dual function was confirmed by law.

In 1960, the Provisional People's Consultative Assembly stipulated that the armed forces were a functional group and as such bore the same responsibility as other functional groups in trying to achieve national aims. A more explicit explanation can be found in another decision of 1966, where it was clearly stipulated that the socio-political function of the armed forces should be regulated to ensure its permanence. And finally the official lawful recognition of the armed forces as a defence and security force as well as a social force is contained in Decision no. IV of the duly elected People's Consultative Assembly of 1973.

The latest and most emphatic law was passed in 1982.

The government has issued the following guidelines for the conduct of the armed forces in connection with their dual function.

1. The policy conducted by the armed forces, Angkatan Bersenjata Republik Indonesia, or ABRI is based on the Constitution of 1945, and not on the policy of any particular group.

2. In achieving its goal, power based on the possession of arms should not be used.

3. In the execution of political aims, ABRI must use the power of persuasion and methods allowed by the 1945 constitution.

4. The army should participate in the political process mainly through guaranteeing that the legislative assembly remains the sovereign body representing the people.

5. Participation in the executive field is only for the purpose of

77

stabilization and dynamization.

6. In deciding the right political course to take, ABRI should consult members of ABRI, who are considered able to give objective advice.

The implementation of this dual function can be defined as any activity, endeavour, or undertaking, pursued outside the jurisdiction of the Department of Defence and Security. The aim is prescribed in the constitution.

Various Indonesian leaders have had things to say about this law.

The commander in chief of the armed forces, General Soedirman, said: "The TNI was born because of the proclamation of the 17th of August 1945 – they have lived with that proclamation and vow to defend the purity of that proclamation to their last drop of blood."

General T.B. Simatupang, once the armed forces chief of staff, said: "The 1945 army generation cannot be blamed for having a dual identity. In one hand they are military and on the other they consider themselves freedom fighters. This situation is the legacy of the history of the birth of the TNI and its subsequent growth. Who can avoid the influence of history?"

General Nasution, ex minister of defence said: "The position of the TNI is as an apparatus of the people, and not as a part of a military regime that holds power in the country. The TNI is a social force, a people's force beside other civil forces."

Harold Crouch, lecturer in Political Science at the University of Indonesia in Jakarta said: "Indonesian officers have always concerned themselves with political issues and for most of the period actively played important political roles."

The people admit that through the history of the war for independence, the armed forces showed their genuine unselfish concern for the welfare of the people. The people wanted the armed forces to continue in this role and beside that to help develop and modernize the country. Development and modernization need technical know-how and a firm mental attitude that generates a driving force. The armed forces fulfil all these preconditions to be a driving force for development and modernization.

The armed forces have a central, responsible leadership, the courage to make decisions in difficult circumstances, discipline, esprit de corps and a technically well organized communications system. Indonesia will prosper if the people, armed forces, and other national bodies and organisations cooperate with each other.

My family. Left to right: My brother, Soewarso, who died in 1947; my mother; my father, Wriyohardjo; my brother-in-law and de facto father, Donowirsastro; my sister and de facto mother; and lastly myself, Soegih Arto.

PART II: MY LIFE

My Childhood

It is such as obey God and his Apostle
and fear God and do right, that will win
(in the end).

Qur'an, Surah Nur, verse 52.

I was born on the 22nd of December 1923, and to this very day, believe it or not, this day is celebrated by every lady throughout Indonesia, involving all kind of ceremonies, receptions, bazaars and other festive activities. Why? Am I that famous and popular? No. The 22nd of December is Mothers Day in Indonesia, hence the celebration. But I pretend that all the fireworks, bazaars and dinners are for me, in my honour. Is that wrong? Not to me.

As I've mentioned before, my name is Soegih Arto, which literally means "plenty money." This has its history. According to Islamic teachings, seven days after the birth of a baby the parents should kill a goat, symbolically cut the baby's hair and give the new-born infant a name. A *selamatan* (thanksgiving ceremony) follows and many people are invited. According to my parents they spent about five guilders on this feast, but donations from friends and neighbours amounted to almost eight guilders. That was plenty of money in 1923, when one kilo of good rice cost you only five cents. Hence my name, Soegih Arto.

We have a popular tradition in Indonesia called the spirit of *gotong royong* or mutual help. It means that neighbours and friends are always ready to help when you are in trouble or when you are organising something, like the name-giving ceremony I just mentioned, wedding ceremonies, or celebrating the circumcision of

82

a boy. There were no catering services at that time, so the ladies of the community came together and prepared food for all the guests at a celebration, which could sometimes be as many as 100 people. Without apparent instruction, the ladies organised themselves – some did the shopping, some did the cooking, some prepared snacks, some decorated the house, etc., etc. They all did it out of good neighbourly spirit and without payment. Payment would be considered an insult.

Now let me tell you about my circumcision. It happened when I was about 14 years old, after I'd finished elementary school, Dutch style. During the Dutch colonial period children would attend seven years of elementary school. This would be followed by three years of what the Dutch called MULO school (Meer Uitgebreid Lager Onderwijs – More Advanced Elementary Education), then three years of AMS (Algemeen Middelbare School – High School). The next step was university.

Sometimes, Muslim boys are circumcised soon after they are born. But some people consider it better to wait until the child is big enough to take care of themselves.

On the afternoon before the ceremony, I was paraded on horseback through my village, accompanied by a drum-band consisting of members of my boy scouts group, the KBI (Kepanduan Bangsa Indonesia – Indonesian Boy Scouts Movement). I wore make-up and was beautifully dressed.

At about five-thirty the following morning, clad only in a sarong, I was carried to a nearby river, entered the cold water and sat there, half submerged, for about half an hour. When I came out of the water I was shivering, my teeth chattered, and my whole body was numb. This was in Sukabumi, a mountain town, so you can imagine how cold it was at six o'clock in the morning. After my cold river bath I put on a beautiful shirt and sarong, but no underpants.

In procession we all walked back to the house. In the garden a small shelter had been specially built for the occasion, decorated with palm leaves. The ground inside the shelter was covered with sand for soaking up the blood after the circumcision, and a chair was placed in the middle. Traditional Sundanese music was played, which helped create an atmosphere of serenity.

My father sat on the chair and I sat on his lap, The *bengkong* (as the man performing the circumcision is called) kneeled before us, took my vital part in his hand and with one deft movement cut my foreskin with a bamboo knife. The cut gave me quite a jolt. I did feel some pain and when I saw blood dripping on the sand, I realised that I had lost my precious helmet. I almost fainted. The presence of my classmates, especially the girls, prevented me from becoming unconscious. All my classmates wanted to see what was left, and I showed them (with pride) what they wanted to see. Even the girls were curious.

I was carried to another chair, next to a table, where an aluminium washbasin was placed. All the guests passed by, offering words of comfort and encouragement, while dropping coins in the basin. Words of comfort and encouragement I did not hear, but the sound of coins dropping gained my fullest attention. What a nice sound those falling coins made; it sounded like heavenly music and made me forget the pain. I had lost something, but gained many things. I gained many coins, which totalled almost 50 guilders – what a fortune!

Nowadays, these kind of circumcision ceremonies are rare. People take their boys to a clinic, and in matter of minutes everything is finished. The days of romanticism and ceremony belong to the past. Today it is business only.

In those days it was quite common that during these kinds of festivities gambling was organised, that is, card play with Chinese cards. For two or three days, the participants sat cross-legged on a mat. A table was never used for this occasion. The winner of every round was expected to put a certain percentage of his or her winnings into a special box. The money in the box would go to the host.

I come from a family of 12 – eight boys and four girls. Although separated from my other brothers and sisters, I had a very happy childhood. Most of my brothers and sisters were "given away" so to say, and brought up by other families. The ones who remained with my parents died very young. Believe it or not, but that is fact. I was brought up by my older sister and her husband, who had remained childless for more than 12 years. Their first baby was born after 13 years of marriage. So I was adopted and considered their first-born.

My brother-in-law worked with the Land Tax Department. He went round the villages in the area and decided how much tax the landowners had to pay. Sometimes, he took me along and that was quite an experience for me. Riding on horseback, while one man held the reins of the horse and another man held an umbrella over me. I felt like a king.

I attended elementary classes in Jakarta, or Batavia as it was then known. I did not like this school very much, because we had to wear shoes; if we forgot, we were punished. Other elementary schools allowed their pupils to go barefoot. At six o'clock in the morning I had to leave home and go by train to school. A monthly train ticket to Kemayoran cost 50 cents. We were called *treinjongens* and *treinmeisjes,* or train boys and girls. Seconds before we arrived at our destination the boys, including me, used to jump from the train before the train had completely stopped. To do this involved special tactics and training, because it was dangerous. But we wanted to impress the girls and win their hearts. And in order to win their hearts no sacrifice was big enough. When I look back at those days I realize it was a silly thing to do. To endanger your life for girls is sometimes not worth the risk. But boys are boys, and adventure is in their blood.

From early childhood I loved uniforms. For ages I could watch the uniformed policemen doing their duty, directing the traffic, with sabres at their sides. They look so handsome and dashing. I especially loved seeing the KNIL men marching past with their drum band. I decided there and then that when I was grown-up I wanted to enlist in the army, or police, because they wore uniforms. Then one day I went to the hospital, and saw doctors in their white doctor's attire. So I decided instead that I wanted to become a doctor. However, because of financial difficulties I entered the teachers college in order to become a teacher, something I had never previously dreamed of. In the 1930s in Indonesia, despite a population of 60 million, the Dutch masters allowed Indonesia to have only ONE government teachers college for Indonesian trainees, plus one for Eurasians.

Although I entered the teachers college, my desire to become a uniformed official never left my mind. Ultimately I became an army officer, thanks to the independence struggle. My family, as far I knew, were not interested in politics. I had never heard any one of them talking politics, or giving their opinion on the political situation; their opinion of the Dutch was always good. The Dutch were the masters, and hence were always right.

I remembered that the Dutch did not allow us to use the word 'Indonesians,' but referred to us as 'Inlanders' or natives. Like aborigines. The term Indonesian contained political meaning in the context of our struggle for freedom. The name implied a national and political identity for us Inlanders.

But my family were not interested in politics. Inlanders or Indonesians, what did it matter? My family were happy as long we had enough money to provide for all our needs, especially so that the children could gain a good education and hence become loyal government servants. It was not that my family shunned politics, but they wanted to live in peace, and enjoy what ever there was to be enjoyed. Thoughts of independence were farthest from their minds. My family knew of the existence of discrimination, like the caste system in the Hindu religion. The Dutch and other whites occupied the highest caste, followed by the Chinese, and the "brownies" (us Indonesians) belonged to the lowest class.

I remember a swimming pool in Bandung, called Centrum. On the entrance in very big letters was written NO ADMITTANCE FOR DOGS AND INLANDERS. We were on the same level as dogs. This was pure apartheid.

I knew we were treated as second class people and yet I was not angry or upset. All of this I considered normal, and perhaps acknowledged the fact that there was nothing we could do. I myself considered Dutch people superior. My mind and my perception were affected by the situation in Indonesia at that time. To me all Dutch men were handsome and endowed with good brains and all Dutch girls were beautiful. Later I realised how stupid and politically blind I was at that time.

When the Japanese marched into Bandung, after beating the superior Dutch in record time, hundreds of people lined the streets, to watch the small dirty Japanese. I kept asking myself, did these small, dishevelled Japanese really beat the mighty Dutchmen? Unbelievable. But it was true. I stood there on the sidewalk, with hundreds of other Bandungers, shouting, "Banzaai! Banzaai!" without having the faintest idea what it meant.

There was a festive atmosphere in Bandung. Electricity in the town was restored after so many months of blackouts. Some people celebrated the Japanese victory, and hailed them as liberators. But I was rather sceptical. I felt there was nothing to celebrate. There were too many questions unanswered.

Had the Dutch lost the war, or had they just lost the battle? Was there the possibility of them returning as our masters? I felt that we had lost the Dutch, but gained the Japanese in their place. Would the Japanese be better than the Dutch? Opinion differed; already we had pro-Japanese groups, but Dutch sympathisers could not be ignored. But the majority had, as usual, no opinion at all.

Political discussions were the order of the day. Everywhere I found groups, talking and deliberating, discussing the future of Indonesia, most of the time in low voices, and frequently looking to the right and left. I joined these groups, listened attentively, but never said a word. I thought the best attitude was to keep my mouth shut. This way I would not make mistakes, nor need to retract anything, because I had not contributed to the discussion.

I've maintained this attitude my whole life. I prefer to listen than to talk: why else do men have two ears and only one mouth? I nod once in a while. Nobody could make out exactly what was in my mind. By doing this I made many friends and practically no enemies.

All the talk, discussions, and predictions conducted when the Japanese first entered Bandung made me dizzy. I could not digest all of this and so decided that the safest way was to join the ranks of the neutrals, the abstainers.

Que sera sera, what ever will be, will be.

A Happy Reunion At Last

Two weeks after the Japanese entered Bandung my school was closed by the authorities for an indefinite period of time. Nobody knew why, or for how long. We were told to leave our dormitory and go home. We had to leave behind an address where we could be reached.

This was a shock to the students, especially for those who lived outside Java, because they did not know whether it was possible for them to go home, and whether there was transportation available; and to add to our troubles, nobody had any money.

The last night we were together in the dormitory, we sat huddled on the floor, each with our belongings packed in one small bag. We were very quiet, hardly anybody talked. We all had lumps in our throats. Six years together, for better or for worse, in health and in sickness, had made us blood brothers. And the worst thing of all was the uncertainty of whether we would see each other again. Although we were all boys, some of us cried openly and unashamedly, our tears flowing freely.

I prayed to Allah. I knew that if I prayed to Allah and asked his help, he would listen: Oh, God do not let us be separated for long. We cursed the Japanese for bringing this trouble on us. I hated them.

The Dutch teachers and staff at the college were in a much worse psychological state, as well as a difficult political situation. They belonged to the nation who had just lost the battle; at least we Indonesians were neutral. They asked for our help. But how could we help them, even if we wanted to? We did not even know what was going to happen to us. It was a strange situation. Now the masters were asking for help and seeking protection from their subjects. For the first time we saw the Dutch as they really were; the master race were not so superior after all.

The Japanese victory made an indelible print on my politically untutored mind. I started thinking about politics, something I had never done before. The Japanese brought far-reaching changes in my way of thinking – I became politically conscious. I began to realise that food and clothing were not all that mattered in life. I started to look at the world with different eyes, I was overwhelmed with questions I could not answer.

One of my friends in Bandung offered me a place to share with him, which I readily accepted. I hadn't much money, and staying with this friend for free solved my problems. There was still plenty of rice in the school's store room, so I decided to bring one bag to my friend's house. This was not stealing, because this rice belonged to the Dutch, who no longer existed as a power. So this was nobody's rice. It was very lucky that I decided to take that bag, because the next day the Japanese came and occupied our dormitory and claimed all the rice for themselves.

There was nothing to do. Although the town seemed more cheerful than before, this did not remain so for long. The uncertainty of our future hung heavily in our minds. We spent much time meeting together to discuss the situation, but the more we talked the more confused we became. People were also talking politics, about the chances of the Dutch returning, about the attitude of the Japanese, and about so many more things. There were more questions than there were answers. I usually joined these groups, but refrained from saying anything. I thought this was the safest thing to do under the circumstances.

After waiting one month in Bandung, without any decision having been made about our school, I decided to go home to Tegal in central Java. I came home to an empty house, because my parents and their whole office had moved to Kalibakung, a Dutch hill station. I followed them.

Kalibakung was a small village without electricity. No cinemas, no restaurants, no newspapers, nothing. I led a quiet, secluded life, and honestly enjoyed it very much. After a week I got used to everything, and even the village girls became prettier in my eyes.

I was one of the few "intellectuals" in the village, so people often asked me about the political situation, and what was in store for all of us. I became a VIP, a role I liked very much, because most of the time this meant free coffee and once in a while a free meal. And, of course, the admiring eyes of the village girls.

I discovered that enjoyment of life is purely an attitude of mind. You make it nice, then it is nice, you grudge everything and complain all the time, then you suffer. I always say "Alhamdullilah" – thank you, oh God. That is the correct way to live. Accept life as it is and remember, it could be worse.

One day, the *Lurah* and his *carik* (village head and his secretary) came to see me, to ask whether I was willing to teach at the village school. He knew I was a student of the teachers college and he was short of teachers. Without a second thought I said yes. Then he was silent, which puzzled me. He should be glad because I had solved his problem. I asked him what the problem was, since perhaps I could help?

"First I would like to express my gratitude on behalf of the people, that you are willing to teach. But we are not sure that we can pay you."

"Oh, that is not a problem for me. I will teach for free. Do not worry. Besides, I have nothing else to do. This teaching job will keep me busy. I need that." And then I added, "If there are adults who want to learn how to read and write, I can teach them in the afternoon."

This teaching job lasted for about two months, because I was called to join a Japanese language course, organized by the Department of Education, for the students of the ex-Dutch teachers' college. This course was held in Leonielaan no. 5 in present-day Jatinegara.

Myself and my fellow students were very happy to see each other again, after so many months. All my friends were there, plus students of the Christian, Catholic and Islamic teachers' colleges. It was a very happy reunion.

The course lasted for six months. We were given eight hours a day of Japanese language studies. We learned how to write the intricate *kanji*, the simple *katakana*, and the *hiragana*. The Japanese were preparing us to become Japanese language teachers.

My Army Life

As I have said already, I liked uniforms. People in uniforms looked so confident, so powerful. A uniform radiates a certain authority that makes people listen and follow orders. No matter how small you are, you look authoritative and you feel confident. When I was a small boy I saw a policeman, himself rather short and small, arresting a big pick-pocket and the pick-pocket did not fight back. So I wanted to become a soldier or a policeman. It did not matter very much which it was, as long as I could wear a uniform.

When I was at elementary school I joined the Indonesian Boy Scouts movement. Every Saturday afternoon, we met for all kinds of training exercises. I was a very serious and conscientious boy scout because I loved it. I had the chance to wear a uniform. I managed to earn a specialist badge as a cook and as a drummer.

My dream of becoming a soldier or a policeman went up in smoke when I had to enter the teachers college. Becoming a teacher was something I had never dreamt of doing. A Dutch proverb says, "Mens wikt, God beschikt" (Men plan, God decides). The reason my parents sent me to attend the teachers college was the cheap cost and the assurance that all graduates were sure of a job afterwards. Teaching was a very prestigious position, and paid well, too. A teacher's education continued for about six years after elementary school. Three years in the lower grade and another three years in the advanced grade. When you passed, you were qualified to teach at an elementary school. The most important requirement to be accepted as a student was that you had to be fluent in speaking, reading and writing Dutch.

All students had to stay in the dormitory and life was very strict. Discipline was observed 24 hours a day. We had to clean our own rooms, make up our beds, and sweep and mop the floors. We would study, eat, and sleep according to fixed and rigid rules. My education was rudely interrupted by World War II, which changed Indonesian life completely. I finished my studies during the Japanese occupation and following graduation became a Japanese language teacher at a high school in Jakarta, though this was not for long.

The Japanese occupation forces decided to create an indigenous army – 100% Indonesians commanded by Indonesian officers. It did not take me long to leave my teaching job, with a monthly salary of 50 rupiahs, and join the *Pembela Tanah Air* or PETA (defenders of the fatherland) with a salary of 60 rupiahs per month. In the army everything was taken care of, such as food, clothing, a place to sleep, everything.

The 60 rupiahs was net income. As a teacher, I had to pay 15 rupiahs for my boarding, plus about five rupiahs for instalments on my bike. Beside that, I had to be properly dressed, complete with tie, at a time when clothing was becoming difficult to get.

What were my motives in joining the PETA?

Certainly not for patriotic reasons. Firstly, I liked uniforms, and secondly, I got a better salary. Some of my friends boasted that they joined for patriotic reasons, which was pure nonsense. I definitely was not going to fight for these Japanese – they were like the Dutch, that is, colonial masters. So I decided to join as an administrative officer. You got to wear the same uniform, you had a samurai sword hanging at your side, and I was sure that the girls would not know the difference between a fighting officer and a administrative officer who sat behind a desk.

After I'd finished my training I was directly promoted to a lieutenant third grade, because of my proficiency in Japanese. My salary was 100 rupiahs. No family to take care of, no costs for board and lodging or clothing. What else did I need? I was in paradise.

I was very popular with the high school girls in Bandung. I discovered that girls liked uniforms without bothering what was inside them. I looked rather smart in my PETA uniform, which more or less looked like the Japanese army uniforms, though we did not smell as bad as they did. It was a very good time. No war, not even news about the war, because we had no way of getting information.

No newspapers or radios. It was a good time for me.

Because of my knowledge of Japanese, I was appointed as a translator to the Japanese army divisional headquarters in Bandung, commanded by Major-General Harada. I got additional benefits like free sake (Japanese wine) – but I do not drink, and cigarettes – but I do not smoke, and *mochi* (glutinous sweet rice cake), which I like very much. The *mochi* was more than welcome. I used it as bait to attract more girls.

According to the official version, the PETA was created because the Indonesians, represented by Mr. Gatot Mangkupradja, asked the Japanese to create a local army, so that the Indonesians could help the Japanese in defending Indonesia.

Although the idea was 100% Japanese, for propaganda reasons it was considered better that this looked like an Indonesian request that had been granted by the Japanese. The Japanese chose Gatot Mangkupradja as the petitioner. On the 7th of September, 1943, Gatot Mangkupradja handed this petition to the Japanese 16th Army headquarters. The Japanese accepted the petition and agreed to create the home guard as soon as possible. The Japanese set the whole thing up, and Gatot was merely an honourable pawn. On 3rd October the Japanese high command issued *Osamu Seirei* no. 44, outlining the creation of the home guard.

I could prove that the home guard was a Japanese set up, because I translated Japanese instruction manuals for PETA, printed in Tokyo in March 1943, long before anyone in Indonesia had any idea of creating an indigenous army. I did not tell anyone about this, fearing I might be accused of treason by the Japanese. But it didn't really matter whose idea it was. We needed the PETA and so did the Japanese, they had their plans, and we had ours.

But why did the Japanese want to have this PETA?

Let me quote from a book written by Dr. Nugroho, a military historian. "The Japanese wanted to create Indonesian units in areas where the Japanese were very weak in manpower. The first reason was the critical war situation. The Allies had begun their counter offensive and halted the Japanese advance in the Pacific. The Japanese feared that the Allies might plan to attack Java and Sumatra. The second reason was that this potentially dangerous area was thinly manned. There were only a few brigades, made up mainly of old soldiers." Dr. Nugroho got this information in an interview with Lieutenant-General (Ret) Inada Masazumi in 1968.

As a home guard officer, you gained many benefits. A sticker was plastered on the front door of my family's house indicating that a member of this house was a member of PETA. When my parents queued for rice, they were served first. When I came home for holidays, the village head came to pay his respects. What a life for a young man only 20 years old.

Next to my house was a Japanese-run brothel for Japanese non-commissioned officers. In the early hours of the evening it was very noisy, they were laughing and singing and getting drunk. After the battle of sexes, it was RIP – Rest In Peace. I could understand all this, because these soldiers were far from home and did not know when they would go home or how long they had to live. The biological urge remained strong in spite of the war.

At first, my motivation for joining PETA was purely commercial, but slowly this changed. I came in contact with politicians, started to hear from them about the desire to gain independence, and also the importance of having a military organization. I gradually became more politically aware and I regretted not having joined the field officers. I understood that we had to fight to gain our independence and once we had gained it, we would have to defend it. The Dutch had never allowed us to acquire military training and experience as a group. I prepared myself to become an Indonesian soldier for our future battles, a soldier with patriotic motivations.

At the headquarters I was the official interpreter, and my daily job was to translate Japanese military manuals into Indonesian for use by PETA, or if there was a conference of battalion commanders I would act as interpreter. Officially I was a member of PETA Headquarters West Java, but I worked in the Japanese divisional headquarters. Our barracks was next to the PETA headquarters, commanded by Colonel Nagai.

There was a small river flowing across the barrack ground, with enough water for us to throw all the waste, human and other, into it. Colonel Nagai decided to build 10 toilets above the river. These toilets were just bamboo boxes, with no roof on top. Over the river we put two planks about 10 inches apart. On those two planks we would squat and do our business. Starting from upstream the toilets were numbered one to 10. Six toilets were for the use of the Indonesians and four for the Japanese. The problem now was which four would be used by the Japanese – numbers one to four, or numbers seven to 10? If the Japanese used the first four then the Japanese waste would have to drift behind Indonesian waste, something the Japanese would not consider, because of their superiority. If, on the other hand, the Japanese used the last four boxes, the Japanese would see the Indonesian waste floating by. It became a serious matter for the Japanese, which gave us a good laugh. There should have been more serious and important things to worry about than whose waste was going to follow whose.

Finally, the commander decided that the Japanese were going to use the first four. End of problem.

Infant Steps in a Free World

Indonesian independence was proclaimed and soon after the PETA and *Heiho* were disbanded and we were all sent home. I stayed on in Bandung. Unlike the time when our teachers college was closed and we had to go home and did not know what to do, this time the future was no mystery. The Republic of Indonesia, the reincarnation of former power and glory, was something we were determined to defend. My future was crystal clear.

The early days of proclamation were difficult for me personally. I was, like so many others, dismissed from the Japanese sponsored home guard, without any clear picture of what was coming or what to expect, except that I was now a citizen of a free country, and determined to defend what was rightfully mine.

I still had some money saved, because my years in the PETA were cheap years, and I could save a lot. There were no expenses for food, clothing, or housing. The only expenses I had to pay out of my own pocket was going out with some girls, who admired uniformed men. That was cheap.

One day I was standing in front of the Bandung mosque, for no particular reason. I did this almost every day, just to kill time. Suddenly an elderly gentleman approached me and asked, "Are you Soegih Arto, the son of Mas (brother) Wiryohardjo?" Wiryohardjo was the name of my father.

" Yes I am."

"I am your uncle, although not too closely related." And then he explained how he was my uncle. I did not pay too much attention, until he asked where I lived. I said that for the time being I was a nomad, moving from one friend's house to another. My uncle said that I could stay with him. He lived in a big house, with only his wife, son and adopted daughter. He said that I was most welcome to stay with his family. I accepted his invitation immediately and without a second thought, before he could change his mind. He gave me his address and said that I could move in whenever I wanted.

I was in the seventh heaven. Oh thank you, God. I considered myself a very lucky man. My housing problems were solved and no more eating at roadside foodstalls. I was becoming a respected citizen. That night I joined the family, who welcomed me warmly. What a nice family. I got a room near the kitchen, small but comfortable, and most importantly, clean. For the first time in so many weeks I had a decent dinner and drank coffee. What a life. I slept like Snow White for almost ten hours, but was woken by the alarm clock and not by a beautiful mysterious princess.

Luckily I was asked to join the BKR (the people's security body) So I had something to keep me busy, but no salary. It did not bother me very much, because there was nothing to buy. One day the BKR in Bandung was approached by Mrs. Aruji Kartawinata, wife of the Siliwangi divisional commander. She needed an instructor to train the Laskar Wanita Indonesia or LASWI, which means the Indonesian Girls Army. I was chosen to become the instructor of the LASWI, a unit consisting of young girls who wanted to join the fight against the enemies of the Republic. I'd had similar feelings in 1942, when for the first time I'd had to teach a class full of young, beautiful girl students at a high school in Jakarta. I was happy, nervous, and excited.

I reported to Ibu (mother) Mrs. Arudji Kartawinata, the commander in chief of the LASWI, and she explained what was expected from me. She wanted me to train the girls, make them ready for front-line duty and be with them 24 hours a day. I had two months in which to prepare them. The age of the girls ranged from 16 to 20 and some were still high school students. Spirits were high and the girls were prepared to abandon their studies and go to the front if and when necessary. Mentally they were prepared not only to work in the field kitchens or in the emergency hospitals, but also to fight with weapons alongside the boys.

I was facing a big and difficult job. I soon found out that training boys was a much easier job than training girls. If boys did not listen to you or tried to violate discipline, you hit or slapped them or kicked them in their ass (this last word and many more I learned from watching American films). But how do you discipline girls you are training? You cannot slap or hit or kick them. There are too many soft parts in a girl's body, and I know that they were not created to be slapped or hit. These parts should be lovingly caressed. What a dilemma.

But what must be done, should be done. No bargaining, and I was prepared to do just that, without slapping or kicking. I started with what the Japanese called *seizing kunwa* – lectures to give them the right motivation. This I considered very important. They should know what they are doing, and why they are doing it. They must be convinced that this was the right path – sacrifice for the sake of the country.

I was with them almost 24 hours a day, and after some weeks they accepted me not only as their commander but more importantly as their brother. We were on the same wavelength. The first test came when southern Bandung, where our headquarters was situated, was shelled by the British. Artillery and mortar shells fell all over the place. They knew exactly what to do. They were pale and nervous all right, but they did not panic. After the shelling had stopped, they helped the passers-by, giving them drinks and helping them on their feet, or tended the wounded. I was a proud man.

While training the girls, I was also appointed as the personnel officer of the Siliwangi Division under the command of Bapak Arudji Kartawinata. Mr. Arudji was a battalion commander of the home guard in Cimahi, a small town to the west of Bandung. He was famous for his inspiring 'motivation' speeches.

One of his famous speeches went like this: "If you have to die, do not die like a hero, die like a watch. If a watch dies, you wind it up, and then it is alive again." One of his platoon commanders was a gentleman named Poniman, who later became army chief of staff and minister of defence and security. Pak Arudji himself entered politics and became deputy chairman of Parliament.

Colonel Arudji made a funny request of me: he wanted me to type out some sort of an identity card for him, because he had to travel to Purwokerto in central Java to attend a divisional commanders' meeting. There were many "warlords" at that time, and many commanders of non-government troops, who considered themselves as the rulers of their respective area. To be on the safe side, Pak Arudji thought that he should have some sort of identification with him. Freely translated, this was what this identity card looked like:

I, the undersigned, Arudji Kartawinata, commander of the Siliwangi Division, declare that Arudji Kartawinata is Arudji Kartawinata and at present holds the position of commander of the Siliwangi Division.

Arudji Kartawinata

Although it looked rather strange, I was satisfied with my product and I knew that no one was in a better position to explain who Arudji was, than Arudji himself. Surprisingly, Pak Arudji signed this document and he passed safely through the screening posts. A unique creation of an identity card and the product of a genius!

One day, a friend who had stolen some radio equipment

approached me and asked whether I had a place he could start a modest radio station and broadcast music and news to the Indian troops north of Bandung. At that time Bandung was divided into two parts. The north was occupied by British troops and the south by Indonesians. I said that he could use my house, because I was there alone. We broadcast news at 19.00 hours and some music afterwards for half an hour. I was promoted to broadcaster in English. With lots of courage and spirit I started broadcasting news in English. I was doubtful whether those Indian troops could understand my version of English. Let us say my English was English brewed and cooked in an Indonesian kitchen, by a cook who still had a lot to learn. In spite of everything we kept on broadcasting.

I had a very good time as member of the BKR. Lots of adventures and experiences fighting first the Japs and then the Indian and British soldiers. Soon we established good relations with the soldiers of the 23rd Indian Division, or to be more precise the future Pakistanis. We exchanged with them chickens and vegetables and gained in return rifles and ammunition. Many of them, especially the Muslims, deserted to our side, bringing along their weapons or sometimes radios. The same happened with many Japanese soldiers. For some Japanese soldiers, joining the Indonesian forces was better than going home as members of a defeated army and facing shame.

One day, the British attacked our position in town and I was allotted a sector to defend. There was a river separating us from the enemy. The British started bombing us with aircraft, artillery, and mortar fire. A while later tanks started to appear.

At the time, I was sitting on a bucket while watching through my binoculars and issuing instructions to my platoon. After a while, I stood up and went towards an open area. I was barely 20 meters from my bucket, when a mortar projectile directly hit the bucket, blowing it to pieces. I trembled and became very pale, imagining what would have become of me if I had remained on that bucket. I kissed the ground I was standing on and thanked God that my life had been miraculously spared. After a heavy exchange of fire, the enemy withdrew. They didn't cross the river.

Then one day my adventures as freelance BKR member abruptly ended. It was around this time that the TNI was finally born, in January 1946. The commander of the 8th Infantry Regiment in Bandung asked me to report to him. When I reported to Lt.-Col. Omon, I was there and then appointed as his ADC, with the rank of captain. Salary unknown. Now I had a job I liked. And beside being an ADC I was also appointed as liaison officer with the British army in north Bandung.

There was a Captain Clark, a South African who became my opposite number. He spoke Dutch, not the real Dutch I'd learnt at school, but South African Dutch, a bit strange to my ears, but I could understand him. I think the difference is like that between British and Australian English. We got along nicely and once I was brought to his headquarters in north Bandung. Coffee and cookies were served. I ate and drank as though this was my every day menu, while in reality this was a real treat for my palate. I wished I had a longer neck, so I could enjoy these snacks longer. They offered me whiskey, which I politely refused.

This position could not be maintained for long, because soon we were in trouble. The British wanted the Indonesian army and armed gangs to leave Bandung, which we refused to do. We were determined to fight and defend our soil. We knew the risk and consequences of this refusal.

Repeating the words of General Ter Poorten, commander in chief of the Dutch forces, who surrendered to the Japanese in 1942, we said: "It is better to die standing than to live kneeling." General Ter Poorten did not keep his word.

So war broke out and we burnt Bandung. This was the famous episode called "Bandung Lautan Api" or Bandung, sea of fire. To commemorate this memorable event a song was composed called *Haloo Haloo Bandung*. The lyrics went more or less like this: "That although we burnt Bandung, the capital of West Java, we are going to take it back. Bandung, a town full of memories." During the Dutch time Bandung was considered the Paris of Java; now it is called the flower town. For the time being, it was good-bye Bandung for all of us. I said in my heart: "I shall return." A few years later I did, but as a prisoner of the Dutch army.

On the 24th of March 1946, we set Bandung on fire; I shall never forget that night. Afterwards, we left town on foot and once in a while glanced back. The burning town made an eerie sight. We could still hear explosions, and sporadic fire. Some units had been ordered to protect the mass evacuation and hold the British at bay.

Behind us was a long, long line of civilians, freedom fighters, members of the army, all leaving town with whatever they could take along with them: their meagre belongings and their children, some chickens, goats, buffaloes, and cows. They all willingly followed the orders of the army to leave Bandung after destroying it, so that the enemy could gain no advantage from the town. They all walked silently to a destination unknown, and into a future nobody could predict. They were sad, yes, no doubt about that. Their life was going to be difficult. But they held their heads high; this was their contribution to Indonesian independence.

The combat engineers expertly planted explosives on all the vital buildings, roads, and bridges. Bandung, the Paris of Java, so cool and beautiful, became a desolate ghost town. It had been a difficult decision, setting fire to Bandung and evacuating. Army headquarters in Yogyakarta had ordered that every inch be defended, while the central government asked the army to comply with the British ultimatum, and leave town, so that the army would remain intact for future operations. The British ultimatum had not requested the civil authorities to leave.

I attended all the meetings involving the preparation to abandon Bandung in my capacity as ADC. Though I kept quiet, in my heart I was mad at the central government for ordering us to leave town without a fight. What else is an army for? I had not joined the army to retreat every time we were given an ultimatum from the enemy. The purpose of having an army is to fight and not remain unharmed. But a mere ADC has very little influence.

Battalion Commander

After leaving Bandung, all army units and fighting forces were placed around the town, so that the British in Bandung were surrounded by Indonesian troops, and regularly harassed by them.

Soon afterwards I was appointed battalion commander of the second battalion of the 10th Regiment. I had a battalion according to the number of soldiers, but not more than a company's worth were actually armed with guns. I can't remember whether I was promoted to major or not. This is not important, since there was no extra salary.

A battalion commander at that time was more than a fighting leader. He was a father in the true sense of the word. I had to take care of my men's families, give advice on non-military matters, and try to get regular supplies of rice and ammunition and uniforms. In short I was the master of a very big household. This might sound strange to Westerners, because such a situation does not exist in a regular army. On one occasion my battalion could not get enough to eat. We got only two potatoes a day per person and were in the front line, facing Dutch troops, and separated only by the Citarum River. I cannot remember clearly how we got through these difficult times. And yet there were no desertions, everybody remained at his post watching the enemy's movements.

One day we were attacked by artillery and mortar fire. With short intervals, the bombardment lasted the whole morning. We got used to it. In the afternoon the Dutch attacked. They crossed the river and moved with their bren-carriers and light tanks. We fought back with everything we had and after three hours, we managed to drive them back over the river. The Dutch did not want to stay on strange territory during the night. Remarkably, we suffered no casualties.

Of the 800 men in my battalion, the average age was around 16 or 17. Ninety percent of them had never had any intensive military training, or worse still, had never seen a rifle before. I was given three months to forge a fighting unit capable of offering resistance. The company commanders had training during the Japanese period and so were considered experts. At least they knew how to shoot. I had platoon commanders who had previously been teachers; I had shopkeepers; I had criminals recently released from prison.

With the help of the company commanders, I drilled these people mercilessly, 10 or 11 hours a day, just like I was drilled by the Japanese instructors. And the soldiers enjoyed themselves tremendously. No complaints, even when we had to march in pouring rain, carrying bamboo spears, our standard weapon.

I decided to disarm the local police force, because I did not think they needed the rifles. Everybody was so busy fighting or doing something useful that there was practically no crime. I told the police chief that we needed their rifles desperately and he understood. I got weapons from other sources as well and by the time my battalion was given front-line duty, I had two companies fully armed.

During lulls in the fighting, I ordered ex professional thieves to enter Bandung to get medicine, or tires, or anything else we could use, such as canned food, and old newspapers or magazines.

Life was not too bad at the front line. Once in while the Dutch bombard our positions with artillery or mortar fire. But most of the time we did not pay any attention, because they did this just to let us know that they were still there. They fired their artillery without aiming at any specific target. It was a pure holiday, without pay. The boys went fishing along the river, while one squad was constantly on the lookout for any suspicious enemy movement.

There were many Indonesians in the town of Bandung who were very friendly and helpful. They collected for us medicine, food, and sometimes scarce articles like soap and toothbrushes. These were sheer luxury items. I usually brushed my teeth with coconut fibre and ash from the kitchen mixed with water as paste.

We kept in constant contact with these Indonesians, who called themselves Republicans, and we had a list of pro-Dutch Indonesians we called 'Nicas' – a short form of Netherlands Indies Civil Administration. We considered these Nicas as traitors and treated them as such when we captured them. But it was very rare for us to capture a Nica, because they did not dare to go outside of Bandung.

The Big Battle

One day I received an intelligence report from divisional headquarters saying that the Dutch were planning to move out from Bandung and attack all our positions. They would begin with aircraft attacks, followed by artillery and mortar fire, and then their infantry would cross the river.

This was welcome news after so many weeks of doing nothing. Although I did not know the exact date of the attack, I started to prepare my sector's defence. The boys were in high spirits. They were bored with their leisurely life. Most of these young lads did not yet realise the danger of a shooting war against an experienced army. Rifles were cleaned, platoons were put in place, and company commanders were briefed as to what they could expect. I told them to be alert 24 hours a day.

One day after the briefing, one of my company commanders went for an inspection of the river, wearing his favourite shiny boots, which turned out to be bad luck. While he was talking to his ADC, an enemy sniper shot at him and he was hit in the knee. He fell down and the ADC panicked. He did not know what to do, because the firing continued and my boys started to fire back. Firing went on for a few minutes, while the company commander lay on the ground in agony. One of the soldiers ran back to the battalion headquarters to fetch our "doctor" – a paramedic with the rank of sergeant. The captain lay there unattended for almost half an hour. The nearest hospital was about 60 miles away. When he eventually arrived at the hospital his knee was infected with tetanus and a part of his leg had to be amputated. My first casualty. Later, I heard that he'd married the nurse who had taken care of him, and in 1951 was elected as village head in his native Cirebon in western Java. His village won several prizes from the governor for cleanliness.

Eventually the Dutch attack began with artillery and mortar fire, but luckily there were no enemy planes in the air. We could do nothing except hide and keep quiet. Artillery and mortar fire continued and I decided to go to the front and see for myself how the boys were doing. Except for one or two who were shaking from fear, the rest behaved quite well and seeing their commander was a big boost to their morale. I told my people to be cautious and shoot only when they could clearly see the enemy. But the waiting, the uncertainty and the feeling of fear made them react differently. They started shooting, just to let off steam. Some also started shouting.

When the enemy started to attack our sector, my two companies stood firm and gave the enemy hell. The boys shouted dirty words at the enemy, as if the enemy could hear and understand them. Enemy firing intensified, but fortunately the Dutch could not bring up reinforcements because they were attacking on the whole front and had no men to spare.

According to my observation, we wounded two or three Dutch soldiers. Though the enemy had established a bridgehead, in the late afternoon they started to retreat. The ordeal was over. No casualties on my side. I called it a big battle, while it might not be according to normal standards.

Courier Service

According to news we were given, there would be a ceasefire, for which we began to prepare. On the 4th of November 1946, a ceasefire agreement was reached. All units were ordered to be prepared to hold talks with the Dutch. The place chosen for Indonesian-Dutch ceasefire talks in the Bandung sector was Dayeuhkolot, a place close to the Citarum bridge. My battalion was very close to that location and so we were responsible for security. We had to take care that the Dutch strictly adhered to the agreement. The ceasefire talks took place on the Dutch side of the river.

About three days before the talks I had to deliver to the Dutch a letter of confirmation from Colonel Hidayat, leader of our delegation. To deliver this letter, I was allowed to bring along 10 soldiers armed only with rifles. A Dutch captain accompanied by 10 armed soldiers would meet me to receive the letter. I selected the smallest soldiers in my battalion and armed them with long Japanese rifles.

On the day agreed I met the Dutch captain, who seemed to be very curious to see Indonesian soldiers close up. He was a pleasant looking man. He spoke Dutch to me, but I pretended that I did not speak Dutch and preferred English. When he knew that we did not understand Dutch, he started to talk about us to his soldiers. It went more or less like this:

"Are we fighting these little boys, my God I feel ashamed. They could be my sons. Look at their baby faces."

Of course I understood every word and almost burst out laughing, but my intention of making them feel ashamed was achieved. In silence I handed the letter to the Dutch captain, we saluted each other and departed. Actually I did not trust the Dutch, so there was a platoon hiding nearby, just in case of trouble. My first ever diplomatic mission was over and I went back to battalion headquarters.

As earlier mentioned, our ceasefire delegation was headed by Colonel Hidayat, a graduate from the Dutch Royal Military Academy in Breda, Holland. Beside me there were two other members in the delegation, one lieutenant-colonel and one major. I was appointed as secretary and security officer. We crossed the Citarum bridge into Dutch territory, where the Dutch military delegation was waiting, headed by a Major Bayetto, a Eurasian, or what we called an 'Indo.'

Colonel Hidayat tried to be friendly and extended his hand, but Bayetto preferred to ignore that and asked us to sit down. Colonel Hidayat was angry at this rudeness. We sat down, and the business was over in one hour and we announced that we were leaving. The Dutch offered us coffee, but we ignored the offer and left.

When I saw these Dutch officers, I no longer felt admiration, respect, or awe, as during the colonial time. They did not look like superhuman beings any more.

Years later, in 1952 to be exact, I met this same major again. He was still a major, while I was already a lieutenant-colonel. He was a lecturer in Military History at the Dutch Staff College and I was one of his students. When we met, he saluted me – he had to, because I was of a higher rank – and we shook hands.

"Major, I have I seen you somewhere before."

He looked at me and then shook his head and said, "Not that I can remember."

"Do you remember November 1946, the Citarum bridge at Dayeuhkolot, Bandung? Do you remember the ceasefire talks?"

"Ah, yes of course, now I remember. Your delegation was headed by Colonel Hidayat, a graduate from our Military Academy, in fact my senior. A very nice man, I should say."

"Yes, I agree, but you refused to shake hands with him."

"Did I, I was not aware of it." He abruptly cut short the conversation and offered me a drink, which I refused. It felt good – a sweet, unexpected revenge, after six long years.

Mystic

God forgiveth not, that partners should be set up with Him; but he forgiveth anything else, to whom, he pleaseth; to set up partners with God is to devise a sin, most heinous indeed.

Qur'an, Surah IV (Nisaa), verse 48.

In the early years of the revolution mystic was very popular. The freedom fighters were trying to compensate for their lack of weapons, training and experience by using mystic. Can you blame them? *Dukuns* (witch doctors) were in high demand, and some did good business. But there were lots of them who did everything for free, just to contribute to the fight for independence.

I had a neighbour, an elderly man, who was called an *orang pintar* or clever man, a name for people who can predict the future. He could also make you invulnerable to bullets. One day I visited this neighbour, Mr. Denda, and after a long chat, he told me that I possessed a kris (a dagger). I was surprised because it was true. He said that I should keep it in a special place, because that kris was very valuable and had mystical powers. In that kris was housed the soul of a lady general from Pajajaran, called Djajapangrengot, who would be my protector. Because of this, I named my battalion Djajapangrengot.

He also told me that when times returned to normal, the kris would become empty and the occupant would return to her special abode. But I must keep the kris clean because, he said, when you are facing danger, she will return and enter the kris to protect you. This lady general would leave behind two black panthers to guard me day and night. I did not know what to believe, but I did not have the courage to tell him that he was talking nonsense. He sensed that I was not quite convinced and so made a comparison with radio waves. If you have a radio and you are tuned to the right wavelength, only then can you hear what is broadcast. Otherwise, you can hear nothing, even if the radio station is broadcasting. He added that he had this "radio" and tuned to the mystical world, and that was the reason why he knew what was going on. I kept silent, because I was still sceptical.

I was still a very young and inexperienced man at that time, so it was only normal that in times of trouble I should try to find strength through mystic. Many members of my battalion wore "magical" amulets, either hanging from their necks or safely hidden in their pockets. Now I know that what I did was wrong. I should have prayed to God and asked for his guidance, not looked for esoteric protection.

Bung Karno, the great Indonesian leader, believed in mystic. He explained why he preferred to proclaim independence on the 17th rather than on any other date. Here is what he said: "I planned this whole operation towards the 17th. Why the 17th, asked one of my friends? I replied, I am a mystic. I cannot rationalize logically why 17 feels hopeful to me. But I feel in my inner self that 17 is holy. Seventeen is a sacred number. This is our holy month, Ramadan, during which we fast. Next Friday is Holy Friday, the 17th. The Koran came to earth on the 17th. Muslims perform 17 rokaats daily. Why did Mohammed decree 17 bows instead of 10 or 20? Because the holiness of the number 17 is not of man's making. When I heard the surrender news, I thought we should proclaim immediately. Then I realized it was God's will for this to fall on His holiday. Hence the proclamation will be on the 17th." Soekarno, *An Autobiography*.

But let us continue with my case. Next I had to decide whether I wanted to become invulnerable. I eagerly replied, yes. My neighbour told me to fast for seven days, excluding the nights. I did what he told me to do. This was during the time when my battalion was resting from duty at the front, so I had plenty of time.

After one week's fasting, I visited him again. He told me there are two kinds of invulnerability. The closed form and the open kind. The open one is very popular, because people can see that you are invulnerable, they see that you are unharmed when the enemy shoot at you or stab you with a knife. You become famous because the enemy can never get beyond the intention of harming you – at the last moment he will lose his courage or miss his aim. The second kind is not obvious or noticeable, but you are still protected. You are safe, but nobody knows that you are invulnerable.

Now which one do you want? It is entirely up to you, I can give you whichever you choose, because it is already written that you will become invulnerable. I am only doing what is ordered by my bosses in the world of mystics, said Mr. Denda.

After much thought weighing the pros and cons, I chose the closed method. He said that I had made the right choice; most people if given the chance would choose the open one.

He went into deep meditation, and when he woke up, he said that I would become invulnerable in due time, but only if I observed two things: firstly, I must be polite and friendly to everybody, and secondly, I must never act arrogantly. At that time I felt cheated and disappointed. Is that all I get, after seven days of fasting? I took my leave and went home. I could not sleep, and kept thinking about those two things. And then I realised how deep the meaning of those instructions were. If I behaved like that, who would be my enemy? I could only gain friends and no enemies. So it was this that constituted my invulnerability.

Mr. Denda added that I would be protected 24 hours a day, by two black panthers, which I could not see, but could be seen by others. One night, a sergeant in my staff went outside to wash his face. While washing his face, he felt that someone or something was licking his buttocks. He turned around to see who or what was doing this and saw two black panthers. He screamed and ran back into the building. I asked him what was the matter? Stammering, his face pale, he told me that two black panthers licked his buttocks when he was washing his face. Henceforth I believed in the mystic, Mr. Denda.

One day, a subdistrict head from Soreang, south Bandung, came to me and gave me a kris, saying that he'd dreamt the night before that he had to give his kris, an ancient family heirloom, to Captain Soegih Arto, because I was the rightful owner. Can you believe this?

One day during a lull in the fighting, a *santri* (religious student) from the eastern part of West Java came to see me with a letter from his teacher. The letter said that he would come to assist me in fighting the enemy. He would bring with him 300 of his students armed with bamboo spears, which would turn into rifles once the fighting started, plus hundreds of trained bees, ready to sting the enemy to death. I had my doubts, but any help was welcome. Three days later the religious teacher, with his army, arrived and I allotted him a sector to defend. When eventually the enemy attacked, nothing extraordinary happened. The bamboo spears remained bamboo spears and so many of his soldiers died against the better equipped enemy. The bees were freed but flew off to an unknown destination without harming anyone.

One last anecdote about mystics. When I was appointed battalion commander, a fellow captain was not very happy. He thought that he should be made commander, because he considered that he deserved it more than me. He was extremely jealous and made plans to kill me during the fighting at the front. I knew about this from my loyal ADC. But what could I do, there was no proof, and so far he had acted very normally. He followed orders as a loyal, disciplined subordinate should. I wanted to test him, I was only waiting for the right time and opportunity. At last it came. The enemy attacked our positions in the night and we were caught by surprise. It was a critical situation. I asked this captain to follow me to the front line to see how our boys were doing. He came along with a sergeant and I brought along my ADC. It was a very good opportunity. The night was rather dark. Enemy fire was heard everywhere, and once in a while the enemy shot flares into the sky. A perfect set up for a murder. I was alert, as was my loyal ADC.

When we arrived at the riverside, my captain suddenly stopped and started crying, his body shaking uncontrollable, tears flowing freely. And then he confessed, and told me his ambition and his plans to murder me. But he could not do it, he had not the strength.

He handed me his revolver, while looking down all the time, avoiding my gaze. I embraced him and we cried together. I was relieved and he became my most loyal company commander. End of mystery.

Much later, when I was commandant of the Army Staff College, I had a Lieutenant Duyshart in my staff, who was a mystic fanatic. He usually visited all the famous graves, slept there in the open air, and fasted every Monday. Besides that, he was a fanatical hunter.

One day he went boar hunting in Banten. He hunted the whole day, but there was no boars to be seen. At around five o'clock he saw a big boar, running towards the sea. He aimed and shot. He saw the boar fall and ran towards it. But to his utter surprise, he saw no wounded boar, but an old lady, lying there moaning from pain. He helped the old lady to get up, gave her water to drink and offered his sincere apologies. Suddenly the lady sat up, and with a smile, said that she was all right, and only pretending to be wounded. She had been told that the Lieutenant was coming, to receive from her the *Besi Kuning*, or yellow iron knife, which makes the owner invulnerable. She said that she was ordered to give it to the Lieutenant, but not for him to keep. She told him that the rightful owner was Colonel Soegih Arto, and in due time the Lieutenant should hand it over to Colonel Soegih Arto. It had to be done like this, she said, because the Colonel is an outsider. After explaining this to Duyshart, she ran to the sea, jumped in and disappeared.

Goodbye, My Friends and Good Luck

At the start of the independence war I did not know the exact definition of a guerrilla war but I felt that what we were doing was nothing more than waging a war of indecision. We kept avoiding the enemy whenever they came in great numbers, and would harass them when they least expected it. At that time we were fighting the enemy in an official capacity, but the task given to me after the Renville agreement was something completely different.

Mao Tse Tung wrote: "Without a political goal, guerrilla warfare must fail, as it must if its political objectives do not coincide with the aspirations of the people and so their sympathy, cooperation, and assistance cannot be gained. The essence of guerrilla warfare is thus revolutionary in character I." We were having a revolution, a revolution to change a political system and our political status. A change which could not be achieved by peaceful means. We had all the necessary ingredients for guerrilla warfare. We had political objectives and the complete and wholehearted support of the people. But most important of all was the our strong political convictions, which ensured the success of our efforts.

One day early in 1948 I got a cable, saying that I had to report to brigade headquarters immediately. Headquarters was some 30 miles away, and could only be reached on foot through dense jungle, since we had no vehicles. I set out, accompanied by my ADC, a squad of bodyguards, and, not to be forgotten, my faithful dog.

We hacked our way through the jungle and after about 10 hours reached brigade headquarters. A message was waiting for me at the village-head's house. I decided to sleep first although the message stated clearly that I had to report immediately upon arrival. After

113

about five hours refreshing sleep and a rice breakfast (or was it lunch?) with salted fish and some chillies, I was ready to face anything.

The brigade commander, Colonel Daan Yachya, greeted me and we talked about everything and nothing. Following this he came to the point. Looking back it was a moment that changed my life and gained me experiences I still treasure. He asked me whether I knew anything about the Renville agreement, to which I gave a negative answer, but I added that I had heard that name before.

He explained the essence of the Renville agreement reached on board the United States' ship Renville, which made nobody happy, especially the armed forces. The TNI troops in the pockets of resistance were to be evacuated to Republican areas in central Java.

The commander in chief of the TNI knew that this was a very painful decision, and he anticipated that the Siliwangi Division in particular would suffer psychologically from the withdrawal. It would be felt as a retreat. But this was our government's decision and hence had to be carried out. So he decided to send special couriers to all field commanders to explain the situation and stress the importance of discipline. The army must show the Dutch that it is loyal to the government.

General Sudirman also left instructions for some units to be left behind to continue harassing the Dutch in western Java and the puppet state of Pasundan. There should be no peace or tranquillity in Pasundan. The Dutch would then soon realise that Pasundan was not popular with the people. This was, in a nutshell, my main job, as explained by Colonel Daan Yachya. I asked him how I was going to carry out this difficult operation. He replied that he knew as much as I did, which was nothing.

This was something completely new. I would have no support from the central government, because the government would deny knowing anything about my battalion. I had to act completely independently. Here is the scenario laid out before me by my commander.

"We will tell the Dutch that Captain Soegih Arto could not be contacted. His battalion has fallen to pieces and is no longer a coherent force. But we are still trying to contact him through couriers. There is one other thing I have to tell you," the brigade commander continued. "You are completely on your own. Officially, you and your men are no longer members of the TNI. If you are captured by the enemy, you will not be treated as POWs, but as rebels. The Geneva convention won't protect you and you could be shot on the spot."

I was silent for a moment. I was not afraid for myself but for the safety of my men, plus this unusually difficult task weighed heavily on my shoulders.

"Do I have a choice?" I asked my commander.

"To be honest, no. We have selected you after careful scrutiny and we think that you are the best choice for this job. But it is still up to you."

"I ask for one thing only," I said.

"What is that? If I can help you I will do so with pleasure."

I said, jokingly, "Just say to me that I am the best choice and that you expect I will do everything in my power to do the job to the best of my ability."

Colonel Daan said what I asked him to say. He thought that I was serious.

We shook hands and I left him in silence. I did not know what he was thinking. But I knew that we were very good friends. I felt very proud and very honoured but a feeling of fear also shadowed me on the journey back to my troops. What if my officers left me, what if my soldiers refused to take this dangerous gamble, what if I could not accomplish my task, what if I was captured by the enemy? There were so many whats and ifs but few clear answers. I felt that my ADC wanted to ask me what our new orders were, but he kept silent. I was also silent, most of the time, only the dog seemed to enjoy herself.

When I arrived home, I told my ADC to call the company commanders and also the district area chief for an urgent conference. I outlined our new duties and held nothing back. I thought that they had the right to know everything, including the dangers. To my utter astonishment, the news was received with joy. The unknown, the adventure, the danger, the fight without rules appealed to them. Except for Lieutenant Gaossulalam, who wanted to join the forces being evacuated, everybody expressed their support and loyalty to me. The civilian district chief was especially happy. Now he knew he would not be isolated. He knew that the army was still there (even if unofficially) and that gave him the moral support he needed. The atmosphere was festive, with everybody laughing and telling jokes and saying what they were going to do to the enemy. There was no trace of fear at all. That was the advantage of being young: I was 24 and my company commanders a little bit younger. I was very much relieved by their confidence and enthusiasm, and my fears slowly ebbed away.

On the other side of the Citarum River was the enemy, the much feared and hated green berets, called the KST (Korps Speciale Troepen – Special Troops Corps) under the command of the notorious Captain Westerling. We all knew that Westerling was a very good shot and his soldiers were very cruel and blindly loyal to the Dutch. Most of the soldiers were Timorese. I did not know that Westerling had just been transferred from southern Sulawesi, where he had slaughtered 40,000 civilians in cold blood.

Much, much later I heard that Westerling had a Turkish mother, and had learned how to read the Holy Qur'an. He cleverly used his knowledge of Islam to attract people to his side. On a number of occasions he visited my village and asked about my whereabouts. But the answer was always negative.

One of the troop assembly areas was a cavalry barracks in Purabaya, a small place about 15 miles west of Bandung. Colonel Kawilarang, the Siliwangi divisional commander, was already there with some units. One day he asked Dutch Lieutenant Ulrichie when they would be shipped to central Java.

The Lieutenant said that it would be soon and that they were only waiting for Captain Soegih Arto, who had not yet surrendered. Hearing this Colonel Kawilarang became very angry, and said that the evacuation had nothing to do with surrender, and that we had not lost the war. The evacuation was a consequence of a treaty signed by the Dutch and Indonesian governments. Kawilarang asked Ulrichie to be careful in what he was saying. The Lieutenant left without answering Kawilarang.

An hour later, a platoon marched into Purabaya. A Dutch sergeant shouted: "Lieutenant, another group of bandits are just marching in." Kawilarang again became angry, and told the sergeant: "We are not bandits or robbers. You are the ones robbing our country."

This shows the attitude of the Dutch toward us – they considered us nothing more than rebels. Years later, some of my friends told me that they were treated like a defeated army because they looked like beggars. Some soldiers had no shoes to wear, some wore shorts, some long trousers, some had helmets, some were without head gear, not even berets. The TNI was in rags. The Dutch must have wondered how such an army was causing them so many problems.

Two weeks after all the TNI troops had been evacuated and West Java was empty of troops, I received a letter from Captain Westerling, which had taken three days to reach me. The actual distance between us was only 15 miles, and the letter changed hands frequently before it reached me, going from outpost to outpost and from one soldier to another.

In his letter Westerling proposed we have an informal meeting, without any preconditions. A meeting just between the two of us in Batujajar, his barracks. He said that it was no use us fighting each other, and that we'd better arranged for a local ceasefire. If no agreement could be reached, he guaranteed my safe return.

I showed this letter to my company commanders and everybody advised me not to accept his invitation. This was clearly a trap, they said. Remember Prince Diponegoro, who was invited by the Dutch to have talks after the Dutch suffered heavy losses. The Dutch also guaranteed his safe return. The Dutch did not keep their promise, and the prince was exiled. How cunning the Dutch were. I decided that since I was not a prince I was not going to accept this invitation and my RSVP was a regret, in very harsh and impolite words.

After I had signed the letter, I moved immediately to another hideout. It was not a difficult manoeuvre. I had nothing to carry except my rifle and my pistol.

I outlined to my company commanders what my plans were. I made each company independent and assigned them a certain location, their operational area, for them to live in and maintain the independent spirit of the people. No company should enter another company's area without specific orders from me. I kept one platoon close to me, for my protection and for courier services. Only the company commanders knew my whereabouts.

Each company was divided into three groups. One group was armed and had fighting duties – it was their job to harass the enemy at every opportunity. I gave the company commanders complete freedom of operational action. I told them not to stay too long in one place and remain mobile. Later, when I became a lecturer at the Staff and Command College in Bandung, I read what Sun Tzu wrote 500 years before Christ. "Mobility is the essence of guerrilla warfare. The people should be organized to provide all means of support needed by the guerrillas."

The second group was a logistics group. They had to ensure that there was enough food stocked in secret places to support the company. It was not a difficult task, because of the cooperation of the population. They gladly donated rice, corn, vegetables, chickens and what not. This group was not armed. This second group was officially the group on vacation.

The third group was the intelligence and territorial group. Their job was to gather information about the enemy, about Indonesians collaborating with the Dutch, and Indonesians sympathetic to our cause. They had to inform the population about our struggle and give contra information to counter Dutch propaganda. This group had to keep up the people's spirit; if they encountered opposition I gave them permission to use force or terror. In due time these three groups would be rotated in their duties, so that all my men would gain experience in all operational fields.

I decided to establish a legal political party lead by politicians who were pro Republic. This party was called PAKRI, the Partai Kesatuan Republik Indonesia (Indonesian Republican Unitarian Party). I sent letters to people who were fighting against the Dutch from within the system in the West Java Parliament of the puppet state of Pasundan. The Dutch allowed a token opposition party to give the impression of a democratic state. These politicians agreed in principle, but told me that they needed time for preparation.

To keep up our spirits, I tried to work on my soldiers minds and imaginations. I created small units named after legendary heroes or dangerous animals. Names appealing to their imagination and romantic spirit. We had a tarantula platoon, an eagle platoon and others. The men felt proud to belong to units with names like lightning, broom of the world, sweeper of the universe, thunderstorm, stinging bees, etc. The symbol of my battalion was the elephant, an animal with extraordinary power and strength and yet so calm and obedient.

Some anecdotes from this guerrilla period are worth relating. One day I went on patrol with a platoon. We visited many villages and talked to the villagers. I was very happy, because though there were plenty of problems, the people still supported the Republic and refused to help the Dutch, despite arrests and tortures.

At about three o'clock in the afternoon we took a rest and I ordered a soldier to climb a tree and watch out for enemies. After about an hour, I ordered everybody to move on to our destination for the night. However, we had forgotten the soldier up in the tree! Apparently he was asleep. When he woke up, he saw some Dutch soldiers resting under the tree and that we had left. He was shocked, fell out of the tree and landed in the middle of the resting Dutch soldiers. The Dutch soldiers were so startled they ran away, because they had never seen a tree bearing human beings as fruit. After a while they recovered from their shock and arrested my soldier. He spent the rest of the war in prison, and rejoined my battalion after independence had been recognised.

One of my squads, after delivering ammunition to a far away post, had to spend the night in the open under the skies. Fortunately, it was a beautiful night. The moon was in its first quarter. The place where they slept was a graveyard, but graveyards were considered safe. When they woke up in the morning, one of the boys saw a skull. In a playful mood, this soldier took a grass stalk and put it into the nose of the skull. To his consternation, the skull started sneezing. He stood up and ran away screaming. The others stopped him and asked what was the matter. He told his story and everybody started laughing on their empty stomachs. That was a good substitute for breakfast.

I cannot guarantee the truth of this story, but it was fun, anyway.

If the stories told above were humorous, the next one was rather sad. We knew from our information sources that our arch enemy Westerling was going to pass a certain area to inspect his troops in Gunung Halu, a nice cool place in the mountains surrounded by tea plantations. At a curve in the road we planted a landmine strong enough to blow up a jeep. One side of the road was a ravine and the other side a slope. I placed five men on the slope to shoot at the approaching jeep if it did not hit the land mine.

At the exact hour the jeep passed, but inside was not Captain Westerling but a lieutenant with two other soldiers. We watched but were unlucky. The jeep did not drive over the planted landmine and passed safely. The boys were so intent on watching the jeep that they forgot to open fire. When they opened fire, the jeep was already out of reach. This unsuccessful attempt made me mad.

The next day a green beret platoon went to the place of ambush. They set fire to all the houses in the area, killed one man and took away some of the villagers' livestock. We were very sad when we heard about this incident. Our mistake had caused suffering to the people. This is the problem with guerrilla warfare. Every time we sensed danger we could not cope with, we left the area. But the people had to stay and bear the brunt of the vengeance of the KST.

The boys decided to take revenge, so we planned an attack on the Dutch barracks in Batujajar. Fortunately it was the dry season and the river that separated us was shallow.

One dark night, the boys crossed the river, surrounded the barracks, and, at about two o'clock in the morning, started shooting blindly in the direction of the barracks; it seemed like all hell had broken loose. The boys shouted while firing their weapons. We could not get into the inner area of the barracks, but the boys managed to wreck a few trucks and jeeps and blew up one water tank. Before leaving, the boys drew the symbol of our battalion, an elephant's head, on the walls, and wrote: "Soegih Arto's elephants are coming back. Beware. Till we meet again." This was our name card.

We withdrew safely and without casualties, because the enemy did not return our fire. This is how we took revenge for the burning of the village.

Achmad Sungkawa

One of my sergeants, Achmad Sungkawa, sent me a letter. He told me about some Islamic troops who called themselves Tentara Islam Indonesia (TII), or the Indonesian Islamic Army. They were also fighting against the Dutch. This army belonged to Darul Islam, a political organization that wanted to establish Indonesia as a Muslim country based on the laws of the Qur'an. Their leader was Kartosuwiryo. His political ideals have already been explained.

Achmad had a platoon under his command, and asked my permission to join the TII, and together with them fight against the Dutch. The courier left before I had the chance to give my answer. Personally I thought it was a good idea. When the Dutch had left Indonesia, and everything was normal, he could return to my unit.

Another reason why I agreed was that at that time the TII were a rebel group fighting the Dutch and not the Republic, so our aims were practically identical. I had not yet given Achmad Sungkawa my official permission, but he acted thinking I would agree. He was very active and caused considerable loss to the Dutch and their allies. Because of his achievements, the rebel leader of Darul Islam promoted him to a regimental commander and also head of the Bandung regency. He was both a successful military and civil leader.

When the war ended and I had regained my command, I gathered my scattered troops, but I missed Achmad Sungkawa. I tried to get some information on his whereabouts and I learned that he was still hiding in the mountains south of Bandung. I waited a few days, but he still did not show up, so I decided to send him a letter asking him to return and report to me immediately.

He sent me letter in which he wrote the following: "Bapak, I have fought side-by-side with the Tentara Islam Indonesia and I think they are on the right path. We must have an Islamic Republic based on the law of the Qur'an. I've decided to stay with them and not to come back to the TNI. But whatever happens, you are still my personal leader and father, only our political ideals differ. Receive my deepest respect and may Allah protect you."

So I lost a platoon and its commander to a rebel organization. But he kept his promise and respected me as his personal father and leader.

Darul Islam, and its army, the TII, became bolder and we had trouble in maintaining law and order. The population lived in a fearful atmosphere and did not have the courage to give information about TII activities and their whereabouts. They said: "If we do not help the Darul Islam/TII we die, because they are ruthless killers. If we do not help the TNI we are beaten. It is better to undergo a beating than be killed."

My battalion became very busy with mopping up operations against the TII. One time I had to ask help from the artillery to soften up an area of jungle before attacking them. When the artillery fire had ceased we rushed to the location, but it was already deserted. We found that the TII had evacuated in haste and we captured rice, goats, and ammunition; there was also a badminton court in the middle of the village. After a careful search we arrested a woman and her son, who had not had the chance to escape with her husband because the son was suffering from a serious illness. We took care of the woman and her child.

All military operations went hand in hand with what we called "territorial operations." In short, "territorial operations" encompassed our intention to gain the people's sympathy and cooperation in fighting the rebels. We provided free medical treatment, we helped repair schools, we helped build roads, etc., etc. With good roads, we could quickly send troops to the various trouble spots. These roads made it possible for us to increase road patrols and pushed the rebels farther and farther away from towns and villages, forcing them to retreat into the mountains and jungles, where food and supplies were scarce.

These territorial operations continue to this day, and are called AMD (Abri Masuk Desa – armed forces who enter the villages). The same activities are carried out with more efficiency, because now the armed forces can use modern equipment. Because of these territorial operations the armed forces are loved by the people.

One day in 1950 I decided to go on patrol with two companies of my battalion, reinforced by a platoon of the mobile police force. We were planning to search the jungles, ravines and villages for rebels and destroy their supplies as well as gauge whether the people were now more willing to help the army. I was on horseback, protected by the police platoon. At around two o'clock in the afternoon I passed a slope surmounted by a banyan tree. When I passed under the banyan tree, all was quiet, but a few minutes afterwards, I heard a commotion.

I turned back to discover soldiers climbing the slope and an unconscious rebel soldier, left behind by his friends, being arrested. I asked the rebel what had happened. Here is his story.

"I was under the banyan tree with a bren-gun and Bapak Achmad Sungkawa was standing near by. We knew that a patrol was going to pass. When an officer on horseback (he meant me) came into sight, I aimed. Suddenly Achmad Sungkawa leapt up, took up his pistol and hit me on the head, saying, 'Don't shoot, that is my leader Bapak Soegih.' I fell on the bren and the bullet magazine fell down the slope. This alerted your soldiers and Sungkawa and his boys fled."

In my heart, I said, thank you Achmad Sungkawa, you saved my life. He saved my life again, two months later, in an almost identical incident when I was driving my jeep to Cianjur. This time there was some shooting, but it stopped very abruptly. In an operation two days later, we captured two rebels and they told almost the same story. Achmad Sungkawa stopped the firing when he recognised me in the jeep.

Eventually Achmad Sungkawa died in an army ambush near Sukabumi.

Big Father Captured

Everybody, including the enemy, knew of my whereabouts, and the name, Big Father, that the people had given me. I was political adviser, spiritual leader, supreme law enforcer; I was everything rolled into one. In some villages I was even considered as a 'wonder doctor,' capable of curing almost anything.

Because of my reputation and high profile security suffered, and my coming and going was easily monitored by the enemy. Another mistake I made at that time was that I received almost anybody, sometimes against the advice of my security officers. I told them, that as a guerrilla leader I should be popular, loved and trusted by the people.

I had two choices; firstly, I could isolate myself and so be safe, or secondly, stay in the open and meet the people and sacrifice security. I chose the latter, which eventually led to my capture.

Early in the morning on the 31st of May 1948, the special police force, BRIMOB, or Mobile Brigade, surrounded my house after capturing my guard. They entered the house armed and ready to shoot and calmly told me to surrender. There were seven of us. There was nothing we could do except surrender. We were ordered to sit together in a corner, while they searched the house. Except my pistol, they found nothing, not one single official sheet of paper or document.

With hands on our heads we were put in a truck. I was very sad, but surprisingly unafraid. What I felt was not fear, but pity for those Indonesian policemen who were working for the Dutch. I could not blame them, not everybody is a patriot.

When we arrived at the Recombas, a kind of governor's office, we were separated. I was kept in that building and my comrades were taken to a nearby police station. My comrades included one of my company commanders, one sergeant major of the medical corps, and four soldiers. I did not know why I was separated from my companions, but I guessed it was because they wanted to prevent us from consulting with each other. I was kept in an office room.

There was a sofa for me to sleep on, toilets nearby, and they gave me a radio to listen to. It was not bad. The meals were good, or at least better than what I was used to. For breakfast I had bread with butter and sugar, things I had not tasted for a long time.

Every day at 10 o'clock an inspector of police began his interrogation. He always opened our interview with plenty of apologies. He asked for my understanding, said he was only doing his job, and had nothing personal against me and other freedom fighters. He respected my status, but he requested for me to cooperate so that the job given to him could be finished easily and quickly.

I asked him what would happen to me when the interrogation was finished. He said that he did not know, but perhaps the government would set me free. It had happened many times before; after a freedom fighter had promised something they were set free, and some even got a job with the government.

I had no contact with my companions and we could not discuss what to say or what not to say. After one whole week of intensive interrogation, I was brought to the MID (Militaire Inlichtingen Dienst), some sort of military intelligence agency. I was kept in an uncomfortable room for two whole days and every day a Dutch sergeant interrogated me. He asked me whether I spoke Dutch, which I answered in the negative. So there were two sergeants, one Dutch and one Indonesian who translated all the questions. This way I gained more time to think, because the questions had to be translated first, as were the answers.

They asked me questions about the position of my units, their weapons, names of the unit commanders, what orders I had given them, and why I had not joined the other troops evacuated to areas controlled by the Republic.

I became very tired after two weeks of interrogation by both the police and the military, but I managed to keep my mind cool and give consistent answers. Several times they tried to trap me, but I managed to avoid falling into it. One day the Dutch sergeant could be very kind, and then he could become very cruel in his questioning; it was a combination of hooks and jabs. Although I was exhausted, he never could knock me down. I thank God, for the strength He gave me and the guidance I felt.

Although at the time I managed to keep my composure, one day I was really shocked when the sergeant showed me what he said to be a captured authentic document.

"This document was captured from a courier on the border between West and Central Java. It contained an order from army general headquarters about your duty to stay behind and create unrest in the new state of Pasundan."

But when I asked him to let me read the document, he refused, saying that there was no need for me to read it because I already knew the contents. I became suspicious and I felt that this was another trap.

When the military intelligence unit decided they could gain no more information from me I was sent back to the police and on the same day taken to Bantjeuj prison, located in the middle of Bandung. The prison is no longer there; today, there is a shopping centre on the site.

❖

My Prison Days

When they took me to prison I was handcuffed to other prisoners, mostly thieves and murderers. They were very mean-looking men, and most of them were still quite young. The oldest in my group of seven was 40 years old.

I was the best dressed among them. When we arrived in Bantjeuj we were ordered to squat on the ground, while the accompanying police officer did the necessary registration. The place where we were told to wait was visible from some of the cells. The people in the cells started shouting "Meat, meat, meat." I did not know what they meant, but soon enough I found out. Meat meant that there were new prisoners coming, who are relatively well clothed. When a new prisoner arrived in a cell the foreman would take away the prisoner's good shirt or any other good thing in exchange for a bad one. The good shirt or pair of trousers was then handed over to the guard and the guard sold them outside, and brought back, in exchange, cigarettes or some other scarce articles, like good soap.

What happened in the cell was no secret to the guards, but they preferred to turn a blind eye and let these things continue. Every cell was headed by a *voorman* (foreman) and this man had near-dictatorial powers. Your fate was in his hands. Usually a notorious gangster or murderer was appointed *voorman* and helped the guards in maintaining law and order.

I was separated from my six men and taken to a community cell. The nearer I came to the cell, the louder was the cry of "meat." Then my fate changed. The foreman of the neighbouring block saw me and ran towards me, shouting, "This is my Bapak. Whoever does him any harm will have to deal with me." Suddenly the call for meat stopped. The same man introduced me and said: "This is Captain Soegih Arto, my boss. So you will all treat him well, because he is a freedom fighter and our leader." He held a hush-hush talk with the foreman of my block, kissed my hands and left for his block. Instantly, I was a VIP. The foreman, Abdul, entered the cell before me. He looked around and saw a sleeping mattress owned by a Chinese man. He said to the Chinese, "Get up, your mattress will be used by Pak Soegih. You can sleep on his palm leaves mat." The Chinese got up from his mattress, gathered his belongings and went to my mat. Here I saw the first demonstration of the power of the *voorman*.

Normally, the cell was designed for 20 persons, but at that time it was occupied by 30 men, including me. It was rather crowded. There was one water tank and the toilet consisted of a hole in the floor, but there was no partition or wall, so everybody did his natural duties for everybody else to see and smell. Otherwise, for the time being I was comfortable, according to prison standards. I had a most favoured position and that was good enough for me. I was allowed to take the first bath in the morning, a real privilege, because the tank was still full. If you were last there was barely enough water to wash your face. Although I was also given first priority in doing my natural duty, that was not always possible, because this depended very much on the situation of my stomach.

In this prison I met a lot of friends from the army and heard many strange stories. A man called Danu was charged with the murder of Achmad, a murder he did not commit. He kept denying the accusation, but he was heavily tortured by the police, sometimes with burning cigarette butts or electrical shocks. He could not bear it any more and he confessed. The police never found the corpse, or perhaps never tried to find it.

About a month later a man was brought in, having been charged with robbery. When he was pushed into my cell, Danu shouted, "That is the man, that is the man!" He was very excited and kept repeating that sentence. I calmed him, and then he told me that the man just brought in was Achmad, the man he was supposed to have murdered. Achmad was silent and kept his head down. Danu explained to the foreman the whole case. The foreman reported this to the boss of the prison. Luckily for Danu, he was set free three days afterwards and left in a happy mood. He took leave from me by kissing both my hands and promised to contact my boys in the jungle.

The most sadistic penalty inflicted in the prison was called 'Avocado Juice,' dealt out to spies or Dutch collaborators. I did not know how the system worked, but every time a man of this category was brought in, the prisoners knew immediately. A short court session was held by the detainees, and the verdict was always the same – 'Avocado Juice.' If you have a weak stomach, do not read the following account.

As I mentioned before, we had a toilet in the cell. 'Avocado Juice' consisted of a mixture of water and human waste, thoroughly stirred. The victim was held lying on his back. Some held his arms, some his legs, so that he could not move at all. Then his mouth was forced open and this avocado juice was poured into it. Not very much, but just enough. He was freed after he had swallowed the stuff. Very cruel indeed, but prison life is cruel. You had to be strong to survive. I could not watch this ordeal. The first time I watched this being performed I vomited.

If the special court decided that the crime committed was not too serious then the accused only got a beating. And then he was told to tell the guards, if they asked (but they never did), that he slipped while going to the toilet.

The guards knew exactly what went on, but never commented. Usually the beaten man was brought to the clinic for treatment. On one occasion an accused told a guard the true reason for his bruises and asked to be taken to the prison boss. The boss came and asked the foreman what had happened. The foreman told the boss that he had slipped on the slippery floor, and the cell inhabitants supported his story. One complaint against 30 hostile witnesses. No chance. He was transferred, but that did not save him. He got another beating, by other cell mates in another cell. The detainees could tolerate murderers, robbers, thieves, rapists and other criminals, but not Dutch collaborators.

In the meantime I was promoted to foreman and I made a pledge to myself to be a good foreman and look after the detainees' well-being to the best of my ability. I hated the dictatorial attitude of the foremen.

Most of the inhabitants were detainees waiting to go to trial. Twice a week, their families were allowed to send food and clothing, because as detainees you did not get a prison uniform. The foreman collected all the food parcels and then distributed them to the rightful owners. My family was far away and they could not send me any food parcels.

I was foreman of block I – a block reserved for intellectuals and prisoners sentenced to death. There were no community cells, everyone got one small cell to himself. It was equipped with one bed and an empty can, in case at night you had trouble with your stomach. One of the cells was once occupied by Bung Karno, Indonesia's first president.

According to tradition, the foreman had the privilege of taking what he wanted from the food parcels, and then hand over the remainder to whom it belonged. I had very sincere intentions in wanting to be a good foreman but this privilege was very attractive, and I decided to continue this lofty tradition. But I never took cigarettes away, and the others were very grateful for that. Of course they did not know that I didn't smoke. Hence I had a very good life.

As foreman I could stay outside my block until six o'clock in the evening. I could go to the library, read books, and could go to other blocks and talk to other detainees.

Slowly I started to behave like the other foremen and became as bad as them. This is a common phenomenon. When you belong to the down-trodden, you hate the guts of the powerful. You promise yourself that when you get the chance and become powerful, you will act differently and be more considerate. But once you gain that position you tend to forget your good intentions and act like those you hated so much. It was the same in my case. Sometimes I think that a man's behaviour depends completely on his position in society.

One day, a beautiful woman was brought in by the police. She was well dressed, tastefully made-up and had a nice hairdo. I asked the police what her crime was. The police told me she was arrested for pick-pocketing. After the usual administrative work was finished she was brought to the women's block. Two or three minutes afterwards I heard shouting and tumult in the women's block. The guards ran to the block and after a while, they came out, laughing heartily. What had happened?

When the lady guard undressed her, "she" proved to be a man, with a well-developed vital organ. The other women prisoners (and I think the lady guard as well) screamed on seeing what they had not seen for a long time. I could not make out whether they screamed from shock or out of sheer delight.

This man-girl was transferred to my block. I spent long hours with him, gaining all kinds of information on how to select victims and pick their pockets. He was not operating alone, they never do. Usually, he said, they operated with three or four friends and each one of them knew exactly what to do. When arrested, they kept their mouth shut and never betrayed their friends. If the arrested pick-pocket had a family, then the group would look after the family until he/she was freed. As a pick-pocket you stayed only three to four months in prison, and then you were free again to restart your activities. I learned a lot from this man: discipline, organization, loyalty, and group solidarity. I came in contact with all kinds of criminals, but what amazed me was that these people were all very disciplined and never caused any trouble. A prison, I think, is a very useful laboratory for psychologists.

I became the uncrowned king of the prison. Everybody knew Captain Soegih Arto. The guards treated me with some respect. One guard became my link with my battalion outside. This guard smuggled all kinds of letters and reports to and from my troops and proved a useful way for me to send orders to them. When I regained my command, I made this guard a corporal in my staff.

Two of my boys worked as distributors in the kitchen. So I had plenty of food from both the kitchen and from the forced contribution from other detainees. One of my boys worked in the office and could read the newspapers so he could keep me up to date with the domestic political situation. One other boy worked in the clinic, so I had no trouble in getting medicine. All in all, I lived like a king.

There were seven young boys in death row, waiting to be executed.

They all belonged to freedom-fighter units. The oldest was 25 years old. All of them were sentenced to death for murder. One murdered a village head for collaborating with the Dutch and causing trouble to the partisans. One had killed five Dutchmen, by cutting their necks with a samurai sword. This was the well-known Brombeek affair, where lots of Dutch men and women were killed.

All these young boys were very proud to be sentenced to death – they did not show any fear and they believed that they would be released soon, because the Republic was going to win. Eventually five of them gained their freedom. Two others were executed - shot by a firing squad of Dutch military police. I remembered the last night of one of these boys, a boy from the island of Ambon. At seven p.m. he was notified that he would be shot the next morning at six a.m. When the prison official asked him whether he wanted to write a final letter to his family he said loud and clear, that he had no family. Then he was asked what he wanted for dinner, and he had his last dinner.

After he had finished his dinner, he called me and asked me to sing his favourite song – *Bengawan Solo* (Bengawan is river). After that he asked all the people on the death row to listen, because Bapak Soegih was going to sing. I could not sing, because there was a lump in my throat, and I started crying. Boy, that was his name, shouted to me not to cry, because he himself did not cry. I started to sing with a choked voice and soon the others joined me. Boy shouted, "Let us sing again, let's have fun, because I am going to die tomorrow." What courage. The next morning at five-thirty the MPs came to collect him. Before he was taken away, he shouted, "Goodbye, my friends. Long live our Republic, merdeka, merdeka." Through a slit in the cell door we all waved our goodbyes. The heroic end of a freedom fighter.

I felt that something was brewing in prison, but I could not put my finger on it. The boys were rather reserved in their attitude – which was very unusual. They were always open and told me everything on their minds. I asked my boys to keep their ears open and report to me as soon as they knew something. After a few days the kitchen boys reported that the detainees were planning a prison break. They were planning to capture the guards, take their pistols, force the arsenal open and then run back into the jungle to continue their guerrilla war.

This was ridiculous, this was mad. They would never succeed. Firstly, the walls are strong and more than three meters high. They could force the main gate open, but then they would find themselves amidst the people, because the location of the prison is right in the middle of Bandung. I had to talk them out of it, by pointing out the odds. I told them that the victory of the Republic was not too far away. But it seemed that the boys had made up their minds and now asked me to lead the prison rebellion, which I refused.

When, after lengthy argument I still refused, one of the boys said, "Perhaps you are getting old and have lost your fighting spirit?"

I replied, "It is not that I have lost my fighting spirit, but basically I am a coward. I never do anything unless there is a 50-50 chance of success. But this is sheer madness, this is suicide. You want to go ahead, please do, but count me out."

"But one of the guards, Pak Samsudin, promised to help us. He knows where the key to the arsenal is kept. He will get the key and give it to us."

"OK, if you have made up your mind, there is nothing I can do, except keep my mouth shut and wish you every success."

"When is this going to take place?"

"On the 17th of August."

While we were talking, this guard, Samsudin, approached us and whispered, "Finish your talk quickly, I will be off soon. I will be on the look out and I will warn you if someone suspicious is coming this way."

I asked who was going to lead this operation?

"I am," said Sanusi, a youth leader of one of the non-government fighting units.

All detainees are allowed one hour walk in the sun in the morning and another hour in the afternoon. On the 17th of August 1949, as the morning walk started, all hell broke loose, the guards were attacked and disarmed. The detainees who were cleaning the offices

133

disconnected the telephones. But something unforeseen happened. A truck carrying five armed policemen and 20 detainees drove through the gate. When they saw what was happening they started shooting and reversed the truck out of the prison and closed the gate. They notified the military and within five minutes military policemen had stormed into the prison, started shooting into the air and the rebellion was finished. The MPs shoved all the detainees back into their cells. After a while two other trucks full of MPs entered the compound and the prison looked like a military barracks.

The rebellion could have been successful, but for the unexpected entry of the police. My block was not involved in the rebellion. In the afternoon the prison official announced the penalties. Two weeks without food parcels or outdoor exercise. This punishment was very hard, especially for the smokers. I suffered too, because I lost my forced food contribution. I had, instead, to eat from the kitchen.

Special Court Trial

One day I was told to be ready at 10 o'clock in the morning, properly dressed, because I had to appear before the Dutch garrison commander, Colonel van Langen. It was a surprise for both myself and everybody else, and we racked our brains as to why the commander should want to see me. The next day a Dutch corporal fetched me. He brought me to the palace of the Wali Negara or state head of Pasundan. A butler ushered me into a waiting-room and served tea and cookies. The tea was served in beautiful cups, unlike the metal cups I was used to in prison. After waiting about 15 minutes, a Dutch officer entered the room and introduced himself as Colonel van Langen. I stood up and we shook hands.

He said: "You are a very lucky man, Captain. The Wali Negara refused to hand you over to Captain Westerling, because you are no longer a military man and were arrested for illegal political activities. You can imagine what would become of you if Westerling had laid his hands on you."

"Thank you, Colonel."

"How is life in prison?"

"Well, I cannot complain. I can read books from the prison library. So I keep myself busy all the time. I have no family, so all in all it is not too bad."

"Well, Captain, you are of course wondering why you were called here. This meeting could change your whole future. Let me explain what we have in mind. We have been gathering information about you, and I must say that everything we've observed is favourable."

I remained silent but attentive.

"We have," continued the Colonel, "a battalion of what we call pre-federal troops in Cimahi. This battalion consists of 100% Indonesian soldiers and officers. It is fully armed and ready for action. The only thing we do not have, yet, is a battalion commander. These troops will be used by the Wali Negara to fight insurgents like Darul Islam. Already some units from the TNI in Tasikmalaya and Ciamis are cooperating with us against Darul Islam. We want you to command that battalion, with the rank of Captain. So what do you think?"

"I am overwhelmed, I do not know what to think. It is a complete surprise. The whole battalion is there, complete with company commanders and platoon commanders. They have been together for quite some time, they know each other. Suddenly a stranger, an outsider, comes in, and takes command. They will also know that I am from the TNI. How will this affect the situation and efficiency of the unit?"

"Don't you worry, Captain, we have thought about all this and we are prepared to take the risk. You just say yes or no."

"Can I have some days to think it over?"

"Of course we know this is a big step, and you need to think it through. Anyway, I give you one week to decide, then we will meet again. Goodbye, Captain, and see you next week."

I stood up, saluted, and shook hands.

Back in prison, I went round and told my friends what had happened and at the same time asked their opinion about what I should do. Their advice and opinions were very much divided, so in the end I had to decide for myself.

I thought to myself, my original instructions had been to fight the puppet regime in Pasundan, and now I was being offered command of an enemy unit. To take this command would be against my instructions, so I must refuse the offer. But how to do this?

I met the Colonel the following week.

I said: "Thank you very much for the trust you have placed in me, but I have my conditions. I am prepared to accept the job, but only if the battalion consists of boys whom I can trust. The Wali Negara should issue a decree asking all members of the 22nd Battalion to report only to me and to no one else. Only then can I do the job, because I can rely on the troops. Otherwise, it will be difficult for me and for the pre-federal unit to accept each other."

I knew that my conditions were not acceptable, but it was a good way of politely refusing without offending the Colonel.

The Colonel was silent for a moment and then said, "I understand what this means. You do not want to take this offer. It is a pity, because this would be good for you. But as I said before, you are free to decide."

He left, and we did not shake hands. I was taken back to prison, and felt happy that I had made the right decision.

A week after I had rejected the Colonel's offer, I received a summons to appear in court on a charge of subversion against the legal government. Well, that was quick, I thought. This charge carried the death sentence.

The Pasundan special court was presided over by just one judge, which was rather unusual. The judge was called Mr. Dirkzwager and the prosecutor Mr. Het Hoen. All seven of us from my unit appeared together. From the prison we were transported by truck and we were chained together. If one wanted to go to the toilet, then we all had to go. I did not mind this treatment, but for our families it was a very sad sight.

I was assigned a lawyer, Mr. Soeranto, to defend my case. He came to see me to map out our defence strategy. I told him that I knew nothing of the law, and that he had full freedom to decide our strategy. His said that we should base our whole defence on me apologizing to the Dutch and that I should express my regret at having fought against them.

Without a second thought I rejected this line of defence, explaining that I had the right to defend my country. I was not the one who was subversive, but the Dutch. We agreed that he would defend and tackle the legal aspects of the case and that I would manage the political side. I wrote my defence in Dutch and was rather proud of my creation. I read it over, and was satisfied.

I thought to myself, perhaps I should become a lawyer when I get out of prison? After 10 sessions and a brilliant defence speech from me, which I felt did not impress the judge very much, the verdict on the 15th of February 1949 was 15 years imprisonment. I laughed when I heard this, though now I don't know why. Perhaps out of fear? The judge asked me why I laughed and I replied that I would be free within 10 months from then. Now it was his turn to laugh. I appealed against the decision.

Later, I was summoned again to appear before the judge of appeal. When I was ushered into a room I saw only one man, sitting behind a table. He stood up and introduced himself as Mr. La Riviera. He asked me to sit down and then we had a long talk.

He was a pleasant and understanding man, this judge. He explained that he understood the aspirations of the Indonesians, especially the young people, the *pemudas*. He said that he asked me to see him because he wanted to know me personally and talk about certain aspects of the freedom struggle. He went so far as to say that if he was a politician he would certainly side with the Indonesians, because he felt that the Indonesians were right; but he did not say that the Dutch were wrong.

The whole conversation was very heartening and refreshing for me, especially coming from a Dutchman and a judge. I knew then that not all Dutch were colonialists, and that there must be enough enlightened Dutch in Holland. We parted as friends and he reduced my sentence to ten years. But I was freed in November 1949, when the Dutch finally recognised Indonesian independence.

In January 1950, Indian Prime Minister Nehru paid an official visit to Indonesia and visited Bandung. A big reception was held in the governor's palace. I was invited as the South Bandung area commander. I was wearing my uniform. As I was walking around, with a drink in my hand, I noticed Mr. Dirkzwager, the judge who had sentenced me to 15 years imprisonment. I approached him, said good evening, but he did not recognised me. I told him my name, and that I was sentenced by him for subversive activities. Slowly the court session dawned on him, and to my surprise he became very pale. He did not answer my greeting, but left abruptly.

Later, I heard that he asked to be transferred to Holland straight after our meeting. I did not blame him, because at that time the kidnapping and disappearance of Dutch officials was a regular occurrence. Actually there was no need for him to be afraid, because I am a very peaceful and law abiding man.

Medan, Here I Come

In 1952 I wore two caps. One cap as garrison commander of Bandung, and the other cap as commander of the 11th Infantry Regiment, located around Bandung. It was a very challenging job, because Bandung was the capital of West Java and also the location of the Siliwangi divisional headquarters.

In 1954 I was relieved from those two jobs, and became deputy commandant of the Army Staff and Command College. I enjoyed my assignment as deputy commandant, because I came in contact with many other officers from all over Indonesia. I was also teaching military history, a subject I like very much. Life here was very regular – no emergencies, no surprises. Everything ran like clockwork. I made a habit of starting classes with one joke from me followed by one from the students, to ensure a relaxed atmosphere.

Then one day a cable arrived from army headquarters saying that I had to prepare myself for a new assignment, as commander of the 2nd Infantry Regiment in northern Sumatra. I was pleasantly surprised, because this would be my first posting outside of western Java since I had enlisted in PETA in 1943. I was a very happy man, and told my family that we were going to move to Pematang Siantar in northern Sumatra.

The official written order came two weeks after the cable, but I still had to wait for my successor, and the marching order. I waited and waited, nothing happened, and in the meantime I had already handed over all responsibilities to my successor. After a month an officer from army headquarters visited me to explain the delay. He told me that the military area commander, Colonel M. Simbolon, objected to my appointment as commander of the 2nd Regiment. He told me to be patient, and that the army chief was negotiating a solution. I was perplexed, I could not imagine why a colonel should disobey the order of the army chief of staff, unless he was planning to rebel. Even more puzzling was the fact that the chief was negotiating a solution, when in fact the power was supposedly all his.

I am a simple soldier. To me, all orders from a superior officer must be executed. If there was any doubt then there should be consultation first, but once it became an official order the subordinate has no choice but to follow those orders.

Simbolon was smuggling rubber through Teluk Nibung. Was this the reason for his objection, the fear that his illegal activities would be exposed when a stranger came into the region? These were baseless fears, because the smuggling was already known by the central government. Was Simbolon planning something else that a new and powerful commander might upset? I did not know what went on at headquarters, but after patiently waiting I was told that my assignment had been changed and that I would take command of the Medan garrison in northern Sumatra instead. I took up this new assignment as ordered.

I flew to Medan, my family later following by boat. When I arrived, my ADC showed me to my official residence. I was surprised, because the furniture was brand new, my car was new, and in the kitchen was a refrigerator. I had never had a refrigerator before.

My predecessor was Major J. Samosir. I took over from him and he was assigned as the new commander of the 3rd Infantry Regiment. I reported officially to Colonel Simbolon and he apologised for the change and assured me that there was no need for me to be suspicious. The only reason for the change was that I was a senior officer and more suited for the job as garrison commander of Medan, the capital city of northern Sumatra. I must confess that Simbolon was a very nice man, both charming and polite. I liked him instantly. I made my courtesy calls to the governor and the mayor and everything seemed all right.

From the very beginning I felt isolated. I had eyes and ears, but was not allowed to see what was going on around me. I started to approach my fellow officers from Java, and this proved to be a very fortunate move that helped me through the turmoil I was later to endure. The commander of the military police was Javanese, as was the commander of the artillery units, the cavalry units, the engineers, and the medical division. The commander of the police was also Javanese.

Defining ourselves by our locality is wrong, I know. The right thing to say is that they were all Indonesians and officers of the army, with the same loyalties. But in truth this was not so. Ethnic feelings were still very strong, in and outside of the army.

In Sumatra, the main ethnic groups are the Melayu people and the Batak people. These were sub-divided into smaller groups, each with their own loyalties and traditions. There were also some Javanese. These Javanese were brought to Sumatra by the Dutch to work in the plantations and had lived there ever since. This was quite a large and compact group. Last but not least, there were the Chinese.

I was the only Javanese troop commander. Many senior officers in this territory knew me, because they had followed the staff courses at the staff college where I was the deputy commandant. This previous position gave me a certain extra authority, on top of the authority I had as garrison commander.

In the first few months life was very enjoyable. My family liked Medan very much. We had a large, well furnished residence. We had a new car. We had everything we could ever wish for. For no particular reason we Javanese often met socially as a group. We played volleyball together, we organised picnics, we arranged dinners. At all these functions I was the senior man, recognised and accepted by all the "expatriates."

I was excluded when the local officers came together and made their pledge on the 4th of December. Was it accidental that of the participants in the pledge, no officer from Java was present? If this was wholly an army affair, why were there no Javanese officers included, though these officers were stationed in northern Sumatra? And yet there were people who claimed that this was not an anti Javanese movement.

My simple military mind could not digest this kind of situation. If you choose to be a military man, then you have to go all out and

141

obey your superiors, because that is where the strength of a military organization lies. It must also be remembered that in Indonesia, the armed forces are a social and political force by law and actively participate in the political life of the country.

Simbolon Takes a Big Step and Slips

On the 22nd of December, Colonel Simbolon broadcast through Medan's radio that he had severed relations with the central government and that he was establishing the Dewan Gajah – a military government responsible for law and order in northern Sumatra. Djamin Gintings, Simbolon's chief of staff, was appointed as military governor.

I was dumbfounded by this action. My first reaction was annoyance with myself for not anticipating this. How could I be so blind? But what could I have done, if I'd known in advance? I could not warn the central government, because all means of communication were controlled by the Sumatrans. I was called to the headquarters of the new "government" and told that I was responsible for law and order in Medan. The situation was tense. I telephoned my Javanese friends, but they knew as little as I did, and warned me that there might be some danger for non-local officers.

On Christmas Eve I went with my wife to visit an old friend from Bandung. We talked about the situation while listening to the radio. And then I heard President Soekarno broadcasting that what had happened in northern Sumatra was a rebellion, and that Colonel Simbolon was fired as commander as of that very moment. Colonel Djamin Gintings, the chief of staff, was ordered by the President to take over, but if unable to do so, then Colonel Wahab Macmour, commander of the 2nd Infantry Regiment in Pematang Siantar, should do the job. I was very happy to hear this broadcast, but did not know what would happen. After a while, my wife and I left for home.

As I neared my residence I saw several cars parked in front. I became suspicious, but I saw that the guards were still there with their rifles. I decided to take a gamble and entered my house. In the sitting room, I saw the cavalry commander and the artillery commander with two other officers, all sitting down, apparently waiting for me. They stood up, saluted me, and then I joined them. Captain Cuk Soewondo came directly to the point, and pointing to Lieutenant Soeharto, said that Lt. Soeharto would explain the purpose of their unannounced visit.

"Colonel, we heard the broadcast of the President ordering Djamin Gintings to take control, by force if necessary. But we believe that that is impossible because Djamin Gintings belongs to the rebels. We think that you, as the most senior Javanese officer, should take the initiative and arrest Simbolon."

I answered, that it was not that easy, because Simbolon was backed by the battalion of Sinta Pohan. Blood would certainly flow. I tried to win time to think of a solution. But the officers were firm in their decision. OK, I said, but let me see your preparations. So I changed into my uniform and together we went to the cavalry barracks on the outskirts of Medan. When I entered the barracks, I saw all the soldiers fully armed, with tanks and trucks ready. We entered the office of the cavalry commander and sat down. When I took my seat, two sergeants with sub-machine-guns took their position behind me. I broke into a cold sweat and I became very nervous.

We talked and argued some more, and Lt. Soeharto became impatient. He threatened, "Colonel, either you lead this operation, or you will not leave this barracks alive. This is something very serious. The President, our commander in chief, has given the order."

Suddenly something flashed through my mind, information gained that morning, to which I had not paid any attention.

"I heard this morning that the chief of staff and his whole gang of Karo Bataks were preparing to overthrow Simbolon, even before there were any orders from the President. We should coordinate our operation with his, otherwise we will fight each other thinking that we were in opposite camps, while in reality we have the same objective."

The cavalry officers saw the logic of what I said, accepted my reasons and asked what we should do. I told them that we were going to Major Sitepu's house to ask him point blank what his plans were. We went in two jeeps to the chief of staff's house, knocked on the door and after waiting quite a long time the door was opened by a pale and trembling Major Sitepu, the chief of staff. He thought that we had come to arrest him for conspiring against Simbolon.

After a long and serious talk, he confessed that he had prepared a coup against Simbolon to be executed on the 26th of December, using two infantry battalions from Binjei and Berastagi. He agreed to hand over command of the coup to me, but he said that the date could not be changed. I accepted his reasoning, because the understanding we reached at his house was at one o'clock in the morning, and so too late to change his previous plans.

The arrest of Colonel Simbolon would be my responsibility, supported by one platoon. I asked everybody present to be very, very careful and guard this secret. I understood that everybody was invited to Colonel Simbolon's Christmas dinner, so I told them to be present so as not to arouse any suspicions. Please act normally, I added. I told Captain Cuk from the cavalry and Major Hanafi from the artillery to be ready for action the next night at 00.00 hours, and not to act before I give the order.

I appointed Major Ulung Sitepu as my second in command. Before leaving, the Major told me that all his troops would wear white ribbons on their shoulder and all troops without white ribbons should be considered the enemy. He told me that the troops had orders to shoot on sight. He said there was no time to change the identification, and he asked me to order all the new troops to wear white ribbons as well. At two-thirty a.m. we left. I prayed God to bless our endeavours.

At the commander's house a nice dinner had been prepared by Mrs. Simbolon on Christmas Eve. This included dog meat broth, a favourite dish of the Batak people. I saw almost all the important officers present, included the conspirators. On the outside they all looked calm and composed, but I knew that inside, their hearts were beating like never before.

The food was good, but it did not taste good to most of us. There were so many things on our minds. What would happen if our secret was discovered and we were suddenly arrested? I did not dare to think of that possibility. I kept looking outside, to check for suspicious actions from the guards. But nothing happened.

At round 10 p.m. Simbolon's ADC approached Simbolon and whispered in his ear. I saw it, but I could not hear what was said. My stomach turned, and I felt I wanted to go to the toilet. Then I heard the telephone ring, and again the mysterious whispering. Simbolon left us to receive the call. The atmosphere became hot and humid. I started sweating. Then Simbolon came out and said that several trucks full of soldiers from the 2nd Infantry Regiment were moving towards Medan, intention unknown. Simbolon asked us to leave and to go to our respective offices. To me he said, "Colonel, I do not know what is going on, or what is about to happen, but you are responsible for the safety of Medan, so act accordingly. Battalion Sinta Pohan is in town and available. You can use them if you think it necessary. Do what you think is right."

I thought I detected some nervousness in his voice, which calmed me down because it meant our secret was still safe.

I went home, changed into my uniform and waited for the development of our plan. At exactly 00.00 hrs, all troops would move. One battalion from Binjei would enter Medan from the west, and one battalion would enter the town from the south. Everybody knew their duty. I telephoned a secret number, and they reported that the western battalion was already in position on the outskirts of Medan. I was only waiting for the report that the southern battalion was ready. A few more minutes and it would be 00.00 hrs, but still no report from the southern battalion. It became 01.00 hrs and still no news. I told my officers that we would move at 01.30 hrs, with or without the southern battalion.

A few minutes before this time, the southern battalion reported for duty. They were all clad in their ceremonial uniforms, fully armed, with their helmets on. The commander explained that they had just finished attending Christmas celebrations in their church. They'd had no time to change.

I gave the GO order, and I went with a platoon to Simbolon's residence. It was dark and empty. Simbolon guessed at the last moment what was going to happen and fled to the barracks of Sinta Pohan. All commanders gathered around me to decide the next step. It was a very difficult time for me. I could not order an attack on the barracks, because the family of the soldiers also stayed there. I could not risk the lives of innocent women and children just to capture one man. I told everybody to wait until the next morning, but keep an eye on the barracks. Everybody went home, to come back again at 10 a.m. the next morning in my office.

I do not know how it happened, but when we were discussing the next step in my office, a report came in that Simbolon, guarded by about one company, had left the barracks for an unknown destination. We had achieved part of our target. Simbolon was out and now Colonel Djamin Gintings should take over. According to Major Munthe's story, Gintings refused to take command because he was not convinced that we had beaten Simbolon. At gun point he was brought to the radio station and forced to read a prepared statement. Now he was officially the territorial commander.

The true story behind these events can now be told. Major Ulung Sitepu and his gang of Karo Bataks were Communist sympathisers, as was the commander of the western battalion. He acted against Simbolon because Simbolon was anti-Communist and a Toba Batak, while Sitepu was a Karo Batak and a Communist sympathiser. They had strong political and ethnic differences.

Sitepu was not motivated by loyalty to the central government. Later, Major Ulung Sitepu was involved in the 1965 Communist coup and sentenced to death.

Simbolon's escape was a blessing in disguise for me. Originally, Major Ulung Sitepu planned to ask me, being the most senior officer, to escort the captured Simbolon to Jakarta. After arriving in Jakarta, they planned to send a cable asking army headquarters to keep me in Jakarta, and Ulung Sitepu would take over. With me removed, all important positions would be filled by Karo Bataks, and hence Sitepu would be in control. A neat scenario, but God decided otherwise.

Revolutions in Sumatra

Army rebellion was a rare phenomena in Java, where we had the biggest divisions, such as the Siliwangi, Diponegoro, and Brawidjaya. But that was not the case on the other islands, which is to be regretted.

The situation in northern Sumatra was relatively calm and stable after Djamin Gintings took over as territorial commander. I enjoyed being in Medan and occupying an important position. During the Lebaran festivals, my house was like a busy shopping centre. Gifts arrived from everywhere, especially from the Chinese community. I had to convert one bedroom into a temporary storeroom. They sent soft drinks, biscuits, sugar, coffee, tinned meat and sardines, fruits, shirts and what not. This was the first time in my life I had been given so many gifts. Partly, this was because I was the only high-ranking Muslim officer in Medan.

This was the nice part of being in Medan. Unfortunately, there was an unpleasant side. One night in August 1958, three NCOs came to see me, on what they claimed to be very urgent business. There was a sergeant-major from my command and two other NCOs who I did not know. They told me that they were representing all the members of the NCOs association. They claimed that the situation had become unbearable because of the actions of the officers from Djamin Ginting's command.

The only remedy, they said, was to get rid of Djamin Gintings and make me territorial commander. I refused immediately, telling them that in the army we have an organized hierarchy and a clear line of command. A territorial commander is not like a village head, who becomes chief after an election victory. We argued a little more, but I was adamant. They left disappointed.

The next morning, while I was having breakfast, I heard a radio broadcast saying that the NCOs proclaimed me as territorial commander, replacing Djamin Gintings. I telephoned my office, but there was nobody there. I contacted territorial headquarters and asked to speak to Djamin Gintings. A voice answered that some NCOs had ransacked the office, arrested some officers, and that

147

Djamin Gintings had left in a hurry for the hills, his native place. I went to my office, but my chief of staff was absent. After an hour I heard another broadcast saying that Djamin Gintings was still commander. Then another counter broadcast, which was again countered, then another counter broadcast. The radio station appeared to change hands several times. It was a very confusing situation.

The Governor telephoned me and asked who the real commander was. I told him, legally Djamin Ginting was still the commander, but de facto I am the commander. Whatever the legal situation, I promised him that I would take care of security. I called all troop commanders and ordered them to maintain the security of the town. The cavalry units, artillery units and military police were all on my side. However, Djamin Gintings surrounded Medan with his battalions.

Communication with the central government was open and under my control. I sent a complete report to Jakarta of what was happening and what measures I had taken to maintain law and order. The army chief told me not to take any drastic steps and wait for his arrival in Medan. In the meantime Jakarta sent planes to Medan, under the command of Captain Rusmin Nuryadin, plus a company of red berets under the command of Captain Benny Moerdani. With these reinforcements in town I could sleep well, knowing that nothing was likely to happen. Tanks were blocking and controlling all roads into Medan, and our artillery were in position. Military police were patrolling the town and the atmosphere was like a garrison under siege, which it was.

I was mystified as to why the territorial commander, Colonel Gintings, had left, merely because of the radio broadcast from the dissident NCOs. He was legally the commander and had all the authority to act and to smooth out this minor ripple. Compare this to the situation faced by General Soeharto in 1965: this was far more serious and yet he acted, despite there being so many unknown factors at that time. What would have happened to Indonesia if General Soeharto had left Jakarta and tried to handle the situation from outside town?

When the chief, General Nasution, came to Medan, he immediately called me and asked for a full report. I told him what had happened. General Nasution outlined his plan. Having known me for quite some time he did not want to blame me, because he knew I was a very disciplined officer. For the sake of prestige and in the light of the military situation outside Java, he thought it not wise to blame Colonel Gintings. So he planned to relieve both me and Djamin Gintings from our respective positions. This avoided putting the blame on anyone in particular. But being the junior officer, I had to be dismissed first. He asked my opinion, and I answered that as a subordinate I would follow all orders, but please do not give the impression that I am ambitious. He understood.

The next morning, General Nasution ordered me to go and ask Djamin Gintings to come down and meet him at the governor's mansion. General Nasution told me to go alone and not to bring any escort. He had told Djamin Ginting that I was coming with my ADC. The road to his place in the hills was swarming with soldiers loyal to him, and I became very frightened. One provocation or one trigger-happy soldier and Colonel Soegih Arto would become history.

Djamin Gintings came down to Medan escorted by about two companies. It was like a triumphant entry of a winning general into a captured town. I have never seen such a heavily escorted official before, not even the President of the Republic. Djamin Gintings acted very coolly when I came to escort him back to Medan. When we entered the town, I gave a sigh of relief and I thought it was his turn to became pale and nervous. He saw the tanks, artillery units and the combat-ready red berets along the streets.

Later, I heard from our communication centre that earlier on General Nasution had asked Djamin Ginting to come down to Medan for talks. Djamin refused and instead asked Nasution to come up and meet him in his mountain hideaway. What a situation. After a lengthy tripartite meeting between General Nasution, Colonel Djamin Gintings and myself, everything was settled, and Medan became peaceful once more.

The peace was disturbed once again on the 16th of March 1958, when operation *Sabang Merauke* under Major Boyke Nainggolan was launched. This operation was a demonstration of support for the formation of the Revolutionary Government of the Republic or PRRI on the 15th of February 1958, in western Sumatra.

Major Boyke began by firing mortars at the airstrip in Medan. At the first sign of trouble, Djamin Gintings left the city again for his mountain hideaway. This gave rise to some doubts. Did he support the rebellion, or was there another reason for leaving town? This was the second time he had left his command in a hurry.

I moved my family to a friend's house, because my residence was very close to the airport, the target of the rebels, and our son had just been born, on the 8th of February 1958.

The next morning I was arrested by Boyke and brought to a camp where to my surprise I saw many "expatriate" officers from Java. I saw the police chief, the commander of the engineers, plus other Javanese officers and civilians who were kept there only because they happened to be Javanese or Sundanese. We discussed why Djamin Gintings had left town instead of acting against the rebels. The rebellion was supported by only one battalion under Major Henry Siregar. There were enough troops for the rebellion to be easily dealt with. His flight remained a puzzle.

Our prisoners camp was close to the rebels headquarters, so we could see and hear lots of activity. At around midnight we saw a car belonging to the American consulate in front of the rebel's headquarters. After a few minutes we saw a white man go to his car and drive away. There followed a big commotion and we saw soldiers running here and there. All vehicles were packed and the engines started. After about half an hour everybody had left, and the place became as quiet as a graveyard. We looked at each other, but nobody had an answer. We could not sleep, the uncertainty was worse than anything.

At five o'clock in the morning we walked outside the compound. No sentries, no vehicles, no soldiers to be seen. We walked further away and still nothing happened. When daylight came we went around town in an abandoned jeep and found the town deserted.

But still we did not dare to go too far away. At 10 o'clock we saw paratroopers dropped in the harbour area and about an hour later, they entered the town. People cheered and we joined in. I met General Djatikusumo, the deputy chief for Sumatra, and he explained that the town had been liberated. The red berets were just passing through to chase the fleeing rebels.

I immediately went home to see my family. Thank God, they were all right but a little bit frightened. My wife had our new-born baby in her arms, and there and then I gave him his name, which is Djayeng Pristiawan Andalaswanto, which means "victorious in the Sumatran affair" (Djayeng = victorious, Pristiawan = affair, Andalaswanto = Sumatra). Before that we just called him Ucok, which means boy.

Why had the rebels left town so suddenly? Here was the story. Headquarters that night sent an uncoded telegram to General Djatikusumo saying that the red berets would be dropped the next morning and another company would be flown in afterwards.

This message was heard by the American consulate, and a member of the consulate went to Boyke to convey this message. That was the reason for the hasty flight from Medan. General Nasution said that the uncoded telegram was sent on purpose, so the rebels could receive it too, with the hope that this would frighten them into evacuating Medan. The tactics proved successful.

Djamin Gintings returned once he was sure that the town was safe.

Another thriller will conclude my Medan episode. The Batak officers of Djamin Gintings thought that I had masterminded the NCOs revolt in order to become territorial commander. A baseless allegation. However, they wanted to take revenge.

One night, a Javanese platoon commander from the garrison guard came to see me and reported that troops under the command of Lieutenant Sempa Sitepu were preparing to kidnap me on the 22nd of December, my birthday. The soldiers were talking in their own dialect, but this platoon commander could understand what was said, because he had spent much time in this region. They planned to kidnap me on my way to the office. I usually left home at about seven-thirty in the morning.

I told him that I could not believe this would happen, but to be on the safe side I asked him to take measures. After he'd left, I phoned the military police commander and the artillery commander and told them what I'd heard. After that I told the soldiers guarding my house to be extra careful. They were all Javanese.

When I woke up the next morning at five o'clock members of the military police were patrolling the streets leading to my house. A telephone call from the artillery commander informed me that one company was on full alert. At seven o'clock the commanders of the various units were gathering in my house, in order to see what was going to happen. But the kidnappers never arrived, because all the tires had been deflated and the batteries of their vehicles removed by members of a Javanese platoon staying in the same barracks.

The Javanese military police commander, Major Soekardi, took one further step; he gathered Javanese labourers from the estates and by the afternoon Medan was surrounded by about 1,000 Javanese coolies. The territorial chief of staff, Colonel Hasan Kasim, was surprised when he saw this huge gathering of armed coolies. He stopped and asked the leader what was happening. They answered that platoons of a certain ethnic group were planning to kidnap the garrison commander. They said that if these people could behave in this anti-Indonesian manner, then they had the same right to do so.

Colonel Hasan Kasim went to his office and ordered all his company commanders to come and see him. They told him the same story. The Colonel decided that a very sensitive issue was becoming steadily more dangerous. He ordered the commanders to restore peace.

During the Christmas celebrations, the commander asked everybody to be mature and act like real Indonesians.

Peace on earth, silent night.

Let's Go Abroad

And your Lord says: call on me
I will answer your prayer. But those
who are too arrogant to serve me, will
surely find themselves in hell in humiliation.

Qur'an, Surah **XXXX** (Al Mukmin), verse 60.

Army life is very exciting, especially in wartime. Since we were fighting a guerrilla war and there were no fixed front lines, the enemy did not know what to expect. This was usually the situation. We were not fighting a conventional war, but instead tried to harass an enemy who was superior in experience and equipment. Essentially, we wanted to give them sleepless nights.

But when the war was over and the situation became more or less peaceful, most of the excitement disappeared. Everything became regular and routine, and worst of all, boring. Once in a while there was some action – going after rebels or conducting mopping-up operations. Sometimes we became frustrated because we could not locate the enemy and I realised, ironically, that we were going through the same difficult and frustrating situation of our previous enemies. The shoe was now on the other foot.

I began to notice in movies the lives led by diplomats. Always meticulously dressed, attending cocktails, organizing dinners, holding talks with ministers or heads of state, chewing cigars, looking very serious. It was so different from what I was used to. Field uniforms with helmets, instead of dinner jackets or tuxedos; riding in open jeeps, with a jungle rifle in your hand, instead of riding in a Mercedes and holding hands with a beautiful spy, like James Bond; shouting commands, instead of hush hush conversations, with your heads together, so nobody could hear. Oh what a life that must be.

Then I looked into a mirror and asked myself – could you become a good diplomat? You are a colonel in the army, you are used to barking commands and getting mad when your soldiers do not do their jobs properly. You're used to patrolling valleys and jungles and shooting at enemies. A diplomat should talk nicely and politely, maintain an icy face in front of opponents, and laugh when he does not feel like laughing. Could I do that? I said to myself, I could become a good diplomat, because I was used to lying much of the time and besides, I considered myself a good actor. I could smile or laugh or cough whenever the situation demanded it. I was convinced that I was a good candidate for a diplomat.

I prayed to ALLAH, the most gracious and the most merciful, with my whole being, and asked HIM to give me the chance of becoming a diplomat. One day my prayers were answered.

Prayer is the heart of religion and faith.
But how shall we pray. What words shall
convey the yearnings of our miserable ignorant
hearts to the Knower of all.
We offer HIM worship and ask for HIS guidance.
And we know the straight from the crooked path
by the light of HIS grace that illumines the righteous.

Qur'an, Introduction to Surah I (Fatihah).

One day in 1959 a cable arrived from army headquarters, ordering me to go to Jakarta and report to the chief of intelligence. I was stationed in Bandung, as chief of staff of the army's training command.

I went to Jakarta and reported to Colonel Imam Sukarto and there I heard the good news. I was selected to follow a military attache's course in Jakarta. Altogether 25 officers were selected. The course would last three months. After that, whether or not you passed, you would be assigned a military attache post somewhere.

154

At last my dream had come true. Thank you, oh God.

I was very serious and studied very hard. I came second in my class. Students who came first and second on the course had the privilege of choosing their country of assignment. Colonel Samosir, who had come first, chose Yugoslavia. I preferred Great Britain. The others would have their posts decided by headquarters.

I told my family the good news and we made serious preparations, especially in learning English. Our knowledge of English was very limited, but that did not dampen our spirits. I then waited for the order to leave Indonesia for our new destination.

While waiting I received a cable, saying that I was promoted to the rank of full colonel. That caused quite an embarrassing situation. At the Army Training Command we had a commandant, a deputy and a chief of staff. All had the rank of lieutenant-colonel. This now meant that I, as chief of staff, outranked both my superiors, and they could no longer give me orders. It puzzled me, but as a good soldier I did not protest. I decided not to go to the office any more, to spare them the embarrassment.

Then another cable arrived. Now I was confused. Had I been promoted to brigadier-general, after only two weeks of being a colonel? Impossible. So with trembling hands, I opened the cable and I read that I had to report to army chief General Nasution, as soon as possible. Why? Was my assignment going to be cancelled? Oh God, that would be terrible. God, do not let this happen to me. I had a sleepless night. I did not tell my family about this cable. The next day I went to Jakarta by car and fortunately slept all the way. I checked in at a hotel, took a bath and was ready to face anything. My fate was in the hands of God.

At about one o'clock I was received by General Nasution. I tried to read his face but could not detect anything alarming. He congratulated me for passing the exam with flying colours and asked me to sit down. He talked about the time when I attended the preparation course for the Dutch General Staff College and passed as number one. I tried to smile, but where was all these leading to? I became more nervous.

"You know, of course, Colonel S. Parman, chief of the Military

Police. He was in the same class with you."

"Yes, General, I know him." Why this question?

Nasution continued. "Although both of you have the same rank, he is more senior than you are, because of his position. His wife is ill and a few days ago, he came to see me and asked whether he could be posted to London, so that his wife could gain proper medical treatment. I told him that London was already promised to Colonel Soegih Arto, but if you were prepared to change to another country, I would gladly oblige. But first I would have to consult Colonel Soegih Arto. What do you think, Colonel?"

I was silent for a few moments and then said, "It is better that you decide, General. I wanted this post very much and my whole family was very happy, anticipating this posting to London. However, I will accept whatever decision you make."

The end result was that I would be posted to Bangkok and Colonel Parman was going to take my place in London. Later I was relieved that I had made this sacrifice, because in 1965 General Parman, at that time the army chief of intelligence, was brutally murdered by the Communists after being tortured. Sakirman, his elder brother, a hardline Communist, knew that General Parman was on the list to be murdered, but he did not do anything to save his younger brother.

I told my family of the change, and they all accepted it and were happy that we were helping a friend. Now we thought of Thailand. Thailand was not exactly strange to us, because in Bandung there was a villa owned by the King of Siam.

And then another cable came. What was it this time? I opened the cable slowly and I read that I had to go again to Jakarta and meet the army chief of staff. What a strange situation, when would all these puzzles end? But then I told myself that I was a soldier and surprises were common. Again I went to Jakarta and reported to Nasution.

He said: "There will be a cabinet reshuffle very soon and the President wants to appoint General Djatikusumo as Junior Minister of Communications. He is now consul-general in Singapore. General Djati has met the President and he proposes that you take his place in Singapore as consul-general. The President agrees and the Foreign Minister has no objections. So, you are going to Singapore as consul-general instead of military attache in Bangkok."

I could not believe my ears, instead of a staff member, I was now going to be head of the mission in Singapore, a city known to all Indonesians. My heart leapt with joy. Why did General Djatikusumo select me as his successor? When General Djatikusumo was commandant of the Army Staff and Command College I was his deputy and we got along great. This must be the reason for selecting me.

When I got home, my wife asked me where we were going this time. She said that in the space of a month we had travelled from Jakarta to London and on to Bangkok.

I answered that I had changed my mind and did not want to become a military attache any more. My wife said: "So now you are going to get an assignment in Indonesia. Well, if that is the case, what can I do. I had hoped that we could get a foreign assignment for a change, and widen our horizons." She sighed with resignation. I enjoyed teasing my wife.

"I, too, wished I could go abroad with a job like head of mission. A small country would do as a start. A country not too far away from home, like Singapore for instance."

"Yah, that would be nice, that would be a perfect place. Close to Indonesia, and a big shopping and trading centre. But let us stop dreaming. What will your next assignment be. Or perhaps you do not know yet?" my wife asked.

"I know what will come next. Since you like Singapore so much I am going to Singapore as consul-general, replacing Djatikusumo."

"Is what you say true, or am I dreaming? Are you teasing me?"

"No, it is real, and we are going very soon, too."

My Days in Singapore

After I was sure that there would be no more changes, I sold my furniture and all the other things I no longer needed. I knew that we

Top: Myself (second from left) and the Indonesian military attache, Soegeng Djarot (on my right), with Thai officials in Bangkok.

Below: Meeting Yusof Ishak, Singapore's Yang di-Petuan Negara (head of state), on the 17th of August, Indonesian national day, 1963.

were going to live in a fully furnished residence. At last the day of departure arrived, and I went to the airport with a family of eight children. This must be the biggest diplomatic family in the history of the Indonesian foreign service. Apart from myself, this was my family's very first trip abroad and their very first flight.

When we arrived at Singapore's Paya Lebar airport, the secretary to the prime minister and members of the consulate general were there to meet us. Singapore was not yet independent, but had some limited autonomy.

We left the airport in the official car, with the red and white flag of Indonesia flying. I can't remember exactly how I felt that morning, but I do remember that I adjusted several times the way of sitting and had trouble deciding what kind of face I should show to the world – serious, content, friendly or what?

Our official residence at 33 Patterson Road was an old colonial building, big and comfortable, with a large garden and a tennis court. The team of household help were all there to greet the new master. There were two gardeners, two drivers, a cook, a dobi, and three men to take care of the house.

I acted as if all these things were normal and that I was used to all these comforts. In reality, I'd had in Indonesia only one household help, who did almost everything from cooking, making up the rooms and washing the clothes, plus one driver from the office. From now on, life was going to run to a strict schedule. Breakfast on time, lunch on time, dinner the same. I was used to having dinner in my shorts and singlet, but from now on this was going to be a fully dressed affair. I wondered if I would get used to it or not. However, after about two months life became normal again. Breakfast, lunch and dinner were taken according to our own routine. The household help soon got used to my more irregular schedule and relaxed way of living.

I did my round of courtesy calls – to the governor, the prime minister, some other ministers, members of the consular corps, and local VIPs. Not to mention the calls and visits to all important shops and restaurants. The children went to English schools and after some time they adjusted themselves beautifully.

One habit I did not change was not smoking or drinking. We were given tax-free liquor and tax-free cigarettes, and yet these privileges did not make me change my habits.

Everyday I went to the office, fully dressed in tie and jacket, and was driven in an official car with the Indonesian flag flying. When I arrived, an office boy ran to the car and held the door open for me. I had a spacious office, with a big table, two telephones, and a small refrigerator full of soft drinks. As soon as I entered my office, my private secretary was ready to receive orders. What a life. I was only a consul-general and yet I lived like a king. A small king perhaps, but still a king.

The Singapore mission had the biggest staff in the world. I had more than 100 people, mostly in the trade and shipping department. Slowly but surely I mastered the intricate procedures of a diplomat's life. I attended national day celebrations, dinners, cocktails, and I organized my own cocktail and dinner parties. At all these events I kept my eyes and ears open, and heard and saw many useful things. As long as you had normal brains and common sense, life as a diplomat was not too difficult. I became very friendly with the three most important elements of life in Singapore: the mixed population, the government, and the British armed forces.

I and my staff regularly visited Malay communities and in an indirect way reminded them not to forget their origins. During those visits I usually talked about our state philosophy, *Pancasila*, and about the freedom struggle. One day the prime minister, Lee Kuan Yew, asked me to visit him. At our meeting he asked me to limit my talks during visits to Singapore's Malay population. I told the Prime Minister that I always talked about the importance of becoming good Singapore citizens.

"That is just the problem," said Lee Kuan Yew. "If they become good citizens, then it is because you advised them to do so. That means that actually they are loyal to you and through you to Indonesia. And if they become disloyal to Singapore, then it means that they are loyal to Indonesia. Either way, we loose. I hope you can accept that." Lee Kuan Yew had the sharp mind of a lawyer and could see things I did not. He explained that he was not going to curtail my visits, but he requested I keep in mind what he had said.

Every year, on the 18th of August, we organized a garden bazaar or open fair, held in the big garden of the official residence. This was to celebrate Indonesian National Day, which falls on the 17th of August. Everything was organized by the Malay community. We had food stalls selling Indonesian specialities, like *soto, gado-gado, sate, lontong,* etc., etc. We had tents erected where Indonesian traditional music and dances were performed, such as dances from Java, Sumatra, Bali, and Sulawesi. Usually we also set up a stall selling Indonesian books and magazines. Many people came to visit our bazaar, because it was open to everybody. Even Europeans came to taste real Indonesian delicacies, which were different from those they usually found in restaurants.

All the Malays, especially those of Indonesian origin, looked forward to our yearly bazaar. It was a good opportunity for them to meet each other, or for the young people to look for dates. The consulate did not spend a cent, everything was paid for by the Malay community and they also did all the work. This was an unforgettable experience for me. It showed how close the Malays still felt towards their ancestral home.

There were a lot of Indonesians in Singapore, working in the trading business. I kept these Indonesians busy, and I rented a big house and started an Indonesian Club. Here they could meet each other, while enjoying Indonesian food prepared the Indonesian way. I also organised lectures, community dances, and this place was also used by the Indonesian boy scout movement. I wanted Indonesians to feel that the Consulate was looking after them spiritually, mentally, and physically. They should not forget that they are Indonesians, even when working abroad. Once an Indonesian, always an Indonesian. Create one big happy family was my motto, wherever I go.

As an army man, I had certain advantages. I had good, in fact very good relations with the British FARELF (Far Eastern Land Forces) and with the Royal Navy. But I knew nobody in the RAF. At that time Singapore had no armed forces of its own.

I was lucky that my Malaysian friend, Encik Yusof, whom I

regularly met at Friday prayers in the mosque, became the first Singapore head of state. I knew the attorney general very well, because we were together engaged in all kinds of Muslim activities. The minister of finance, Dr. Goh Keng Swee, was a golfing friend.

Backed by good official relations between Indonesia and Singapore, my work in Singapore was quite pleasant. Our foreign minister, Dr. Subandrio, made frequent stopovers in Singapore and he always asked me to arrange meetings with Lee Kuan Yew, and because of that, meeting the prime minister was easy for me. I realised how important personal relations were, and how valuable personal approaches could be.

Relations with other heads of mission posed no problems, as I was a very easy-going man, and these relations resulted in me getting all kinds of useful information. Was I a spy? No, of course not, I did not look actively for information, the information came to me, voluntarily.

The most difficult part of my job was how to treat my newfound friends. From the time that my posting as head of mission in Singapore was known, my number of friends swelled to astonishing dimensions. People I did not know before, people who had met me only once at a party, people claiming to be friends of my friends, they all tried to gain a place in my heart. I knew in reality that these people were friends of my job, of my position. Once the position and power had gone, the friendship would also melt away like snow in the sun. But I did not want to disappoint these new friends, so as far as I could, I helped them. It cost energy and sometimes money, as well as some frustration. Sometimes people think that diplomats are posted abroad to provide them with a service, and some demanded help even for their personal needs. This category of people I despised most – they never asked, they demanded.

For a great country like Indonesia the office we occupied in Singapore was below standard. I decided to ask my government to build a beautiful building, housing the consular offices and other Indonesian business enterprises, like Garuda, Pelni, Panca Niaga, and others. I also had a permanent theatre and showroom in mind, so we could show our films and/or our products. Beside that, we planned to open an Indonesian restaurant. For this we found ourselves a nice strategic spot bang in the middle of Singapore in Orchard Road, and surprisingly the government agreed to my plans. We borrowed money from the Bank Indonesia Negara 46 and as soon as we got the loan we started building. I sold the residence in Patterson Road and bought a very big and beautiful house in Grange Road, once owned by a Chinese Indonesian. It had a very big garden and two tennis courts.

But then disaster struck. On the 15th of September 1963, we broke our diplomatic relations because of the *Konfrontasi* (confrontation) with Malaysia and had to depart Singapore. We were given seven days to pack our things and leave. The Indonesian government gave us three months salary, and with that we started shopping. The Indonesians bought everything they could lay their hands on, and the shops in Singapore did some good business. I chartered one ship to carry all our goods to Indonesia. The Singapore government was very understanding and cooperative, so we did not encounter any problems. Within a week all Indonesians had left Singapore.

I left Singapore after four enjoyable years. Goodbye Singapore, till we meet again. Rangoon, here we come.

Rangoon

Together with General Djatikusumo, who also had to leave Kuala Lumpur because of the confrontation, I reported to the foreign minister and to President Soekarno.

For the time being I was assigned as adviser to the minister of finance. I laughed when I got this new assignment. I knew nothing about finance, I only knew how to spend money. Later I discovered that I was there to act as a scarecrow, to scare away the commander of the Palace Guard, Cakrabirawa. He kept coming and asking for more money for his regiment, despite the budget of the Palace Guard already being almost as big as the budget for the whole army. When he met the Minister of Finance he always said, "The President knows about this," but he never mentioned whether the President had agreed to it or not. And it was very difficult for the minister to refuse these additional requests.

Now the commander had to go through me, and I always checked with the President as to whether he knew about the request made by the Cakrabirawa. I never dreamt that I would ever work as a scarecrow. But a job is a job, and it has to be done. And for this particular and special purpose I wore my uniform, everyday. And then one day, my promotion to brigadier-general came through, so I had one star on my number plate, and became an even bigger scarecrow.

One day I was called to the foreign office to meet with the foreign minister. From the lips of Dr. Subandrio I heard that the President had agreed to appoint me as ambassador to Burma. I was not very happy on hearing this, but being a military man I obey orders without questioning them. I had been in Burma before as ADC to Dr. Hatta, the vice-president. And what I had seen then, in 1956, was not very promising. I'd heard that the situation now, in 1964, was even worse. On our way to Rangoon, we stopped to buy provisions in Bangkok, mainly because my wife was at that time expecting our tenth child. According to information from various friends there was little to buy in Rangoon.

The chief of protocol, who met us on arrival, had never seen such a large diplomatic family. Including the nurse, our party consisted of 12 people. The official residence was rather old, and the car had seen better days. The office was small and cramped, and the furniture prehistoric. A real shock after Singapore. Our household staff numbered a mere 12 members.

I had to wait about three weeks before I could present my credentials. And what a ceremony that was, compared to what I was used to experiencing in Jakarta. In Jakarta, the new ambassador would be escorted from his residence to the palace by police on motorcycles. On arrival at the palace, both the ambassador's and the Indonesian national anthems would be played by a military band in ceremonial uniform. The new ambassador would then inspect the guard of honour. Escorted by the chief of protocol, he would then enter the palace and present his credentials to the president. Speeches followed, plus introductions to the foreign minister and other dignitaries. The ceremony was closed with a toast.

Now let us compare what happened in Burma. On the day of presentation I donned my general's uniform and waited for the chief of protocol to arrive. I could not hear him coming, because he was alone and there were no police or military escort on motorcycles. When we left for the palace, there was just one lonely policeman riding in front of us. On arrival at the palace, I could not see a guard of honour, let alone a military band. I was met by the ADC, a second lieutenant, and he brought me upstairs. After waiting a minute, President Ne Win entered alone. We shook hands and I gave him my credentials, followed by a cup of tea, which marked the end of the whole presentation of credentials.

While waiting to present my credentials in Burma I was without official status or role, and was, so to speak, non-existent. One day, I heard some running and the guard shouting. I looked out, and a Burmese lady was running towards the residence and the guard was trying to stop her, but without success. It looked like she new her way around the embassy. When she was inside the house I met her, and she asked for my help. She told me that the government was chasing her and wanted to kill her. Her father, a freedom fighter, had been killed, and his body was now in the palace. She asked for asylum.

As I had not yet presented my credentials, there was nothing I could do. I telephoned my charge des affairs, Akosah, to come and take care of the situation. Mr. Akosah came as soon as possible and he took charge of the situation. Ultimately the lady, who turned out to be the famous film star, Wim Min Than, and had starred with Gregory Peck in an air force film during World War II, was handed over to the police.

My wife, who had never experienced a situation like this before, was extremely shocked, even to the extent of giving birth prematurely to our son. Both were healthy, and I gave my son the name of Djoko Birmo Saptoputro, which means "son of Burma."

165

Food was scarce and everything we needed was imported from Hongkong. If we needed anything in a hurry, then we went to the American Embassy shop. I remember once that when we needed fish for our dinner party, we had to go to the Ministry of Agriculture to get a permit to buy fish. With this permit, the cook went to the fish market and bought fish. Shops, except perhaps book shops, were almost empty, people just went there to enjoy the cool of the air-conditioning. People went to the office in their national dress, that is, shirt and sarong with slippers. It was very hard to buy ties or find a tailor who could make Western styles of clothing. Because of these sparse conditions we saved quite a lot of money, which was the good side of my assignment in Burma.

Cultivating personal relations with Burmese officials was very difficult and sometimes near on impossible. They avoided outside contacts and maintained only the most essential relations. From a "friend" in the foreign office I heard that every time a Burmese official attended a cocktail party or dinner, they would have to submit a written report to the authorities of what had transpired. This made them reluctant to accept invitations from embassies because of the extra trouble and work.

On their national days members of the diplomatic corps were invited to a garden party at the palace. Here was a beautiful garden. All the guests were received by the foreign minister, after which we mingled and had drinks and snacks. After one hour or so the arrival of President Ne Win was announced, but he remained quite separate from the rest of us. There were no handshakes or offering greetings to the president. After a while the president and his entourage left and the party came to an end.

For security reasons, ambassadors or members of their staff were not allowed to go beyond a radius of 15 miles from Rangoon. If you wanted to visit the provinces you generally could not get a permit. But you could go on your own; they would not prohibit that. And when you came back safe and sound, then the foreign ministry issued a visit permit. This meant that if something happened during these trips, it was your own responsibility.

During my tenure I could only visit Mandalay, but when I

wanted to pay my respects to the governor of the region, I was instead received by his secretary. This was so different to what we were used to in Indonesia. Ambassadors visiting the provinces were treated as guest of honour and the governor himself would receive him.

On the 30th of September 1965 the Indonesian Communist Party staged a coup and murdered the top generals of the army headquarters. I did not know anything about this, because there was no official communication from the foreign office. On the 28th of September 1965, the Chinese ambassador invited my family for dinner. When I say family, It included the children as well. Such an extended invitation seemed very strange, but I thought that the Chinese ambassador, having previously worked in Indonesia, wanted to meet my family. After the dinner a film was shown and afterwards the ambassador gave little presents to my children. A very unusual situation.

On the 1st of October I attended national day cocktails at the Chinese embassy. The Ambassador was very friendly, which was understandable after the previous dinner invitation. But I was surprised when he asked about General Nasution and whether he had been found. The dinner invitation was strange but this question added to the mystery.

That night, I telephoned my friends in Bangkok and Singapore and everything became clear. I found out about the coup attempt by the PKI. The army suspected that Communist China had had a hand in it. This explained the friendliness of the Chinese ambassador – he knew something I didn't.

Among the murdered generals was the army chief of intelligence, General Parman, and soon afterwards I was called home to take the position of army chief of intelligence.

To India with Love

In 1974, after serving more than seven years in Indonesia following my assignment in Burma, the government planned to send me to

167

Top: Presenting my credentials to President Ne Win of Burma.
*Below: Receiving the Indian vice-president on our national
day at my residence in India in 1976.*

London as ambassador. This was welcome news, especially after my earlier upset. But again it was not to be. For the second time my assignment to Britain was changed for the same reason as before, and I had to make way for a more senior officer, a four-star general. There was nothing I could do because of his seniority.

I was called by the minister of defence and security, M. Panggabean, and from him I heard officially that from London I had been switched to New Delhi. Not bad, I thought. Now I was going to be in a country of 700 million people, a country that had produced the *Mahabharata* and *Ramayana*, two of the great legendary works of world literature.

I had been to India in 1956 as ADC to the vice-president, Dr. Hatta, and what I had seen then made me keen for more. I fell especially in love with Kashmir. Who has not heard of Mohandas Karamchand Gandhi, the Mahatma? One night on that visit, while functioning as ADC to Dr. Hatta, I attended a cocktail party. I was dressed in my military uniform, called a "monkey dress." I thought I looked magnificent. But when I arrived at the party I felt like I was not dressed at all. Next to the Indian officers I looked terrible. They looked so brave, robust and courageous. I remembered the film "The Prince and the Pauper." The Indian officers in their ceremonial dress were the princes and I was the pauper. Of course my opinion was based only on appearances. The military qualities of the Indonesians were certainly not inferior to the Indians. I hoped that there would never be an occasion to test this.

One thing is certain, and that is that Indonesian officers are more experienced in areas outside the usual jurisdiction of the armed forces. We are not only a defence force, but a force for social change. We have the opportunity to become civil administrators like governors and mayors, we can become diplomats, or we can get involved in trade and commerce. All legal and according to the law in Indonesia.

We had a few sultans in Indonesia, but India had 565 maharajas, nawabs, princes and rajahs, each one of them absolute rulers of their territory, some of which were as big as some European countries (the Nizam of Hyderabad or the Maharaja of Kashmir) and some as small as a London park, or worse still as big as a cow pasture.

Then there were the palaces and historic buildings, like the Taj Mahal, and many other famous temples. I was as keen to leave for India as reluctant as I had been to leave for Burma. I read so many interesting things about India, some beyond my wildest dreams. It was to be regretted that some ancient customs had fallen into disuse. But there were still many, many things to watch and enjoy. What a life it must be, to be a maharaja or a prince, with beautiful palaces, jewels, fleets of cars, elephants and, of course, wives.

The Maharaja of Baroda had a unique collection of jewels, including the Star of the South, the seventh biggest diamond in the world. The Maharaja of Kapurtala, a Sikh, had the biggest topaz in the world set in his turban. The Maharaja of Patiala had a pearl necklace insured for one million dollars. This same Maharaja had, until the turn of the 20th century, the custom of appearing naked once a year before his people, wearing only a diamond breastplate, his organ fully erect. This pose was suppose to radiate magic powers and drive away evil spirits.

Elephants played a very important role in the lives of the maharajas and princes. A nobleman's standing might be measured in the numbers, size or ages of the elephants he possessed. Sometimes, elephant fights were organized – the elephants would fight each other until one was killed. A unique show was regularly held by the Raja of Dhenkanal in eastern India. People here could see the public copulation of two elephants.

In modern times cars replaced elephants as a token of esteem, and the favourite make was, of course, Rolls Royce. Palaces and historic buildings became famous tourists destinations, such as the Taj Mahal. The Maharaja of Kapurtala was convinced that he was Louis XVI, the French king, in his earlier life, and decided to build an exact replica of the palace of Louis XVI.

The throne of the Nawab of Rampur was surrounded by white marble sculptures of nude women. Because they had plenty of time, the favourite pastime of the Indian nobles were sex and sport. The harem was an integral part of the palace and always filled with dancing girls and concubines, sometimes as many as 300.

Beside all this, which was available only to the privileged few, there were temples, caves and buildings for the common people to see, admire and enjoy. The Ajantha Caves, the Elephant Caves, the Kajuraho temple, as well as many other historical and natural sights, made India a culturally rich country. I wanted to see everything whenever I had the opportunity.

Some of my children could not go with me to India because they were studying in various universities. From the first moment we set foot in India, we felt that this was going to be a pleasant tour of duty. I didn't have to wait long before I was given notice to present my credentials. First I had to pay a courtesy call to the foreign minister, whom I had already met when he'd paid an official visit to Jakarta. I also met the chief of protocol, who explained in detail how the presentation of credentials ceremony would be performed. I became very excited, and what a difference it was going to be after my experience in Burma.

The whole Indonesian diplomatic staff and their wives were invited to watch the ceremony. This was something completely new for me. Our country had recently designed a special costume to be worn at official functions, and this was my chance to wear it. I had a dress rehearsal in my room, and I must confess that I looked very dashing, in my national ceremonial dress complete with medals.

When I arrived at the palace gate, I switched to a horse-drawn carriage flanked on both sides by Bengal Lancers in full ceremonial uniform. A magnificent sight not to be forgotten. All those tall, bearded soldiers on horseback, carrying lances topped by small flags. After that, I inspected a guard of honour of Gurkha troops. The presentation of credentials was held in a special room; I made a speech of thanks, followed by a speech from the president. Afterwards, my wife and I were invited for a private chat with the president and his wife. And the whole ceremony was closed with a joint photo taken with the President and his staff.

Relations with India at that time were improving. Previously, Indonesia had had very close relations with China and Pakistan, both of whom were not very much liked by India. But after the

Top: My sixth son, Toto, presenting to the president of India a boy scouts plaque at an Indian boy scouts jamboree.

Below: Before presenting my credentials I was welcomed by the military staff of the president of India.

attempted Communist coup and the severing of relations with China, relations with India improved. From the very beginning of our struggle for independence India had supported us politically, and Indonesia had in very difficult circumstances managed to send rice to help India fight famine.

When organizing the Asian-African Conference, India, under Prime Minister Nehru, was one of the sponsoring countries, together with Sir John Kotelawala from Sri Lanka, Mohammed Ali from Pakistan, U Nu from Burma, and, of course, Ali Sastroamidjojo from Indonesia. This famous and historic Asian-African Conference was held in Bandung from the 18th to the 23rd of April 1955. African and Asian representatives were invited, even those who had yet to achieve independence, such as Gold Coast (later Ghana) and Sudan. They didn't even have official flags, so they wrote 'Sudan' on a piece of cloth for identification.

The aim of the conference as outlined in Bogor was as follows:

1. To promote goodwill and cooperation among the nations of Asia and Africa, and to explore and advance their mutual as well as common interests and to establish good relations.
2. To consider the social, economic and cultural problems and relations of the countries represented.
3. To consider problems of special interest to Asian and African peoples, e.g., problems affecting national sovereignty and of racism and colonialism.
4. To view the position of Asia and Africa and their peoples in the world today and the contribution they could make to the promotion of world peace and cooperation.

Another fact that made India and Indonesia close was their membership in the non-aligned movement. India and Indonesia, along with Afghanistan, Algeria, Burma, Cambodia, Ceylon, Zaire, Cuba, Cyprus, Ethiopia, Ghana, Guinea, Iraq, Lebanon, Mali, Morocco, Nepal, Saudi Arabia, Somalia, Sudan, Tunisia, United Arab Republic, Yemen, and Yugoslavia, were the original members.

Then war started between India and China, and Indonesia slowly became good friends with China and even created a political axis, Jakarta-Peking-Pyongyang. Fortunately this was only temporary.

India became close with the Soviet Union. When ambassadors sent to India celebrate their national days, the vice-president and the foreign minister of India would attended on behalf of the government. However, the Soviet Union's national day was also attended by the prime minister, to indicate the special relationship of the two countries.

Unlike my stay in Burma, I had the opportunity to visit the provinces and meet the governors. I also visited the military institutions, armament factories, and, of course, the famous places of interest earlier mentioned.

In New Delhi we had a diplomatic enclave, where most of the missions were situated. Our compound was rather big and strategically located. Everything was in one place, the chancery, the ambassador's residence, and the military attaches' flats.

In my time I managed to build a Balinese *gapura* (gate), which was very beautiful and looked exactly like an original, although the stone carvings were done by Rajasthani sculptors. For the official opening of this Balinese gate, I invited a high priest from Bali. Bali, like much of India, practices the Hindu religion. The whole ceremony was witnessed by the Indian minister of culture and the diplomatic corps. The minister commented that the Hindu ceremony performed was purer in style than the kind they usually had in India. Following the ceremony, the high priest asked to be brought to the River Ganges to collect holy water to take back to Bali. He was very happy to have seen the holy River Ganges.

After almost four years in India, I was called back to Indonesia and began my retirement. I felt very happy to have had the opportunity to be ambassador to India.

Surprises of My Life

My life as a government official abroad was normal, regular and most of the time monotonous. Executing my duties as a chief of mission was very exciting at the beginning, but after a few years the novelty began to wear off. Dinner parties did not excite me any more, let alone cocktails. Attending national day celebrations became routine and as I am not a good talker, I mainly played the role of listener. I must say that I am a very good listener, I rarely make any comments or deliver criticism. That's why people liked me. It takes a strong will to listen and smile even when you hear people talking bullshit – sorry for using such a strong word – about their own brilliant performances and blowing themselves up like a balloon.

But I enjoy arguing, because I think I have a sharp mind. When I get the chance to defend a standpoint I usually do it well. I am not a thinker, I do not belong to those who can discuss and analyse things. I am an executive type of person, who feels instinctively the main points of an issue and how to put them into operation. Do not ask me to talk about abstract things, about philosophy or ideas. This is not my field. But order me to do this or that. This is my strength.

However, my missions abroad were not always monotonous, because once in a while I was given a "surprise" assignments, which added colour and excitement to a routine existence. These surprise assignments came straight from the President, and only Subandrio, as chief of the Central Intelligence Board, knew about them. These assignments were:

1. Buy West Irian for US$ 1.5 million.
2. Arrange a meeting with the Malaysian prime minister.
3. Talk to the British government and try to stop the *Konfrontasi*.
4. Take up the post of Governor of Jakarta.

Buy West Irian

After a prolonged war and lengthy discussions in 1949, the Dutch finally recognised our sovereignty and handed to Indonesia the whole region previously known as the Dutch East Indies, but minus West Irian (now called Irian Jaya). This caused disappointment to all Indonesians, and became a thorn in relations between Indonesia and the Netherlands. The island of New Guinea, 808,000 square km, is the second biggest in the world after Greenland. Politically, the western half of the island was a province of Indonesia, while the eastern section was the independent state of Papua New Guinea.

This island was discovered in 1512 by a Portuguese sailor and the name Guinea was given by Yunigo Ortiz de Retes, a Spanish adventurer, in 1545, because this island seemed so similar to Guinea in West Africa. Most of the island is covered with thick rain forest, which covers a central mountain range stretching, spine-like, from east to west. The highest peaks here are Jaya (5,030 metres) and Trikora (4,750 metres). Irian Jaya is the home of many rare birds and animals that the government is trying hard to protect and preserve.

One day in early 1962, I received an urgent cable from the foreign office telling me to report to Soekarno immediately on arrival in Jakarta. I was at that time consul-general in Singapore. When I arrived in Jakarta I contacted Mr. Nasution, secretary to Soekarno, reporting that I had arrived. Nasution told me to come and see the President the next morning. The President will see you in the veranda of his residence, he said.

This veranda was a very important place for the President, because he informally conducted many important activities here. Read what President Soekarno said about this veranda in his book, *Soekarno: An Autobiography*:

"On my porch, unshaven, relaxed and often in pyjamas, I make crucial decisions regarding life and death. I appoint ambassadors, pardon criminals, pass laws, examine the latest figures on rice production, hold strategy meetings with my generals on our Malaysian 'confrontation,' and curse those who deserves it. Yelling, incidentally, is good for me. It helps me lose weight. I'm so busy working my mouth that I don't think about eating. Individually and collectively we discuss everything from the tensions in South-East Asia to the newest emergency in our country. Each gets his turn to whisper his problems into bapak's (father's) ear."

The veranda meetings were usually closed at nine o'clock because the President then took his bath, shaved and dressed. He usually wore his traditional Indonesian black velvet cap, or *pici*, while during the veranda talks he wore nothing, so you could see his almost bald head.

When everybody had left, he called me.

He thanked me first for sending those Chinese volunteers to Indonesia. I had trained about 15 Chinese volunteers in Singapore – ten boys and five girls. They all wanted to go to Irian and fight the Dutch. Before leaving Singapore, they were interviewed by the newspaper and it was good propaganda for our cause.

He was in a good mood and inquired about my family and my health and told me to watch my diet, because I was becoming a little too fat. After these preliminary talks, he came straight to the point and we started talking about West Irian, or Irian Jaya.

I knew how important it was to gain Irian for Indonesia, and it had become one of the three most serious concerns of the cabinet, along with national security and the material welfare of the people. Our economic situation was very bad, and Prime Minister Juanda wanted to know from the President which he thought was top priority of these three aims. The President said firmly and clearly that Irian was top priority and that economic improvements could wait.

After these preliminaries the President came to the point. He said he wanted me to go to Hongkong and meet a Dutchman, who was prepared to help in attaining West Irian for us, without a fight. The Dutchman's motives were mainly commercial. However, he was doing it also because he thought that the Indonesians would take better care of Irian than the Dutch. Kartono Kadri, and police colonel Samsudin from the Central Intelligence Board were detailed to accompany me. But I was in charge.

The President outlined what I had to do. Essentially it was a business transaction. Someone wanted to sell Irian and we Indonesians were prepared to buy it. Since this was a business deal, I was given the power to promise the Dutchman up to 1.5 million US dollars, if Irian became ours.

"Do you have any questions?" asked the President.

"To whom do I report, sir?"

"Directly to me and not to anyone else, except Subandrio. When can you leave?"

"Any moment, sir. But I'd like to go to Singapore first and continue to Hongkong from there. Those other gentlemen can join me in Singapore. Should I report to the Foreign Minister before starting this mission?"

"No need, Subandrio already knows about this, because he made all the preparations. So, To (that is what he called me), good luck. The eyes of Indonesia are on you. If you succeed, it means no blood will be spilt, but if you do not, then we will have to fight for what is ours. Do you realise how important your assignment is? Good luck, and come back with good news."

After meeting my assistants in Jakarta, I left for Singapore. The three of us agreed to leave together for Hongkong from Singapore four days following. I asked our consulate in Hongkong to book rooms in the Hilton for all of us. We arrived in Hongkong the same day as our Dutch contact.

We met him informally in a restaurant and decided that our first official meeting would be in his hotel room, with the following meeting in my room in the Hilton Hotel. When we introduced ourselves, the Dutchman laughed. I was very surprised, and asked why he laughed.

What a coincidence, he said, we have the same name. I asked how he could know the meaning of my name? He answered that he was born in Kediri, eastern Java, and spoke Javanese quite well. My name, Soegih Arto, means 'rich' in Javanese, and his name is De Rijke, meaning 'rich' in Dutch. He brought with him his female secretary, a young, beautiful Dutch girl.

Our first meeting was attended by him and his secretary, while on my side I was assisted by Mr. Kartono Yadri. Samsudin acted as our security and did not join us.

The agenda of the talks was as follows:

1. Drafting a resolution to be passed by the Nieuw Guinea Raad (New Guinea Parliament), on their desire to merge with Indonesia.

2. Financial matters.

During the talks Mr. De Rijke put forward his conditions:

1. The TNI should stop its infiltrations into Irian.

I replied that if there were infiltrations, they would automatically end when Irian became Indonesian territory. It is uncommon for armies to infiltrate their own territory.

2. Irian should become a special territory.

I answered that this could be discussed once Irian was an integral part of Indonesia. We already had two special territories – Yogyakarta and Aceh.

3. The existing foreign Christian missions should be allowed to continue their activities.

The Indonesian Republic is based on the *Pancasila*, which preaches religious tolerance. So there would not be any problems with this request.

4. Irian should be allowed to use its own currency.

I replied that this was a very unusual and irregular request and that he as a politician knows the answer to that.

5. Irian should have its own flag.

My answer was the same as to proposal number four.

After we'd finished our discussions, we drafted the resolution, which took quite some time. Although the talks were lengthy, they went well. We started talking at 10 a.m. and finished at around five in the afternoon, with a lunch break in the middle.

We agreed on the steps to be taken. Mr. De Rijke was chairman of the Nieuw Guinea Raad, the so called parliament. We drafted together the motion to be adopted by the parliament, calling for merger with Indonesia. Mr. De Rijke would take care that this motion would pass. We finished the meeting that day, agreeing to meet the following day in my room.

The next day, Mr. De Rijke arrived promptly at 10 o'clock as agreed and after making some small talk, we opened financial negotiations. The atmosphere was pleasant, and we were all happy with the result of yesterday's talks. After a while he proposed something that surprised me very much. He asked to discuss the financial matters in Javanese dialect, so that his secretary would not understand what was being said. I asked him whether she would not become suspicious? He assured me that he could handle her. I did not know then that his relations with her were personal as well as business. Later I heard that they married and moved to Australia.

In short, I proposed that I would hand to him US$500,000. He rejected this offer outright. He said that he was doing a very dangerous thing, and that he may be killed if people knew about this. Secondly, he would have to bribe those members of the parliament who were not sympathetic to Indonesia. He had four or five influential members in his mind, and it was very important to get these members on our side. I had US$1,500,000 with me, but I continued to bargain and ultimately we agreed on the sum of US$750,000. I heaved a sigh of relief, having saved half of the money.

We then discussed when to deliver the money and how. Over this issue we had a heated debate. He wanted the money transferred to his bank account now. I replied that this might be rather difficult, because I had no guarantees that the motion would passed. I told him that I wanted the resolution to be accepted first and announced publicly, so that the whole world would know about it, and only then would I transfer the money. He said that that was impossible – what if the Indonesian government cheated him? I replied that he might cheat us. We talked for a long time, but could find no method acceptable to us both. In the end we agreed that we would meet again after I had consulted my government about the method in which the money should be delivered. Mr. De Rijke pointed out that he was playing a very dangerous game. People might get suspicious if he went to Hongkong so often. We understood each other's position and we took leave from each other with the solemn promise to keep everything secret.

I returned to Indonesia, and reported directly to the President what had passed between myself and Mr. De Rijke. He was happy about the wording of the resolution. The President told me to come back after two days, because he was going to talk with Subandrio.

When I returned two days later the President told me the whole thing was off but thanked me for what I had achieved. Obviously I was very surprised because I considered my mission to be important, and I did not expect the project to be dropped just like that. Later, much later, I heard that the Communists, who were getting stronger every day, did not like this move because it was an unpublicised and clandestine operation. Hence it would not be clear to the world who had initiated the negotiations, and the Indonesians would appear passive, with the initiative appearing to come from the New Guinea Parliament. The Communists wanted the Indonesians, and in particular, the President, great leader of the Revolution, to gain world recognition for this initiative.

The Communists were very active in building up the image of the President so that he would become more popular with the people. The Communists hoped to increase their own power, and more importantly, reduce the power and influence of the armed forces, who were their one and only rival in the struggle for political hegemony. General Nasution, army chief at that time, said in his book, *The Call of Duty,* that he did not know that the President was trying to gradually wrest control of the armed forces from him. The programme of the G 30S/PKI was to dominate the army, and then use that position to grab the country's leadership. This strategy started at the time of the *Trikora.*

Indonesia was pursuing a doctrine of active revolution led by Bung Karno, who was President for life, Supreme Commander in Chief of the Armed Forces, and held the additional title of Great Leader of the Revolution. He gave ministerial rank to the chairman of the people's council and the chief justice. According to the 1945 constitution, ministers are but assistants to the president. So with one master stroke Bung Karno gained control of the executive, judiciary and legislature.

Not long afterwards, the Mandala War Theatre was created for the liberation of West Irian and Major General Soeharto was appointed as commander. We were going to fight to regain West Irian.

After prolonged negotiations an agreement was reached on 15th of August 1962, under the auspices of the United Nations and the good offices of the Americans. On 1st of October 1962, the Dutch transferred control of West Irian to UNTEA (United Nations Temporary Executive Agency). From this time until the 30th of April 1963, UNTEA stayed in West Irian. A vote by the people to freely decide to join the Indonesian republic was held between 14th of July and the 2nd of August 1969. In November 1969 the United Nations endorsed the results of this referendum.

In our efforts to get Irian back, we must not forget how big a role the *Trikora* played. *Trikora* embodies three commands of the people, i.e.:

1. To foil the Dutch creation of puppet state in New Guinea.
2. Hoist the red and white flag in West Irian.
3. Prepare for a national mobilisation.

One day Mr. Kartono Kadri, my representative in this secret mission, went to West Irian as secretary of the Indonesian chief administrator. He met Mr. De Rijke and they talked about what had happened in Hongkong. Mr. De Rijke was naturally eager to know whether other people in Indonesia knew about what went on. Mr. Kadri assured him that everything had been kept secret. In spite of Kadri's assurance Mr. De Rijke left West Irian and crossed to Papua New Guinea and then to Australia, where he became an Australian citizen and settled there with his former secretary, now his wife.

Confrontation with Malaysia

In early 1959 amongst a very limited circle of army intelligence officers, a very serious discussion was held on the following topics:
1. Indonesian foreign policy.
2. Indonesian security.
3. Potential enemies.

Lengthy discussions were held on the foreign policies of the major powers and their aggressive attitude, and what Indonesia should do in response to these potential dangers. China and Japan were considered of primary significance in this discussion.

Four reasons were mentioned why China might be dangerous. Firstly, the Chinese leadership was following an expansionist policy. Secondly, China had the capability of becoming a nuclear power. Thirdly, China produced consumer goods and hence needed big markets, both inside and outside their country. And lastly, China was pursuing an aggressive and expansionist Communist ideology.

Why might Japan become a potential danger? According to close observation, Japan could become an economic giant, which has since been proved to be true. The signs were already there and could pose a danger to our national and economic security.

What was Indonesian's defence against these potential dangers? Indonesia had to find a way to contain China, but not by creating military bases and outposts like the superpowers, since that was far too expensive for a country of limited means. The consensus was to build a strong defence around Indonesia by creating strong nationalism in neighbouring countries, so that they would not easily be infiltrated by foreign ideologies; if attacked, they would then have the spirit to defend their sovereignty. It was important that their military power be developed. This was at that time considered the best defence for Indonesia, since it could be achieved without costing Indonesia too much money.

In 1961, on his way back to Indonesia, Subandrio stopped in Singapore for a two day rest. I had a very serious meeting with him, in which he explained a theory he had had in mind for quite some time. The theory was very logical and I could accept it's sense. He said that our major potential enemy was China for reasons mentioned earlier. Subandrio was, by the way, chief of the Central Intelligence Board, so he would know all about this secret meeting in 1959. He further explained that one day, China would look southward and set its eyes on Indonesia, because of the immense natural resources as yet unexploited.

So what could we do to defend ourselves? If China decided to go south, they would most probably use the land route, because their sea transportation was inadequate to service such a big operation. Thailand would be easy prey for the Chinese, because of the Thais' strict policies of neutrality. They would probably let the Chinese pass through their territory, as they had with the Japanese in 1941. This meant that the next Chinese target would be Malaya. We must not forget the existence of the Malayan Communist Party, whose members were mainly Chinese.

One of the things Indonesia could do was to create a military crisis in Malaya by infiltrating the Malay Peninsula and starting a petty war, thus providing the Malayan army with combat experience, as well as increasing nationalistic feelings. But what excuse could be given for such aggression on Indonesia's part?

Subandrio said that this was his idea and that he had not yet discussed this with any other official. He asked my opinion and I answered that what he'd explained was very logical. I pointed out that it would be very difficult to find a reason genuine enough and acceptable to the world. After this discussion Subandrio asked me to keep everything secret, because he did not want to create a scandal. I promised my lips were sealed.

I cannot prove this, because there were no other witnesses during that discussion. I was there alone, and people might say that I've made these things up. I do not mind, because for me it is important that my Indonesian friends know the one so far unknown but crucial aspect of the *Konfrontasi*, although it sounds fantastic and unbelievable. But I believed that there was logic in what Subandrio confided to me. The role he played in the Chinese sponsored coup of 1965 was from pure personal ambition, as well as being a miscalculation on his part. He thought that both as a domestically and internationally well-known and experienced politician he was sure to have an important role to play. He was no Communist, which was proved by the Special Military Tribunal's investigations.

But Subandrio should not have ignored history, especially what had happened in Egypt. In the beginning the revolutionary powers placed a well-known general as its frontman, General Naguib, but soon afterwards Colonel Nasser thought that he was ready to take over the leadership, and that was exactly what happened. This could also happen in Indonesia, if the leaders of the PKI felt that they were firm in the saddle, and no longer needed Subandrio. Another thing which puzzled political observers was why Subandrio took the side of the Communists, while before the coup Subandrio was already the most important man after President Soekarno. Perhaps Subandrio calculated that Soekarno's power was declining and the Communists were on their way up. He did not want to miss the train, and perhaps his aim was the presidency.

In May 1961 the Malayan Prime Minister, Tungku Abdul Rahman, proposed the formation of a federation consisting of Malaya, and the then British territories of Singapore, Sarawak, and North Borneo (now known as Sabah).

Subandrio, upon hearing this, said in November 1961 that Indonesia had no objections at all, as long as the people of the British territories agreed. In 1962 an understanding was reached between Malaya and Britain, to the effect that in 1963 Britain would free the northern Borneo territories of Sarawak and Sabah, and Singapore. Indonesia's chance came in December 1962, when the People's Party under A.M. Azhari started a rebellion in Brunei, with the aim of uniting into one country northern Borneo with Indonesian Kalimantan. This rebellion did not last very long, but provided Indonesia with the opportunity to express its doubts that the Borneo territories were willing to merge with Malaya.

On the 8th of January 1963 President Soekarno opposed the formation of Malaysia and Subandrio issued a similar statement afterwards. In February 1963, Soekarno explained to a gathering of the National Front, that the formation of Malaysia was to secure the continued supply of oil, tin and rubber for the imperialist powers.

The atmosphere between Indonesia and Malaya grew hotter and hotter. Dr. Subandrio cabled to me in Singapore to arrange a secret meeting with the prime minister of Singapore, Lee Kuan Yew, not in his office, but somewhere outside the city. This meeting should be kept top secret. The secret meeting took place in a house of one of Lee Kuan Yew's friends, attended by only Subandrio and Lee Kuan Yew. I acted as a security man, and sat outside. The meeting lasted for about 45 minutes.

Afterwards, Subandrio was not in the mood to explain what went on, and I surmised that the meeting was tough. From what I could gather later on, Subandrio expressed Indonesian opposition to the forming of Malaysia, unless the voice of the northern Borneo people was heard properly through a plebiscite. Subandrio asked Lee Kuan Yew to convey the Indonesians' views to Tungku Abdul Rahman. If the Tungku did not heed Indonesia's warning, then there might be trouble, which Indonesia did not want. Subandrio said that Indonesian bombers could reach the Malayan skies in less than five minutes.

Not long after this secret meeting in Singapore I got a cable from the palace saying I must try to persuade the Malayan prime minister to go to Tokyo for a meeting with President Soekarno. I offered my objections, because we had an embassy in Kuala Lumpur, and the ambassador, Mr. T. Razif, was a seasoned diplomat. Why not appoint Mr. Razif to do this job? I got an angry cable back from the foreign minister, saying that this was a personal order from the President and I'd better do it. There was an addendum to this cable, ordering me not to report this to Mr. Razif in Kuala Lumpur. So I drove up to Kuala Lumpur from Singapore, which was very tiring. After two meetings at the Prime Minister's residence, he agreed to go to Tokyo to meet President Soekarno. I was very pleased and I thought that my mission was accomplished.

One day before Bung Karno's departure for Tokyo, I got a telephone call from the Malaysian prime minister's office informing me that the prime minister had decided not to go. No reason was given.

I told Jakarta that the PM's trip was off, reason unknown. Jakarta answered that the President would not change his plans. Later I discovered that Tungku Abdul Rahman felt insulted by the President, because during his Lenso Community Dance party in Bogor Palace, the band played the Indonesian song, *Terang Bulan*, which has the same tune as the Malaysian National Anthem. I thought that it was not very tactful of Soekarno to allow the band to play this song, especially since the government of Indonesia had already issued a ban out of respect for independent Malaya. The Malayan ambassador was present at the dance evening, and the Tungku gained the information from his ambassador.

I did not know what to do. Jakarta said try again, and whatever the results I should go to Japan and join the President's party. I talked to Mr. Ghazalie, later to become the Malayan foreign minister, and asked his help in persuading the Tungku to attend, because this meeting in Tokyo was very important. When in Tokyo, I got a call from the Malayan Embassy saying that the PM was actually coming. I was happy and directly reported this to Soekarno and Subandrio. Subandrio was very happy, and impulsively he kissed me and told the Indonesian ambassador to Japan, General Bambang Soegeng, to give me US$500 as a bonus. There was nothing the ambassador could do, and as a good soldier I did not protest.

Tungku Abdul Rahman arrived in Tokyo in a KLM plane. I met him on behalf of President Soekarno, and the Malayan ambassador and the chief of protocol of the Japanese foreign ministry were also present. I did not know the exact results of the discussion, but this talk in May 1963 seemed to cool down the temperature a little bit.

Another meeting was organised in Manila from the 7th to the 11th of June 1963, attended by Tunku A. Razak representing Malaya, Subandrio representing Indonesia, and Emanuel Palaez for the Philippines. This meeting was at the initiative of President Diosdado Macapagal. This meeting produced the Manila Accord, amongst which certain important decisions were reached:

1. Agreement to the formation of Malaysia if the support of the people of northern Borneo was assured by the United Nations.
2. The Philippines claim to Sabah would not be dropped.

3. A proposal for a meeting of heads of governments by, at the latest, July 1963 in Manila.

The heads of governments accepted the Manila accord and the summit talks went ahead from 30th of July to 5th of August. After the meeting, the heads of governments issued the Manila Joint Statement:

"In line with General Assembly resolution no. 1541, principle nine, the will of the people of Sabah and Sarawak must be known first. Before the formation of Malaysia a referendum should be held, in which the following points are stressed:

1. The formation of Malaysia should be the main question.
2. Lists of the electorate should be accurately compiled.
3. Elections should be free and without any pressure or coercion.
4. Counting of votes should be done correctly."

The three heads of government agreed to appeal to the British government to find peaceful means to solve the Philippines claim to Sabah. If Sabah is included in Malaysia, this occurrence will not lessen the Philippines claim.

Steps were also taken to initiate the formation of MAPHILINDO (a cooperative organisation that included MAlaya, the PHILippines and INDOnesia).

To ascertain the wishes of the people of northern Borneo, the UN secretary general was asked to send an envoy to this area. It was also agreed that Indonesia could send observers, but Britain rejected the number of Indonesian observers and obtaining visas was made difficult. At this meeting, the President was assisted by a big delegation. Besides the foreign minister, ambassadors from the Philippines, Thailand, Australia and myself were included.

Even before the signatures on this accord had dried, Tungku Abdul Rahman, without any consultations with the other heads of governments, announced that the Federation of Malaysia would be formed on the 16th of September 1963, though it was almost impossible to know the results of the referendum at that time. The Manila Accord stated clearly that the formation must be executed after the people's wishes were known. The Tungku clearly violated the Manila Accord. Confrontation was inevitable and started officially on the 15th of September 1963. The Indonesian missions in Kuala Lumpur and Singapore were closed and all Indonesians returned home.

I was not unduly worried, because all of this was according to the scenario explained to me by Subandrio. But one day I heard a story that confused me very much. A very close friend of mine from the army told me that he had orders to witness a test of a so-called Indonesian-made nuclear bomb off the south coast of Java. It was announced in all the newspapers that the Indonesians themselves were able to create their own nuclear bomb, and if necessary this would be used in the *Konfrontasi*. Hearing this I was perplexed, because that was not part of the original plan. From my friend I heard that this bomb was actually from Communist China, but he was under oath not to disclose this information.

After a while, the presidents of Indonesia and the Philippines felt that a meeting was in order and this meeting took place in Manila between 7th and 11th of January 1964. The communiqué issued after the meeting stated that MAPHILINDO was a good forum for solving Asian problems, by Asians. Therefore it was regretted that only two countries attended this meeting. President Soekarno explained the aim of confrontation, i.e., that it was not an aggressive policy and certainly not an attempt at territorial expansion. The main aim was to oppose the neo-colonialist policy of foreign powers, who were confusing the procedures to be used in the referendum to create Malaysia. The confrontation was essentially a defensive policy.

Allow me to quote what President said about the *Konfrontasi* in *Soekarno: An Autobiography*:

"In August 1962, when the heads of state of Malaya, the Philippines and Indonesia met in Manila to strengthen existing friendship among the Malay brothers, I agreed to accept Malaysia provided a UN-sponsored unbiased determination of the people's will in northern Borneo was first undertaken. From the beginning of the survey there were daily insults. It was agreed that the Philippines and Indonesia would send observers, but the British colonial government, unconcerned about preserving the good will of her big neighbour, delayed the visas, and the sounding of public opinion began before our observers arrived."

Mission to London

In 1965 while serving my term as ambassador in Burma, I received an urgent call to go to Jakarta and report to the President. No details were mentioned, I was mystified as to the purpose, but again as a good soldier I went as ordered. Although I had been in the diplomatic service for quite a while, my military habits and attitude remained as strong as ever. Soldiers never die, they just fade away.

Before going to the palace, I went to see Subandrio, and asked what the President had in mind this time.

He said, "It has something to do with the confrontation. I cannot tell you more." Afterwards I realised why he could not explain more fully, because the secretary general of the foreign office was there.

When I arrived at the palace, the President still had one guest, a Mrs. Walandouw, a politician. I shook hands with the President and Mrs. Walandouw and waited for my turn. When we were alone, I noticed that the President had aged and lines of worry showed on his forehead; he looked very serious. It pained me to see him like this. I loved Soekarno and admired him very much. The way he charmed the women, the way he talked, the way he argued, the way he dressed. He spoke fluently Dutch, English, French and German. He was able to talk about politics, art – almost anything, and he knew a lot of jokes, mostly dirty ones. What I loved most about him was that he was so human. He was a human being who happened to be a great leader, but in spite of all this, stayed human, a man who could make mistakes. I think he realised now that he had made a mistake by beginning this confrontation.

He slowly explained: "The confrontation is beginning to put us in a very difficult position. I am now looking for ways and means to end this in an honourable way."

"But I read in your book that you would never accept Malaysia, because its existence is a personal insult."

"Yes, that is true, but many things have happened since then. There are many things you do not know. To you I am honest, and to you I say that there must be a way to end this confrontation. But it must be in an honourable way – we must not lose face. I give you full powers to promise the British anything you like, if you succeed in persuading them to stop the confrontation. The initiative must come from the British and then I will respond to their appeal. That is the plan I have in mind. Do you think you can do that?"

"Please give me time to think it over. I want to consult Mrs. Felice Leon Soh, the lady I brought from Singapore to meet you."

"Why her?"

"I think she has connections with certain parties in the British government and secondly, she sympathises with the Indonesian cause."

"OK. Do what you think is best, I leave it entirely to you."

"But Pak, how can I play a bona fide diplomatic game if I have no money?"

He started laughing. I was happy to hear him laughing and forgetting his worries even if it was only for a moment. He asked me to follow him to his bedroom. We entered an old fashioned bedroom, with a colonial bed, half of which was covered by books and magazines.

"Pak, why so many books on this bed? This space should be occupied by a beautiful woman, not books."

"Ha ha ha, now you are talking my language, and now I know why you need money."

He went to a closed cupboard, opened it and then started counting money. I could hear all this clearly, and anticipated a lot of money. After a while he gave me a wad of bank notes and without looking at it, I thanked him and took my leave. When in my car, I looked at what I'd got from him. I could not believe my eyes. There was about US$200, no more, mostly in one dollar bills. What a miser Soekarno was.

From the palace I went again to the foreign office, reported to Subandrio what had transpired in the palace and complained about the amount I had received from the President. I asked Subandrio to donate some more funds. He laughed and told me that I should be happy to get that much. But he gracefully donated US$500 dollars.

Perhaps it needs some explanation as to why the President sent me to London rather than Malaysia. The British Ambassador to Indonesia, Mr. Gilchrist, whose name became well-known in Indonesia because of the so-called Gilchrist papers, once said to the secretary general of our foreign office that if Indonesia wanted to talk about Malaysia it had better talk to Britain, because Britain was in charge. Another reason, perhaps, was the unsuccessful secret mission of General Sukendro, as related to Harold Crouch in December 1975. In April 1965 Sukendro went to Malaysia, with the tacit approval of Soekarno, to explore possibilities for a summit meeting. Although Malaysia showed some interest, they were not prepared to meet Soekarno's conditions. Sukendro's mission failed. Now Soekarno was trying again, but this time dealing directly with London, and with me as his ambassador.

After two years of confrontation the domestic situation in Indonesia had deteriorated both economically and politically. President Soekarno, the great political strategist, sometimes neglected the economy. To my mind politics and economy are identical, and equal attention should be given to both.

1964 and 1965 were years of secret peace negotiations. But the secret missions were not the monopoly of President Soekarno, because the armed forces also tried very hard to find an honourable settlement of this issue. The armed forces were most concerned about the developments in the confrontation affair. They had just successfully completed the Irian mission, and now they had to face confrontation with Malaysia. Beside this, General Yani knew of the planned PKI action. So the years 1964 and 1965 were very crucial years and the army needed to prepare itself for the coming decisive battle.

Outside the army, some civilians also tried to improve the situation. At the end of 1964 there was a meeting in Bangkok attended by Mr. Tan Po Goan, Indonesian ambassador, B.M. Diah and his wife, Oei Tjoe Tat, and Mr. Kartono Kadri from the

Central Intelligence Board. Tan Po Goan said that the Communists, under the patronage of the President, were practically ruling the country. He asked Oei Tjoe Tat not to associate himself with Subandrio, because if the people decided to hang Subandrio, he would hang too. Oei said not to worry, because he was playing his own game. The whole gathering asked Oei to try to find a solution that would ensure Soekarno didn't lose face. Tan Po Goan said that he could introduce Oei to Lee Kuan Yew and together try to find a solution.

Peace attempts were also made by the Malaysians, mainly by civilian members of government. Malaysia was represented by Tan Sri Gazali bin Syafei, secretary general of the Ministry of Foreign Affairs; Tun Razak, the foreign minister; and Mohammed Sulong. Gazhalie participated in his capacity as chairman of Malaysian national security, and not as secretary general. Indonesia was represented by Ali Moertopo and L.B. Moerdani, and some civilians, such as Yeri Sumendap, Daan Mogot, Pesik and Des Alwi. All these groups operated separately and did not know of the existence of one another.

In conclusion there were two other people trying to find a solution with the British government; firstly, General Parman, the army's Chief of Intelligence, sought contact with the British armed forces. He had previously been military attache in London. Secondly, there was myself trying to contact the British Foreign Office.

In Singapore I had a meeting with Mrs. Felice Leon Soh and she promised to help me. She advised me to go to London and wait for her there and when everything was arranged she would contact me via the embassy.

I stayed two days in Bangkok, just to gather some more information, and was contacted by the deputy prime minister of Singapore, Dr. Toh Chin Cheye, and Mr. Rahim Ishak, a younger brother of the head of state. We had a long talk in my room about the confrontation, but nothing definite was decided. It was just an exchange of ideas, but nevertheless very useful. Not long afterwards Singapore separated from Malaysia and became an independent country.

On my way to London I stopped in Paris to meet our military attache, Colonel Soempono Bayuadji. To my surprise and evidently to his surprise I also met General Parman, the military chief of intelligence. He was not quite frank with me, but he indicated vaguely what he was doing in Europe.

In London the ambassador, B.M. Diah, had officially returned to Indonesia for consultations. The charge des affairs was a stranger to me, but after I explained that I had a mission from the President he gave me his full support, and I could use the ambassador's empty office space and live in the residence.

Mrs. Felice Leon Soh did all the necessary groundwork, following which I met an official from the Foreign Office, a Mr. Silver. I do not know whether this was his real name or not. I found the meeting tough going because my bargaining position was rather weak. The Indonesian economy was in disarray and if we continued the confrontation it would become worse. I could not disclose this fact, or that the army was only half-heartedly pursuing the confrontation, or that the Communists were the major benefactors of the situation. I tried very hard to cling to the English saying, "My country, right or wrong."

After much skirting round the subject, I realised that we were getting nowhere. I was facing a Westerner, who are usually very businesslike and to the point. We Oriental people like to approach subjects indirectly and circuitously, gradually getting to the point.

After lunch I decided to start talking business and told him frankly the intention of my mission. I told him the real situation in Indonesia, mapped out the political situation, and outlined what I wanted to achieve here in London. Explaining how serious the situation was in Indonesia, I felt like I was taking off my clothes one by one and ultimately stood naked before him. Not a very pretty sight for him, I was sure. I felt that he was laughing at me, and who could blame him?

He replied that he could not understand why the initiative should come from the British. The Indonesians had created the problem and now wanted the British to publicly beg for reconciliation. He went on in a typically British way. No traces of anger but very cool and cynical. As he spoke I felt that he was lashing me with a whip, slowly and painfully. I could not stand it any more. There and then I decided to end the talks and go back to Indonesia and ask the President to appoint someone else.

I had heard that the President was going to pay an unofficial visit to France so I waited in Paris to report to him. There was no clear reaction from the President after my report. It was received in the same way as my report on Irian. Apparently the President knew about efforts made from both sides, from Malaysia and Indonesia; he already considered this a face saving device, although officially he knew nothing. Unofficial contacts were stepped up after the abortive Communist coup and eventually Indonesia and Malaysia became friends again. The confrontation ended.

Governor of Jakarta

This story ends my surprises. After my failure in the confrontation mission, I went back to Rangoon and wondered what the consequences of this might be for me personally.

But, I thought, I have done everything I can. My weakness was that I could not stand the cynical style of my opponent's talk. I wrote to Mrs. Felice Leon Soh informing her of the results of my meeting and thanking her for everything she had done. What I feared most was that the President might loose faith in my capabilities. But what could I do?

At the end of July 1965, I got a cable from Jakarta telling me to report to the President. What could it be this time?

My life was full of surprises, but again as a good soldier, I went to Jakarta. Before meeting the President I went to see Subandrio to gauge what the President had in mind. What Subandrio said topped all the surprises so far. Subandrio told me that the President wanted me to become the governor of Jakarta, the capital city of Indonesia. The governor of Jakarta at that time was Major General de Soemarno, who was concurrently the minister of domestic affairs. I could not believe my ears, it was too good to be true.

195

I was silent for quite a long time, and my silence was interpreted by Subandrio as a sign of reluctance. Subandrio tried to persuade me to accept this assignment. He said: "If you want to become a player in the political sphere you must be known nationally. That is very important. You can do all kinds of jobs outside, but if you are unknown nationally, you have no chance. This a good chance for you. Grab it. You know, of course, that the position of governor of Jakarta is a very senior one. Very important and very prestigious. You see now that the minister of domestic affairs is occupying this position. This should indicate to you how important it is."

"It is not that I am refusing this appointment, but I am still surprised. Why me?"

"Yes, why me, you ask. Why did the President select you to do the Irian job? Why did the President select you to do the London job, in connection with the confrontation? This is because he trusts you and because he likes you. Is that not enough reason?"

"Yes, Pak Bandrio, I understand, but I am still surprised, though pleasantly."

"But do not think that you have an easy task ahead of you. The old man (the President) is sometimes difficult to handle. And do not forget that you are also responsible for his safety. Do you know that he sometimes disappears, just to have food at the road side, accompanied only by his driver? Not to mention his other escapades. You have to be alert and ready, 24 hours a day."

"It seems that I am going to be his nurse rather than the governor of the capital."

Subandrio laughed heartily. "Go to Bapak, listen, and talk as little as possible. Good luck."

I had a strong feeling that Subandrio was behind all this and that he was my sponsor. One thing I knew, and that is that he liked me very much. I had no objections, after all he was the foreign minister and the first deputy prime minister, which meant the number two man in the Republic.

I went to see the President. When I arrived at the palace, the verandah was empty, except for the ADC. He met me and said that the President was in his bedroom, but that I could go in.

I replied, "Assalamu Alaikum."

The President asked me to come in. He was shaving and continued shaving while talking to me. He asked: "Did you see Subandrio before coming here?"

"Yes, Pak, I did."

"So you know why I called you?"

"Yes, Pak, I know already."

"Do you want this job?"

"I am a military man, Pak. Whatever you order, I will do. And I will do my best."

"Your job is to make Jakarta clean; I want a clean city. A city everybody will be proud of. The garbage problem is becoming more and more serious every day. Now I order you to find a solution to that problem. Jakarta must become an international city and yet must maintain its Indonesian character. International means that it must have a good infrastructure and facilities, such as roads, communications and transport. You will have to work very hard here in Indonesia. Won't you regret leaving your soft ambassador's chair and exchange it for a hard working chair?"

"No, Pak, I am sure I am not going to regret it. I would be very happy to be working again in Indonesia. I have been away from my country for about ten years now. But when do I start, Pak?"

"Soon, very soon. Go back to Rangoon and wait there for your transfer."

"Thank you, Pak. Thank you again for your trust in me and I hope I will not disappoint you."

"OK, goodbye."

We shook hands and I left.

But I was still curious about this sudden appointment and I tried to get some more background information.

I contacted my good friend, General Soepardjo, who later became coordinating minister of peoples welfare and minister of domestic affairs. He offered me the following explanation: General Yani, the army chief of staff, smelled something was going to happen, something big, which might change the course of the Republic. He suspected the Communists to be planning something, but what exactly, he was not sure. Yani thought that he'd better be prepared for whatever might happen. At that moment the governor of Jakarta was an army doctor, with the rank of major general. If trouble came, it would be better if the governor was a field officer with experience of handling military crises. General Yani's choice for the job was me.

Long after the coup was over, Frans Seda, chairman of the Catholic Party, related the following story to me. Frans Seda, a Timorese, was an outstanding and honest politician and holder of various ministerial posts. The following story supported the suspicions of the army chief:

Late in 1964, the religious political parties, like Nahdatul Ulama, Parkindo (a Christian Party) and Partai Katolik (Catholic Party) felt that the PKI was growing stronger and stronger every day and was misusing Bung Karno's position and influence. These political parties separately contacted General Yani to exchange information. These meetings were conducted in the utmost secrecy.

Later on, contacts were made between these political parties and they decided to form a combined body for regular consultations. Nahdatul Ulama selected Z.E. Zubchan and the combined Christian parties selected I.J. Kasimo and Frans Seda. Later on, Mr. Hardi, ex prime minister and member of the Nationalist Party, joined this group. They talked of the political situation and the coming clash between the Communists and the army as being only a matter of time. All parties agreed that the conflict would start in Jakarta, as the political centre. All previous rebellions starting outside Jakarta had failed, such as the Communist coup in Medan in 1948 and the Darul Islam resistance movement.

But the talks did not result in concrete steps or decisions on what to do. So, one day Mr. I.J. Kasimo and Frans Seda decided to talk seriously with General Yani, and try to find some solution to this problem. After hearing those two gentlemen, General Yani told them to contact General Nasution, because he was the number one man in the armed forces. General Yani told Frans Seda that whatever Nasution decides, the army would unequivocally back him, on condition that Bung Karno as President would not be harmed.

These two gentlemen went to meet General Nasution, but Nasution replied that there was nothing he could do, because Soekarno was his boss and the supreme commander in chief of the armed forces. The two gentlemen conveyed to Nasution that the army guaranteed no harm would come to Soekarno personally or in his position as President. Even with that firm guarantee Nasution was not prepared to act. Had General Nasution acted there and then, the Republic might have been spared a catastrophe. Mysterious are the ways of God.

But how could the President agree to my appointment? General Yani was well liked by the President so as to balance the influence of General Nasution. I did not know exactly what General Yani told Soekarno, but the fact was the President agreed to my appointment. Subandrio agreed because he was a politician, and went along with the strongest. Besides that, he had a grudge against the deputy governor for reasons I did not know. If Subandrio knew about the coming plans of the Communists, he must have felt comfortable because he saw in Soegih Arto an ally, a confidante.

So we had here a unique situation: Soegih Arto was trusted by the anti-Communist army and trusted by a Communist sympathiser like Subandrio. I had experienced a similar situation before, back in 1956, when I was commander of the Medan garrison. The Communists saw me as a progressive officer while the Muslim parties saw me as a dedicated Muslim and naturally anti-Communist. None of them understood that basically I was a military man, who did, acted, and thought what my superiors told me to.

On my way back to Rangoon I stopped in Bangkok and ordered three uniforms in the style usually worn by the governor of Jakarta. I laughed at myself, because this was a little premature. In Rangoon I waited impatiently for my orders to return to Indonesia and assume office as governor. I sent several cables to the foreign ministry and to the army headquarters, but received no answer.

And one day I read in a Jakarta newspaper that General Soemarno had been reassigned as the governor of Jakarta. There goes my prestigious job. I had been fired before even assuming office. What had happened? I had been sponsored by the deputy prime minister, by the army chief of staff, and it had been agreed by Soekarno. I had the strongest sponsorship possible. I felt helpless. But all my actions were, thank God, because HE and only HE knows what is good for me. This has always been my attitude, and whatever happens I always say, "Alhamdullilah," meaning, thank you God. If something bad happens, I say, thank you God, and if something nice happens, I say, thank you God. This attitude has saved me from all kinds of bother and frustration.

Later, when I assumed the post of army chief of intelligence, replacing General Parman, who had been brutally murdered by the Communists, I discovered the reason for my aborted governorship. After the coup, we confiscated all the archives we found in the Communist headquarters. We found a piece of paper in the handwriting of D.N. Aidit, the Communist chief. It was addressed to Nyoto, another Communist leader. In it Aidit asked Nyoto to contact the President and request him to cancel his plan to appoint General Soegih Arto as governor of Jakarta. The Communists had another candidate, the deputy governor of Central Java. How powerful the Communists were. They were practically running things and could manipulate almost anybody.

This was my third failure in connection with assignments direct from the President. Firstly Irian Jaya, secondly the confrontation deal, and lastly I failed again with the governorship of Jakarta. But when I look back, I have reasons to thank God. Suppose I was appointed and the following month the coup had happened, with me still new to the job? It would have been a difficult and confusing situation.

But God knows best what is good for me. Instead of Governor of Jakarta, I became the army chief of intelligence, and four months after that, attorney general of the Republic. Alhamdullilah.

Top: Shaking hands with President Soeharto.

Below: Meeting President Marcos during a get-together of all the chiefs of missions, during the Asian Athletic Championships in Manila in 1968.

Minister Attorney General

Say 0 God!
Lord of power (and Ruler). Thou givest power
to whom Thou pleasest and Thou strippest off power,
from whom Thou pleasest.
Thou endurest with honour, whom Thou pleasest
and Thou bringest low, whom Thou pleasest
in Thy hand is all good. Verily, over all things
Thou hast power.

Qur'an, Surah III (Ali Imran), verse 26.

Strange are the ways of God. Certainly it was in my case. One day in early April 1966, I was called by the army chief of staff, General Soeharto, and from him I heard the startling news that the President had chosen me to become minister attorney general, replacing General Sutardio.

In my whole life I never dreamt that I would occupy such a high post, in fact the highest possible for anybody not aiming to become president or vice-president. Sometimes I dreamed of becoming minister of foreign affairs, but becoming minister attorney general is something that had never entered my mind. The foreign affairs job looked so challenging. Coming into contact with foreigners, especially those who disliked Indonesia, was indeed interesting. Explaining to them the real aspirations of Indonesians attracted me very much. I am rather good in defending existing ideas, but I am no good in creating new ones.

I remember that when I was a small boy, my dream was to become a sergeant in the Netherlands East Indies Army or a police inspector patrolling the town on a motorcycle. Everything in uniform attracted me. And look what happened to me. I retired from the army with the rank of a three-star general, something so far above my target of reaching sergeant. Beyond expectations, I became an ambassador in civilian life. And now I was going to be a minister.

When I failed in my Irian mission, I was not greatly sad, because it was Allah's will. When I failed in my confrontation assignment, I accepted it with resignation, because Allah knows what is best for me. When I failed again to become governor of Jakarta, the only thing I said was Alhamdullilah, thank you, oh Allah.

I reported to the President to receive my brief. He was not so talkative these days, for reasons I knew. He was in a very difficult political position, he was fighting a losing battle, and he felt that the end was near. People's trust and admiration for him was waning, some quarters even openly expressed their suspicion that one way or the other he was involved in the Communist insurrection, or at least knew about the coup.

He had no one to turn to, because everybody was trying to save themselves and had jumped from the sinking ship. But right up until the end of his time in power, his attitude was proud and defiant. I still could not understand why he had lost his political touch. If he was only prepared to condemn the PKI, history would be different. Unlike in 1948, when within 24 hours he condemned the Communist uprisings, in 1966 he hesitated to take the step that could have saved his political career.

In fact in 1966, political support for Soekarno was still great. A cabinet meeting in January 1966 issued a statement supporting the President. Similar statements came from the army, the Marine Corps, various political parties and the active body of the militant students. A chain of loyalty roll calls were held all over Indonesia in the months of January and February, but strangely enough Bung Karno ignored all these. He not only ignored the forces which expressed their sympathy for him, but worse, continued to take steps which further antagonized public opinion.

On the 21st of February 1966, he reshuffled his cabinet, kicked out all the ministers who were known to be anti-Communist, and replaced them with Communist sympathisers. Now the people, especially the students, were really angry. On the 24th of February, the day of the swearing in ceremony of the new cabinet, the palace was surrounded. No one could get in or out. The new ministers had to be transported by helicopters. Fighting broke out and in the shooting a student, Arif Rahman Hakim, was shot dead. At the burial of Arif Rahman Hakim, a very large crowd turned out, and showed beyond any doubt the power of the students. The President still ignored this mass demonstration. But the students restrained themselves and again affirmed that they had nothing against the President.

The Marine Corps issued a statement expressing their blind loyalty: "If Bung Karno says black, then it is black for the Marine Corps, if it is white according to Bung Karno then it is white for the Marine Corps." The Air Force issued a similar statement: "The Indonesian Air Force, hand in hand with the revolutionary people, will always be loyal to the Great Leader of the Revolution and do whatever he commands."

On 10th of March, one day before the SUPERSEMAR, a meeting of political parties was held at the palace. This meeting was at the invitation of the President and was held behind closed doors and heavily guarded. The President demanded a declaration of loyalty and condemnation of the actions of the university and high school students. The political parties complied half-heartedly. But according to the minister of information, this declaration came voluntarily from the political parties, because they realised the seriousness of the political situation.

Parties attending the meeting, which lasted for more than six hours, were Nahdatul Ulama, Front Marhaen of the Nationalist Party, the Catholic Party, the Association of Freedom Fighters, the Muslim Party (PSII), the Christian Party, Indonesian Party Partindo, and Muhammadiah. Reading this we were given the impression that all parties were solidly behind the President.

Offensive action by the President continued. Assisted by Subandrio, he recommended the formation of the Barisan Soekarno. According to Subandrio, terror from the students must be met with equal terror from the government.

Two distinct camps were emerging. Firstly, there were the old guard, who clung to President Soekarno and were assisted by Subandrio. Secondly, there were the newly emerging forces consisting of the army, especially the Strategic Command, the red berets, and last but not least the students. As in the turbulent period of the 1945 revolution, action units sprang into existence. The students organized themselves into KAMI, the woman into KAWI, the university graduates into KASI, the teachers into KAGI, the high school students into KAPPI etc., etc. (KA means *Kesatuan Aksi* or action unit.)

My position was difficult, both politically and psychologically. I still honoured Soekarno as an elder and father, and as a man who had done so much for Indonesia. To my elders I practise the Javanese philosophical principle of *Mikul Duwur, Mendem Jero*, meaning that you give to your elders the highest honours possible, and bury their shortcomings as deep as possible. This was my attitude towards the President. But politically I didn't agree with the President on many issues. I realised that the students and other organizations opposing the President were right in their demands and had to be protected, because they constituted the future generation of Indonesian leaders.

In trying to find the right solution I wanted to avoid chaos at all costs. This was going to be a difficult to achieve, because as the person responsible for the restoration of law and order, I had to take resolute steps.

I started my job in an atmosphere of political controversies and uncertain leadership. De jure Soekarno was still the lawful President, but people no longer trusted him. And Soeharto was just a minister but he had in his hand the SUPERSEMAR, so de facto he was chief of the government. These two men could not always see eye to eye on political matters.

The army, navy, air force and police were divided. On top of these difficulties the economy was in a shambles. The students made three main demands, the so-called *Tritura*, the three demands of the people. These were: disband the PKI, change the cabinet and lower prices of goods. Inflation was as high as 650%. The price of basic commodities like rice rose tenfold. Production was only 10% of its potential capacity and the financial deficit was about 50% of the budget. When Soekarno was asked about this, he answered, "I am not an economist, but a revolutionary. If a desert country can solve its economic problems then so can we."

No previous job has given me so many worries, before I had even started. And I entered my task without any preparation or training. After two weeks of intensive meetings with my staff, I started to get an idea of how the office should work to gain maximum results. Firstly, we needed to improve the organization to be able to meet the challenges of those times. I needed competent officers – the right man in the right place. Choosing the right people was a very important step, because, as we say in Indonesia, it is the man behind the gun that decides failure or success.

The only thing I could do with myself was try to become a good manager of this institution and a good father to all my personnel. I was rather strong in management, and I felt I had plenty of experience. Throughout my career I have never been a staff member, except those few months as chief of intelligence of the army. I've always held commanding positions, whether in the army or diplomatic service. My experience in the army and diplomatic service must be used to my advantage. I had a lot of experience in handling people, especially in the diplomatic service and other small government bodies. I knew nothing of law and had never studied law, let alone run a law enforcing organization, but I had plenty of experts to rely on. I had four deputies to assist me in the field of prosecution, intelligence, administration and procurement. All of them were qualified lawyers.

The next step in my work program was to become a good father, loved and trusted by all my staff. The whole institution should become one big family, helping and loving each other.

As a father I would guide all members, so that they would do their job with a sense of responsibility. I have discovered that a man's performance depends very much on how his boss treats him. His own ability is, of course, an important factor, but the attitude of the boss is also crucial. I always tried to encourage the feeling that

I needed him or her to do my job well.

My three guiding principles had a Javanese philosophical base. Firstly, *Rumangsa Handuwemi.* This means a sense of belonging. My staff should feel that the institution belongs to all. We all have a share in it, and so are all responsible for its welfare and standards. Secondly, *Wajib Melu Hangrungkebi.* This means that we all have the moral responsibility to defend and uphold the honour of our organization. Thirdly, *Mulat Sarira Hangrasa Wani.* This means that you must have the courage to scrutinize your own performance and improve where necessary.

In my previous jobs I always encouraged suggestions and input from my staff, and most of the time I tried to give them the impression that the decisions taken by me were their ideas. This helped to boost their creativity. As a father I had very close relations with everybody on my staff, but I still maintained a certain distance. A commander is a lonely man. He has no favourites, and has to treat everybody equally, although sometimes it is very difficult, because as a person you have your favourites.

I encountered lots of problems and opposition in my work. Being a general helped to solve these problems, because the prosecutors knew that I was backed by the mightiest organization at that time, i.e., the armed forces. In spite of this, one group planned a "coup d'etat" against me. A group asked the help of a major general with a law background to oust me from my position and replace me. He agreed, attracted by the promise of the prosecutors to back him as minister attorney general. What a dirty thing to do to a fellow general.

This group, under the leadership of the general, went to see the President, and explained that General Soegih Arto was not suited for this important job, because he knew nothing about law. They had a better candidate and that was the general accompanying them at that moment.

The President listened quietly, then said: "The reason you want General Soegih Arto out is that he has no legal education and training?"

The spokesman replied, "Yes exactly, Bapak."

Then the President said, "OK. But then look at myself. I have not even graduated from high school, so I am not suitable to occupy this high position, because I am not well-educated. Do all of you want me to step down, for the same reasons?"

One of the rebel prosecutors told me afterwards that they felt as if they'd had ice water poured over them. The next day the President called me and told me the whole story. I thanked him for his support and confidence in me. The whole office came to know what had transpired between the rebels and the President and knowing that the President was solidly behind me, it was smooth sailing from there on.

One of the first things I did was to create a district attorney's office in all the capitals of the provinces, and in all the capitals of the regencies establish a prosecutions office. The chiefs of these prosecution offices were included in the advisory councils of the governor of each region.

I was so immersed in my problems that I forgot the pleasant aspects of being a minister: the power, authority and glamour, plus the minister's uniform – white shirt and white trousers with two gold stars on the collars. I also must not forget the deluge of so-called friends, coming from all parts of Indonesia. But I was used to this because I had the same experience when I became consul-general in Singapore. These were friends of my position, who I would lose as soon as I lost the job.

There were people who said that I was the most powerful man in Indonesia after General Soeharto, which was not true. I could understand why they said this. In the first months of my job as minister attorney general I was also chief of Military Intelligence, chairman of the Coordinating Board of the Armed Forces Intelligence, and chief of the Central Intelligence Board. What great responsibilities for a man barely 43 years old.

There were three major national problems that I had to tackle simultaneously. Those problems were smuggling, corruption and the aftermath of the Communist coup. Those three needed urgent and full attention, while there were also a number of minor problems. We worked according to a guiding principle, *Ambeg Parama Arta*, which means that we must identify priorities, or first things first.

One of the problems that caught people's attention was the existence of revolutionary funds. I had to find out where the money came from, where it went to and who was responsible for it. Part of the revolutionary funds were deposited in foreign banks abroad. Another problem was the creation of deferred payments, as well as special deferred payments.

President Soekarno was a man with grand dreams, but unfortunately there were no funds available to make his dreams come true. His projects aimed at gaining prestige or what we called *Proyek Mandataris* had to be funded, so he created what he called a revolutionary fund for this purpose.

All business people who were given a 'special deferred payment' project, had to donate to the revolutionary fund. There were no fixed regulations to say who could get a SDP project, or any fixed regulation as to how much they should contribute. It all depended on the President and the governor of the Central Bank.

The funds gathered were not enough to build all the projects born out of the imagination of the President, so a 'special budget' in rupiahs and foreign currency was created in 1965 on the instructions of the President. Money from this special budget was deposited in the State Bank and the foreign currency in the Dutch bank Indovest Amsterdam and could only be drawn by the President.

It was harvest time for business people close to the President, and they benefited from these special regulations and enriched themselves. It was my job to find out what exactly had happened and whether there was any money left.

The Buru Project, an Aftermath of the PKI Coup

After the unsuccessful Madiun coup in 1948, Aidit left Indonesia for North Vietnam, and came back in July 1950, with his best friend Mohammad Hatta Lukman. The Communists were very lucky, because after the 1948 coup the party was not banned. Aidit could openly and legally begin his activities anew, according to a well prepared plan. Firstly, he and his close friends Lukman, Nyoto, and Sudisman succeeded in gaining the PKI leadership. Then he gave the Communist Party a face lift, so they would look like a nationalist, anti-colonial, pro-religion, pro-democratic and generally responsible party, opposed to the use of violence in their pursuit of political objectives. The jackal camouflaged its looks with that of a well trained house dog.

The next step was to rewrite the history of the Madiun Coup. Aidit must make the PKI acceptable to the other parties, so the PKI wrote a distorted version of the Madiun rebellion. He wanted the people to forget that they had changed the red and white Indonesian flag for a red Communist flag, and the Indonesian national anthem for the 'Internationale.' According to the new lie, they fought because they were attacked by the treacherous Hatta government, and had to defend themselves. But they never explained why the government attacked them.

Their next step was to build a force which they could use to master the country, and destroy uncompromising potential enemies like the army and Islamic organizations. In building this force, they tried to attract rural folk, primarily labourers and farmers.

Various units were organized: Permuda Rahyat (the youth's party), Gerikan Wanita Indonesia (GERWANI – the women's party), Sarikat Buruh Perkebunan Republik Indonesia (SARBUPRI – the plantation workers' party), Sentral Organisi Buruh Seluruh Indonesia (SOBSI – the labourers' party), Lembaga Kebudayaam Rakyat (LEHRA – the artists' party), and Barisan Tai Indonesia (BTI – the farmers' party). They tried to woo the existing parties, such as the Islamic political parties, to test their support and establish their friendliness to the Communist cause; if found to be unfriendly, then they should be destroyed.

Shrewdly Aidit made good use of Soekarno's weaknesses to build up his image, so that they could use him as a shield and cover. It was not a very difficult job, because Bung Karno was already a very popular figure, and the recognised leader of the Indonesian people. His charisma and charm had gained him much support. Bung Karno had proved that he was an uncompromising nationalist and the builder of Indonesian nationhood.

Aidit manage somehow to become very close to the President. Aidit supported every political decision Bung Karno made. Bung Karno was so impressed by the support and loyalty of the Communists that he said, "The PKI is both family and friend, and if they die I will miss them."

The biggest remaining problem was how to get the cooperation of the armed forces, especially the army. The army had fought the Communists in 1948 in Madiun. One of the reasons that units of the army in the outer regions had rebelled against the central government was that they thought the government was dominated by the Communists. That the army was anti-Communist was no secret among Indonesians. It was this anti-Communist stance that became the reason for the United States ending their support for rebel movements, because the Americans did not want the army to be weakened fighting the insurgents. The Americans believed that only the army could successfully curb the activities of the Communists.

The army had their roots in the population, from the smallest villages to the largest cities. Army organizations covered the whole country, which could not be said of the other forces, except perhaps the police. But the police was never considered a fighting force, but were an organization created only for law enforcement and to fight crime.

It was a very difficult task for Aidit. He gained some support in the air force and navy, but the strongest force, the army, proved to be hard to penetrate. However, the necessary ingredients to take over the government were in the hands of the PKI. They were backed by the President and had some popular support. It was just a matter of time. Everything seemed to be ready for the big step.

Mao Tse Tung won the revolution because he had his own army. Thinking along those lines, Aidit wanted to create his own army, by arming the farmers and the labourers, which he was going to name the "Fifth Force," alongside the four services already in existence, i.e., the army, navy, air force and the police. Chou En Lai promised 100,000 "peace rifles," so that the Fifth Force could disturb the peace with their peace rifles. The TNI flatly rejected this idea, saying that there was already the Civil Defence Corps under army command and which had already been trained and could be armed at short notice. In spite of the failure to penetrate the army, the PKI felt that they were becoming stronger and stronger, and as a consequence they became more and more brutal, showing their true colours. They started to terrorize their opposition. The atmosphere became very tense. Guy J. Pauker wrote in his book, *The PKI's Road to Power*, that "... this can only mean that the party had decided to prepare openly for a possible armed clash with its opponents."

President Soekarno conceptualised NASAKOM as an organization that would bring together all parties into one big working forum. The NAS group consisted of several parties based on nationalistic ideas, the A (Agama) or religious group consisted of Islamic and Christian parties, while the KOM group consisted of the Indonesian Communist Party, the only solid homogenous part of this set up. In a nation of about 100 million people in 1965, the Communists and their affiliated organization claimed to be 20 million strong, which meant one in every five Indonesian was a Communist or a Communist sympathiser.

And then Allah stepped in. The President fell ill, and his life was in danger. This unexpected occurrence upset everything. The PKI feared that the army might step in and take control, and if they did, it would mean the end for the PKI. So they decided to act fast, even though their preparations were not yet completed. It was a race against time. It was now or never.

In the early morning on the 1st of October 1965 the PKI kidnapped the army chief of staff General Yani and several other generals, but none from the air force, navy or police. All these generals were tortured and later brutally killed. Only General Nasution escaped. The Indonesian people were caught by surprise, but not for long. The commander of the strategic command acted and soon the coup was history. After much fighting, on the 12th of March 1966 the PKI was declared dead. It was Allah's will that the Communists should disappear from Indonesian soil, something that followed years later in other Communist countries.

But the aftermath of this short coup lasted for many years. One day I was asked to see President Soeharto to discuss the problem of the Communist detainees.

"Good morning, Bapak."

"Morning," answered the President. He continued, "About two months ago, I asked you to think of some sort of a rehabilitation programme for the Communist detainees, category B. Please report your progress. But before that I want to hear how many detainees we have."

"Yes, Pak, we have at this moment around 115,000 detainees, or to be exact, 116,637 men and women, consisting of 4,926 category A people, 11,611 category B, 25,969 category C, plus another 74,131 who are still under interrogation to determine their category. This is our latest report."

The category A people were all going to be prosecuted before a special military court, because we had collected enough evidence for a trial. The category B people were those whom we suspected were involved in the coup, but of which we could prove nothing definite. Category C people were the fellow travellers, and they would gradually be released after some time.

The President instructed me to arrange a rehabilitation programme for the B category people based on three principles: firstly, that existing laws and regulations must be observed; avoid creating desires for revenge through ill treatment. Secondly, the detainees must be treated humanly. Thirdly, National stability must be maintained. The President also instructed me not to treat the whole family as guilty otherwise we would make more enemies than we already had. A clear difference in treatment must be made between the guilty person and his or her family.

For this rehabilitation program I set up a committee, chaired by one of the deputies, with members from the armed forces, the department of social affairs, the department of home affairs, the department of agriculture and the department of justice. After lengthy studies, meetings and discussions the island of Buru in eastern Indonesia was chosen as the most ideal place for this rehabilitation project. This island is about 13,000 kilometres square or twice as big as the famous tourist island of Bali, has fertile ground and a population of only about 45,000 people. It is located far from Jakarta, the political centre of Indonesia.

The idea was to bring the B category people from Java to this island, let them work the land, so that within one year they would be self-sufficient in food.

We built barracks along the river to house about 10,000 people and simple houses for the staff and security guards. We also invited agricultural and cattle experts to teach these people. And most important of all in this rehabilitation programme was the presence of religious teachers. Roughly 51% registered themselves as Muslims, 17% as Protestants, 30% as Catholics and about 2% as Hindu or Buddhist. Surprisingly, there were no unbelievers. For all these people we had built 17 mosques, 15 Catholic and 13 Protestant churches, plus 10 Buddhist shrines.

Six doctors and 16 paramedics looked after the health of these 10,000 people, which was a better average than in the rest of Indonesia, where one doctor looked after more than 7,000 people. The mortality rate was 0.27% in one year. In a relatively short time, Buru became self-sufficient and the surplus was sold to other islands so money started flowing into this community. Compared to other transmigration programmes of the government this Buru project achieved self-sufficiency in a short time. One of the reasons for the success was that the product of 10,000 working people in Buru was consumed by only 10,000 people, while in a transmigration programme the product of one man was usually consumed by his whole family: himself, his wife and an average of three children.

After a few years, the barracks were torn down and houses were erected, wives began to arrive to join their husbands, schools were erected and life in Buru became fairly normal. In December 1979, all detainees were given back their freedom. They could stay in Buru or they could go back to Java. Many people decided to stay and continue as farmers or traders.

It had taken 10 years (1969–1979) of hard labour, observation, intellectual and spiritual guidance and indoctrination before the government considered this project to be finished and closed.

My Family

Myself and my wife, Imas Djamilah, married in January 1950 in a very small village just south of Bandung. Just a few days before my marriage, Captain Westerling, a retired KNIL officer, attacked the Siliwangi divisional headquarters and killed several staff officers. But his plans to conquer Bandung failed. Because of this occurrence, security in Bandung was far from being stable. It was a wedding under very unusual circumstances. Westerling's rebellion was not yet completely quelled and there were still plenty of Dutch soldiers roaming around.

At our wedding I was dressed in shorts, riding boots, and with a steel helmet on my head. We were married in the house of a sub-district chief, guarded by a heavily armed company of the Police Mobile Brigade. You never knew what might happen.

There were no guests and no reception. Only members of my staff were present to act as witnesses. Very unusual, but nevertheless legal, and we officially became man and wife. I was seven years older than my wife. I had known her for about two years before the marriage. When I was sentenced to 12 years in prison, I told her that I would not object if she wanted to look for another boyfriend. But she said that she was going to wait for me, no matter how long. That was the wisest decision she ever made in her life, and she never regretted it.

After 14 years of intensive joint operations, nine children were produced – three girls and six boys. All first class quality material. Seven children were born in Bandung and Jakarta, while numbers eight and nine were born in Singapore and Rangoon respectively. We had also adopted another boy, a son of my younger brother, who was killed in the Communist rebellion of 1948.

Since my name means *rich*, I tried as far as possible to give names to my children according to the circumstances in which they were born. One girl was named *Dewi Fajar,* meaning Aurora, because she was born at dawn; another girl was named *Sri Milatini* (Milat is a military attache), because she was born while I was attending a course for military attaches. A boy was named *Djajeng Pristiawan Andalaaswanto,* meaning "victory in the Sumatran affair," because we had got through the troubles caused by the rebels in Sumatra. Another one of my sons is called *Djokobirmo Saptoputro,* meaning "the young man from Burma who is the seventh son." So mine is a big, fertile family.

My wife came from a family of 13 and I myself from a family of 12. At the time of writing I already have 13 grandchildren from seven children and I hope many more will come. Three of my sons are still single, the girls are sold out. I have modern progressive ideas about marriage. They themselves must decide who is going to be their lifelong partners – after all, they are the ones who are going to suffer. I have only one condition, which is non-negotiable: their partner must be a Muslim. I do not mind whether she or he is black or white.

I have said that I have a big happy family, but there is one thing I regret up to this day, and that is that none of my boys wanted to follow in my footsteps and become an army man. Seven boys with seven different jobs – a doctor, an architect, a banker, a nightclub manager, a travel bureau manager, etc., but not one army man. I said to myself, well, you cannot have it all.

Bringing up 10 children is not an easy task. But we managed it somehow. None of the children have been involved in student riots, or drugs or any other mischief. They all finished their education in a normal span of time. I could say that I have done my duty remarkably well and deserve a medal for productivity and good maintenance. From the material point of view, I am not a wealthy man. I cannot give them great wealth. What I have given them is training and education in order to acquire skills and knowledge, so that one day they can stand on their own feet. The prophet Mohammed SAW said that the best income is what you gain as a result of your own work. When I look back to what I was and what

I had in 1950 and compare then to now, I can only kneel before God and thank Him for being so kind to me and my family.

However, disaster has struck. One day I fell into coma, which according to my family lasted for about five days. When I woke up, I was in an intensive care unit. At the time I did not remember anything, and when my wife visited me, I asked her what was wrong with me. She said that my blood-sugar rose to 600 and that was the reason for my coma. I had diabetes melitus. I was very much surprised, when I heard I had diabetes, and very serious too. I had never heard of this disease before. I was in a very critical condition. The whole family gathered at the hospital, even my children from Switzerland and Hawaii travelled to be with me. They were prepared for the worse. My wife and my children and their friends kept vigil day and night, and slept in the corridors of the hospital. What a nice expression of love and loyalty to their godfather.

My right half was paralysed, I could not speak properly, and people had difficulty understanding what I said. I could not write down what I wanted, because I could not even hold a pen. But I have a very strong will to survive, and I followed all the doctor's orders to the letter. Then suddenly I had the desire to go to the holy land, to Mecca and perform the *Umroh*, or let us say the small Hajj. I performed the rites on a chair and I prayed with my whole heart and being. When I came home my health improved and then I decided to go again. After the second *Umroh* I regain my speech and I could walk. A miracle for me, and for other people who knew the seriousness of my original condition. They could not believe their eyes. Thank God. Alhamdullilah.

Now I am as healthy as before. I play golf regularly, I can drive again and I feel great. But I maintain my discipline in taking medicine and doing regular exercise.

And they will say : praise be to God
who has removed from us all sorrows:
for our Lord is indeed
oft-forgiving ready to appreciate.

Qur'an, Surah XXXV (Fathir), verse 34.

*Top: My family. From left to right: Erlangga Tribuana (An-An), our second son;
Djajeng Pristiwan Andalaswanto (Wawan), our fourth son; Hario Paramisura Legianto
(Toto), our sixth son; Sri Milatini Respatiningsih Hastawati (Tini), our third daughter;
Dewi Fadjar Titisari Suparti (Dewi), our first daughter; myself; my wife, Imas
Djamilah; Pudjihastuti Peniloka Sumihartiningsih (Pupu), our second daughter; Bunbun
Djolodrio Arijunani (Bunbun), our first son; Bambang Tridjaja Asmara Apriparwoto
(Bambang), our third son; Hari Pahlawan (Hari), our adopted son; Djokobirmo
Saptoputro Soegih Arto (Koko), our seventh son.*

Retired

In 1979 at the age of 56 I officially retired, although at the time I was still ambassador in India. Looking back, I was not too much disappointed with my career. It was neither brilliant nor spectacular, but it was above average, and that was good enough for me. For most of my fellow generals retirement was a nightmare – a complete psychological change. You knew it had to come, you knew nobody could escape this fact, and yet some of us still hoped against better judgment that they still could go on. To adjust from a position of power to a toothless individual, from a somebody to a nobody, is indeed painful, unless you are realistic and accept the inescapable.

Fortunately I was prepared mentally for this to happen. I told myself that this was unavoidable and that one day all of us had to step down and make way for the younger generation. My it-could-be-worse attitude and my saying, Alhamdullilah, thank you, God – a saying for all occasions – helped me a lot. I tried to make the best of it. I always told my children be happy – that is what you must look for, not wealth, not power, but happiness. So in my retirement I practise what I taught my children. I found it was not too difficult. During my working life I always tried to be a father, a good manager and a leader, and avoid being a boss. A boss leans on his authority while a leader counts on goodwill. I am convinced that understanding, love and affection can achieve more than just power.

In 1943 I had joined the Japanese sponsored PETA, so I had had 36 years of continuous service in the army when I retired as a lieutenant general. I had never dreamt I would do so well. I had also been 10 years in the foreign service as head of mission and another seven years as attorney general. I had no enemies, but on the other hand only a few friends. I mean real friends, friends for bad or for worse, in health and in sickness.

Some of my friends became frustrated with their life after retirement. They could not adjust themselves to the new conditions. They are born losers, while the right attitude is to be a winner. If you are a winner, you see an answer in every problem while losers see problems in every answer. They saw some of their friends becoming rich, very rich, while they remained poor. They felt that they were the people who had established the republic, who had sacrificed everything they had, and put their lives at stake. They questioned why they should remain poor when others had become rich. When they saw people riding around in beautiful cars, living in big houses, surrounded by big gardens, people who during the war of independence ran away and joined the enemy, who never suffered for lack of food and sleep, their sense of justice revolted. How is this possible, and why? We fought, we suffered, we sacrificed and we stayed poor. They ran away, they avoided war, they avoided sufferings and now they live a life of luxury. *C'est la vie.*

I joined the Veteran's Legion and was asked to head the foreign relations department, so in a sense I was the foreign minister of the veterans. This was a very interesting position. I headed delegations to several countries, to the World Veterans Federation, and once I led a delegation to the United Nations to participate in a disarmament talk.

My biggest achievement was the formation of the Veterans Confederation of Asean Countries or VECONAC, in which I occupied the position of secretary general. It took long discussions and lots of travel before this came into being but it was rewarding. In my contacts with foreign veterans organizations I came to understand that the word 'veteran' has a different meaning in Indonesia compared to other countries. In Indonesia 'veteran' signifies the freedom fighters who fought for independence, whether they came from the armed forces or from the armed militias. Outside Indonesia, veterans means retired armed forces members. So the Indonesian Veterans Legion is becoming smaller and smaller, because there are no new members coming in. For the retired members of the armed forces we have the PEPABRI, a retired armed forces association.

In around 1983, myself and seven friends came together and created the *Hasta Mitra* or eight friends, a loose organization created for the sole purpose of nostalgia. At certain intervals we and our wives came together to have dinner, talk about old times, and have fun. The eight members were:

His Highness the Sultan of Yogyakarta, Hamengku Buwono IX, ex-Minister of Defence, Vice-President of the Republic and Chairman of the National Olympic Committee. He was unanimously elected as the Godfather.

Mr. Suprayogi, retired lieutenant-general, ex-Coordinating Minister of Public Works and Deputy Chairman of the National Olympic Committee.

Mr. Radius Prawiro, ex-Governor of the Central Bank, ex-Minister of Trade and now Coordinating Minister of Finance and Economy.

Mr. Frans Seda, Chairman of the Catholic Party, ex-Minister of Finance, ex-Minister of Transportation, ex-Minister of Plantations and Ambassador to Belgium.

Mr. Soerono, retired general, ex-Deputy Commander in Chief of the Armed Forces, ex-Coordinating Minister of Politics and Security and now Chairman of the National Olympic Committee.

Mr. Ashari Danudirdjo, retired lieutenant-general, ex-Minister of Trade, ex-Minister of Light Industries, and ex-ambassador to the USA and Japan. Now President Director of Bayer Indonesia.

Mr. H. Boediardjo, retired air marshal, ex-Minister of Information, ex-ambassador to Cambodia and Spain and now a successful businessman.

Mr. Soegih Arto, retired lieutenant-general, ex-Attorney General, ex-ambassador to Singapore, Burma and India and now a small businessman.

Unfortunately, the Godfather passed away and our loose organization became looser. The driving force was no longer there, and then I accelerated my business activities. Not too big, just to keep me busy and to earn enough to run my household. Big business means big worries, although it could bring big money. I did not want to jeopardise my health just for the sake of money. I do not want to become the slave of money.

I was surprised when starting out how little I knew about business, I mean business as it was done in reality, not as it was explained in books. I learned how very important personal relations are. The saying, you scratch my back and I'll scratch yours, is still very much alive. Success depends a great deal on how much you are prepared to spend to convince officials to see things your way and not on how much you learned from books.

Big business people paid high officials in certain key positions a regular fee, so they could gain advanced information on what was going to happen, especially in government policy.

Money and power goes hand in hand. The businessman must have money to gain power and the civil servants must have power to get money flowing into their pockets. All kinds of cunning devices are created to avoid breaking the law, and everything is done legally and according to regulations. I had to follow the existing customs, otherwise my business would have failed. I observed what was going on, I knew it was wrong, but I had no power to stop it, as everything was strictly legal. Well I said to myself, when in Rome, do as the Romans do.

Actually it is not difficult to detect who is abusing his power to get rich. The government knows how much officials are paid. Based on that knowledge, questions could be asked as to why officials can have expensive cars, houses or villas. Suppose a president director of a state-owned enterprise has a salary of four million rupiahs a month. Let us assume that he spends two million on his household. This means that he can save two million every month or 24 million a year. But look, after barely one year in that position, he already has a Mercedes Benz costing 200 million rupiahs. How is that possible?

When I was attorney general, I was asked to head the Indonesian Track and Field Association. I did not know at the time why they had asked me, but I saw so many prominent people who had little or no experience in sporting matters becoming chairman. The answer to this puzzle is that those prominent people are good for fund-raising, and funds are a chronic problem faced by all sporting organizations.

I thought that this situation was not right and that sports organizations should be headed by people who know about sport, who are able to improve quality and performance. Funds should be provided by the government and the people. Suppose we asked everybody to donate 1,000 rupiahs per year, we would be able to accumulate 180 billion every year. A thousand rupiahs a year is a very small sum for most people; the rich could donate much more.

Fund-raising activities should be organised, and funds collected must be allocated to the organizations which need it. Most of the time the big business people are put in a very difficult position. All kinds of organizations regularly ask for donations, and refusing is rather embarrassing. One day there is fund-raising for the Red Cross, then another day for the cancer prevention society, then for retarded children, then for the boxing association, then for this or that sports organization, and this can go on and on. Some businessmen are happy to donate, especially when asked by a high official. Every time he is asked to donate, his business mind starts to calculate how much profit he can make out of it. Some give donations as a way of advertising, and ask reporters to take pictures when they hand over the donations. Can you blame them?

FOSKO

I joined FOSKO (Forum Studi dan Homunikasi, meaning Study and Communication Forum) because I believed in its ideals: that armed forces people, even when retired, still have the duty to help the government with concepts and ideas.

FOSKO consisted of 25 army generals, one police general, one air force marshal and one navy admiral, all retired. When the people showed their confidence and asked Soeharto to start his next term as president in 1978, we felt that this was an expression of the people's confidence in the armed forces. Hence we felt we had a duty to support General Soeharto and his programmes, because Soeharto's success is also the success of the armed forces.

We came together regularly to talk about politics, economics and all kinds of problems faced by the country. We wrote our ideas and opinions down and submitted them to the government. We did not consider ourselves a pressure group, but more along the lines of an unofficial think-tank. We thought that as retired people, we were closer to the people and we had time to consider things at leisure. We were not paid and received no services or privileges for our work. I was unanimously elected as the liaison officer between FOSKO and the government, who were represented by Admiral Soedomo, a senior officer.

Following a meeting, I would report to Admiral Soedomo what went on at our meetings. Then I conveyed the government's opinion on certain matters to the FOSKO members. It was a tiring job but nevertheless very important. Relations were good.

However, people who did not like FOSKO started to report to the government things which were not true. There was even a report that FOSKO was planning a coup. Ridiculous. How can 30 retired officers, without any followers and without any funds, think of starting a coup? A coup against whom? The government became suspicious and FOSKO was disbanded. A useful link between senior officers and the government ceased to exist, which was a pity.

Top: The Hasta Mitra after the demise of HRH the Sultan of Yogyakarata. Standing, left to right: General Soerono; General Suprayogi; Air Marshal Boediardjo; Mr. Radius Prawiro. Sitting, left to right: Mr. Frans Seda; myself; General Ashari Danudirdjo.
Below: Relaxing with HRH the Sultan of Yogyakarta and his wife.

225

❖

Farewell Press Conference

My farewell press conference was held sometime in January 1993, alas only in my dreams, attended by over 100 national and international press people. There were representatives from Reuter, AFP, Tass, PTI, IRNA, MENA, Antara, Bernama and not to be forgotten CNN, the eyes and ears of the world.

I am a big and popular politician and considered a wise statesman. I am used to the big crowds. I am loved and respected by the press, because I always tell them the truth. But to be fair, I must confess that I do not always tell the whole truth. Sometimes it is not possible to tell the whole truth, because it is still considered confidential, or the time is not yet ripe for everything to be known. In the beginning I used to give 'incentives' to the press people to write what I wanted people to read in the papers. But now, there is no need to do that any more. Everything I say or do is hot.

When I enter the hall, I am greeted with a standing ovation. I did not know that I was so popular. Cameras start rolling and light bulbs flash, temporarily blinding me. I taste again the fruit of popularity. After a while it becomes very quiet. Everybody looks at me with expectation, because I am going to speak on all kind of topics in an open and frank manner. I never hide anything from the press except when it is necessary. I never say NO COMMENT. The press love me for this.

I open the conference with these words: "This is my last conference, because after today I am going to go into complete retirement. I am 70 now and this is as good a time as any to leave the political world and enjoy the rest of my life. By leaving this position, I create a vacancy for the young people to fill. I have the greatest confidence in the younger generation. We cannot hold on to our positions forever. There is a time to come and a time to go,

226

and it is time for me to go.

"The older generation must know when it is time to leave the arena gracefully and make room for the younger generation. The younger generation continue to rise, and if there is no outlet then it can become like compressed air and one day the pressure is so big it goes booom!, exploding like a bomb. Now the age limit has risen. When I became a cabinet minister I was 43, but now most of the ministers start at an age close to 60.

"I have served my country to the best of my ability. My success or failure is not for me to decide. Before we start, allow me to thank the press for the cooperation extended to me during my tenure. Thank you, good-bye and may God bless you all."

Great applause greets my opening and my final speech. Here follows some excerpts from the rest of the interview.

"Your Excellency, we heard that ... "

"Let me interrupt. I do not want to hear 'excellency.' In Indonesia we address our seniors or people we hold in esteem as Bapak, which means father. The word Bapak is more meaningful than excellency. Bapak radiates love, affection, concern for the well-being of your family. And more importantly, you are a father as long as you live. You are an excellency only for the time you have a position, after that you are a nobody. So call me Bapak. OK?"

"We've heard you have an interesting definition of politics. Can you elaborate?"

"To me, politics is power and a politician's target should be to retain power for as long as possible. How to do that? Simple: by trying to get as many followers as you can, and secure their loyalty. So when you want to become a politician, you must master the technique of how to gain popular support and when you have achieved this, how to hold on to it.

"Take elections. The more votes you get, the more followers you have, and consequently greater power. Elections are preceded by campaigns, but campaigns are not an accurate barometer of strength. I have seen people attending and wearing the campaign shirts of one party and the next day they do exactly the same for another party. For some it is a matter of income. You get pocket money and a free shirt if you shout the right slogans. The following day you do the same for another free shirt and pocket money. At the end of the campaign you have shirts from all parties. What are you? A real nationalist, because he stands above all parties.

"Simple people live for their stomachs, as in primitive times. Food is their primary need. When they become more advanced, then they start thinking about things around them. About the mystery of rain, about thunder, about floods and so many other frightening natural phenomena they cannot make sense of. They cannot explain these things, but begin to divide things into good and evil. Their feelings began to dominate their life. They try to find answers to the mysteries occurring around them, but they cannot find a solution. They try to appease the mysterious powers through rituals and offerings. And so religion comes about. Then they want to improve their lives, so they start to use their brains. Many previously mysterious occurrences become clear and explicable. All kinds of things are invented. They taste the comforts of life, and then they want more; greed is born, and with greed, politics. They realise that with power you can get what you want.

"Politics has little to do with truth. Political truths change from day to day. Political truth for one group is not necessarily the same for another group. Until a few years back Communism was the political truth for most of Eastern Europe. But not any more. Why has this changed? Simple, because there are not enough followers any more.

"Telling lies, political lies that is, or giving promises that are difficult to fulfil is part of the game. Doing down your opponents is normal practise. If you watch the political fighting between presidential candidates in America, then you realise how much truth there is in what I say. The Indonesian newspapers once reported that President Bush, during the last presidential campaign, said that his dog knows more about foreign policy than Bill Clinton. What a clever dog. The good thing about Indonesia is that for the top jobs we do not vote for individuals but for the parties or ideologies."

"What do you think of Indonesia's political future?"

"I am convinced that the political future of Indonesia is bright. We are peace-loving, we do not want more territory than we already have, we do not want to play a world police role, but we are very concerned with the situation in neighbouring countries. With limited resources at our disposal we are always ready if the United Nations ask our help to maintain peace and stability. We are recognised as a political force, hence the successful non-aligned conference and our solid position in the ASEAN organization. We have a national leadership that has the confidence of the people, we have our armed forces doing more and more peace work, such as repairing roads and building bridges and schools."

"How long will this political stability last?"

"What a strange question. First of all, we not only have what you call political stability in Indonesia; what we have is national stability. This is a more comprehensive sort of stability. There is stability in the economy, in culture, in religion and in society. In short we have stability in all fields. Indonesians are unified. We take a comprehensive approach toward all our problems. But the leaders decide on priorities. And here President Soeharto is a master. Pak Harto knows or perhaps feels instinctively how to select and decide priorities. Or as we say in Indonesia, "Ambeg Parama Arta,' or first things first. Another thing Pak Harto is good at is selecting the right advisors and ministers. We are optimistic that we will maintain this stability."

"But sometimes racial clashes occur."

"In my political dictionary there are no races, only nationalities living in lawfully recognised countries. I only can find races in my cultural dictionary. If there are clashes, then that is normal because differences exist.

"We want unity and if we want unity, then the main problem is not to eradicate those differences, because that is impossible and unnatural, but to find ways and means of how to use these differences to create unity, expressed through our motto, Unity In Diversity.

Racial differences, in the cultural sense, add beauty to the Indonesian garden. Clashes occur, but this must be viewed as an expression of personal discontent taking some followers along and not as general unhappiness of a whole race."

"Is there any friction between the indigenous peoples and the Chinese?"

"I think there is, but nothing we cannot control. In Malaysia they have a so-called multiracial society, consisting of Malays, Chinese and Indians. If they can live peacefully together then so can we. We have the *Pancasila*, which teaches tolerance. Problems in Indonesia in this context cannot be bigger than in Malaysia. In my opinion, in Indonesia the problem is not of a racial origin but is perhaps economic, in that the Chinese are usually wealthier and so are resented for this. The Chinese community try very hard to fully integrate into Indonesian society. Most of them have changed their original names to Indonesian ones. In the beginning we had a division between the Chinese (called non-Pribumi) and the indigenous people (called Pribumi) resulting in different treatment and different privileges. Now there are no more differences and everybody is equal before the law."

"What is the status of women?"

"Women are treated as equals in Indonesia. You can see for yourself. Emancipation is not a hollow slogan, but a reality. We have women in the army, navy, air force and police, in business and in education. We have women in all the professions. But sometimes I fear that it could go too far, and when that happens then family life will suffer. We consider family to be the pillar of society. And women make up the core of family life, their educational influence on the children is tremendous, because they are patient, caring and loving.

"Our prophet Mohammed was once asked who we should love most in this world. The prophet answered, your mother. And after that who? Again the prophet answered, your mother. After that? Your mother, he answered again. And after that? He answered, your father. This shows clearly the important position of the mother in a household. The saying, that paradise is in the feet of your mother, is another illustration of this point. Men and women are created differently. This we cannot change or deny.

"What is the right balance between the demands of nature and the desire for emancipation? That is very difficult for me to say. I can only appeal to the ladies and say, that whatever you do, do not forget your nature."

"What do you think of *Pancasila* ?"

"I Honestly do not think about *Pancasila* in a critical fashion. I accept it and try to implement it. I am not a thinker, I am a doer. I am convinced that *Pancasila* is the best policy we can have at this moment as a state philosophy. It has proven it's worth as a shield against extreme influences, from abroad or domestically. Extreme Muslim groups tried to change the state philosophy, but failed. The Communists tried twice and failed twice. *Pancasila* is not something that is suddenly born. It has a long history and is ideal for Indonesian social conditions.

"Bung Karno dug it up in June 1945. He is not the inventor of *Pancasila*. Indonesia is very lucky to have *Pancasila* and that is why we will defend it at all cost. Do not change *Pancasila*, do not even try. Failure will be the only result. The government is making every effort to make *Pancasila* a living reality, accepted and implemented by the whole population, from all walks of life. The implementation must be out of conviction and not because it is forced upon them.

"The government have spent millions and millions of rupiahs to popularise *Pancasila*. We have an institution giving courses to all people on the subject, called BP7. They organise two-week courses on the subjects of *Pancasila*, the 1945 Constitution, and the broad outlines of the state's development. Thousands of people – businessmen, pressmen, politicians, religious leaders, and political leaders – have followed these courses and continue to do so. Some people say that the government gives more attention to *Pancasila* than to religion. I do not agree with this view. But even if it was true, it can be explained. In my opinion, *Pancasila* is a state ideology, so it is understandable that the government apply every effort to make it understood and accepted by the people, for their own welfare. Religion, in my opinion, is something personal. It is a personal relationship between an individual and God. Some do it this way (Islam), some do it in a different way (Christianity) and some do it that way (Buddhism or Hinduism). This is not the case with Pancasila. We expect every citizen to understand and implement it in the same way, regardless of race or religion."

"What about corruption – can it be controlled? In a similar vein, I have been invited several times to attend wedding receptions. What do you think of these extravagant receptions, where millions are spent? Have you been able to control it?"

"I have asked the same question myself and still cannot find a satisfactory answer. Corruption is not a specific Indonesian phenomena, it happens everywhere. If by control you mean we should completely eradicate it, I say NO. If by control you mean that corruption is reduced, then again I am inclined to say NO. If by control you mean that we should do everything possible to fight it, then I say YES. There is a strong political will to fight corruption, because of the harm it creates.

"In my opinion the basic reason for corruption is greed. As a proof I can say that many cases of corruption are committed by people who are wealthy and do not need more money. Corruption will be there as long as there is greed. Good laws and regulations alone cannot prevent corruption, but a combination of good laws and regulations and the right mental attitude can. During the Puasa month, people who are fasting do not smoke or eat or drink even when they are completely alone and nobody can watch them. Why? Because they know God is watching. If they thought that God was always watching them, then I think lots of crimes, included corruption, could be prevented. This is, however, easier said than done.

"Now about those wedding receptions. The government tries very hard to curb such extravagances, but so far the results are negligible. This show of wealth can create social jealousy and can become a threat to social stability. I am not talking about wedding receptions held by businessmen, because their income can cover that. But what I am concerned about is wedding receptions held by fixed income earners, for instance government officials and members of the armed forces. Everybody knows exactly how much they earn every month. If you take that into account then it is not possible for them to have such big receptions, costing hundreds of millions of rupiahs. Where does the money come from? We can guess as to the source. It must have come from donations. Is this government official not going to violate some regulations to repay the donor? Your guess is as good as mine. This is a very delicate problem, and should be tackled wisely. I can say no more, because this is a mystery to me, to you, and to most people."

"What do you think of Indonesia's economic future?"

"The bleak global economic situation will make its influence felt, but we have to maintain our optimism. Problems are increasing, we have to take care of more and more people – our population was 176 million in 1989 and was about 186 million in 1992. But job opportunities are also growing. Our labour force in 1989 was 77 million, but now we have almost 84 million. Our export earnings are about US$6 billion from oil and gas and about 12 billion from other products. But our imports are still high, amounting to about US$15 billion.

"The most important thing is that international confidence in Indonesia is still high, so getting foreign loans is still possible. The government, however, is trying to lean more on its own power. If US$1 billion in short funds loans are withdrawn by the overseas owners, then our foreign exchange reserves will still be about US$8.6 billion, a sum sufficient to finance our imports for several months. Investment is, on the other hand, declining sharply. Domestic investment fell from Rp.44 billion to only 22 billion in 1992, while foreign investments fell from US$8,778 million to about 4,706 million. So all in all the situation is not so bad.

"J.P. Coen, a 17th century Dutch governor-general, once said, 'Ende despereert niet,' or never despair."

"How do you feel about freedom of the press?"

"I am 100% behind it. But you also must recognise that in this world there is not such thing as unlimited freedom. We live in society and have to honour other people's freedom as well. Indonesia is an independent country, but this does not mean that Indonesia can do whatever it likes in the society of nations.

"Freedom is essential, because freedom creates creativity, and creativity is needed for development. Anyone or any group in this society, including the press, has the freedom to express their opinion. In a *Pancasila* democracy there is an honourable place for expressing differences of opinion. The settlement of differences of opinions must be done through talks and deliberations and not through the use of power.

"In my opinion freedom of the press consists of two things, i.e., freedom to report facts, whether good or bad for the government, and writing opinions or comments. Opinions should be based on facts as much as possible. Journalists should not write editorials or opinions based only on facts supporting their opinion while conveniently ignoring other facts which might be detrimental to their view.

"I think that a free press is beneficial to the government, because in this way the government can feel the pulse of the people, and calculate the best steps to be taken. We all know that there is no government that can satisfy the whole population, and even democracy can't guarantee satisfaction for each and every one. You are free to criticize, but this freedom to criticize does not mean the same as being rude. The language used must still be polite and keep to the point.

"I expect the press to put forward alternatives when they criticise government policy. Saying this or that is not good, but failing to offer alternatives in not mature. If you know what is wrong then you must also know what is right. If the press thinks that the people should know what is wrong, then the people should also be told what is right. This is what I consider constructive criticism."

"How do you rate the performance of your press?"

"All I can say is that it could be worse and it could be better. Press people should read more and expand their knowledge, so they can ask deeper questions and get the background on everything. They must have the interrogative capacity of a legal prosecutor. What I do not like in newspapers is when sources are not revealed. This is just bullshit (sorry!). This is cowardice and they should be responsible and reveal their sources. Another possibility is of course that there was no source, and that the press just made up the story. In Indonesia we have the Indonesian Press Association. This organization is working very hard to upgrade and educate their members and in due time we will have a professional class of reporters and press people."

"In Indonesia you can have a president for life. What is your opinion of this?"

"Bung Karno, the first president, was elected president for life by the Provisional Peoples Council (MPRS). That was against the constitution, so the mistake made during the Old Order was corrected by the New Order, and by another decree of the MPRS.

"A president can be reelected for another term of five years. Article 7 of the 1945 constitution clearly states that the president and vice-president hold office for five years and after that can be re-elected. As long as the constitution is considered valid, then we should live by it. The constitution does not limit how many terms a man can hold office as president or vice-president. Pak Soeharto was elected and reelected because of his performance and popularity. The people have complete freedom to elect anybody they please. So you cannot blame Pak Harto if he is continuously reelected. I have never heard of Pak Harto campaigning and exhorting people to elect him. Indonesia is not like America, where candidates praise themselves as the best. So the president is not elected for life, but for five years."

"How do people perceive Bung Karno nowadays?"

"I personally think that a lot of people still admire Bung Karno and hold him in high esteem; I belong to those people. Because of one fatal political mistake, we should not forget what he has done for the people and the struggle for freedom. He began his political life when the Dutch were at the peak of their power. He had the courage to proclaim our independence in very difficult and uncertain circumstances with Bung Hatta, and dug up the biggest hidden treasure for the Indonesian people, *Pancasila*. For this reason it is impossible for Indonesians to forget him.

"Some people liken Soekarno with Karna, a character in the Indian epic *Mahabharata*, a courageous man of high moral values, ready to even sacrifice his life if necessary. Bung Karno is also like this. Soeharto or Harto on the other hand means 'wealth.' So Indonesia is very lucky to have had a man like Soekarno, who built a solid Indonesian house, and Soeharto, who is now furnishing this house so that the people can live comfortably. In a nutshell, Soekarno built the nation, while Soeharto tried to give the nation wealth and comfort."

"You have been an ambassador in foreign countries for quite a long time. What is your most memorable experience?"

"First of all I would like to stress that you must be accurate. There is no need to say ambassador in a foreign country, because you can not be an ambassador in your own country. What I liked most as a diplomat was having the chance to meet people who do not like Indonesia. This gives me a chance to explain and to argue, which I like best. I am happy when I can make him or her understand the motives behind Indonesia's actions, why Indonesia is doing this or doing that. My first target is just to make my adversary understand. There is no need to agree, because he or she is bound by the policy of their own country.

"Sometimes I am engaged in heated debates, arguments and counter arguments. As ambassador you must be able to defend the policies of your country, and to do that you have to learn a lot, by reading lots of books and newspapers. So in a sense the press also contributes to the education of an ambassador. Because of this the press must always be accurate and up to date."

"You told us that you are 70, but you look so young and healthy. What kind of sports do you do?"

"Do not flatter me, I am 70 and I look 70. If you say I look healthy, then I reply yes. How do I achieve this? By avoiding stress, and accepting life as it is. To avoid stress, I always say Alhamdullilah. Part of staying healthy is maintaining the right state of mind. Feeling rich or poor is also a mental attitude. If you feel rich then you are rich, if you feel poor even when you have everything you need, then you are really poor. Being rich is an attitude of mind.

"I also play sports and control my diet. Food is essential, but when you are careless then food becomes the source of disease. My sport is walking, and I try to walk at least 30 minutes a day. Twice a week I play golf. I think golf is a very good sport because this is a game where you have to control your emotions. You have to master the technique and at the same time control yourself.

"Controlling yourself is very difficult. I am a diabetic patient so sport is very essential. Diabetic patients must observed four things: take the medicine prescribed by your doctor, regularly and according to the right dosage; exercise regularly; do not overeat and stick to the number of calories advised by the doctor; and finally, maintain your spirit of survival."

The Curtain Falls

No kind of calamity can occur, except by the leave of God.
And if anyone believes in God, God guides his heart,
for God knows all things.

Qur'an, Surah LXIV (At-Taghaabun), verse 11.

CUT! LIGHTS OUT! CAMERAS STOP!

Now I have come to the end of my story. Looking back I am quite satisfied with my achievements – satisfaction caused by the knowledge that I tried my best in whatever I was doing. The result is not up to me. There are so many things I wanted to have, so many positions I wanted to attain, but knowing my limited capabilities, I am satisfied with what I have achieved. This is what has brought me happiness.

Bung Karno said: "Put your ideals as high as the stars." That I did, but I never could reach the stars and yet I am happy. That is what counts. In life I have always looked for happiness and nothing else, although I dream of wealth and position. In my dreams I am a wealthy man, a very powerful man, with the world in the palm of my hands.

But does wealth mean you are free from worries? As a wealthy man you have your worries. As a poor man you have worries, although of a different kind. You are well-known, you have worries, you are unknown, you have problems. Power means additional worries.

But when you are happy, then you are happy, with a minimum of worries. I discovered that everything depends on your own mental attitude. If you think you are rich, then you are rich. If you think you are still poor, although you own a fleet of cars, villas and a big bank account, then you are indeed poor.

As for material wealth, I see so many people still poorer than I am and suffering more. I am better off. As for achievements and success, I try to look towards those who have done better, so their achievements can become a spur in improving my own efforts.

Dear readers, having finished reading my book you will probably have discovered that I am basically a coward. You are right to think that I am afraid of taking risks. I never do anything that does not guarantee at least a 50% chance of success. I never gamble. I must feel solid ground under my feet before I move. This does not count of course in my military life. In that I do what I am told. In a sense this again proves that I am a coward, since I have not the courage and will never have the courage to go against my superiors. I am a very disciplined soldier.

This is the reason why I could never understand how army officers could rebel against the government during the PRRI and PERMESTA periods. I understood their cause, perhaps even agreed with their arguments, but I could never approve of the way they acted. In my opinion, if, as an officer, you do not agree with your superiors, you should tell your superiors in a polite and correct way or in extreme cases hand in your resignation. Using your weapons, which were paid for by the taxpayers, and risking the lives of your soldiers to satisfy your personal ego is wrong. There is only one authority that should command the national army and that is the national government.

I joined the freedom fighters because I was fighting for my rights as a citizen and to gain independence for our country. I did nothing spectacular during my military career. But I am a dependable, disciplined officer, with no ambitious ideas or revolutionary notions. Basically I am a pragmatist and action oriented – I am a doer and have not much interest in abstract thinking or theorizing. Do this or do that – action is where my strength lies. I knew that as a *pemuda* I should be dynamic and full of action. That I was. I never left a job unfinished, unless ordered to do so by my superiors. I tried to listen respectfully to my elders, because they had experience. Young and old should go together, they need each other. There is no need for the young to criticize their elders, or any need for the older generation to be sceptical of youth – they should understand each other. The only difference between them is that they live in different times, with their own specific problems and conditions.

I believe that the past was the responsibility of the elders, the future the responsibility of the youngsters, and the present is a joint responsibility. The wisdom and experience of the older generation must go hand in hand with the dynamic idealism of youth.

I believe strongly in *Nasib* or fate. In the moral and spiritual world, we should, under all circumstances, hold firmly to the belief that nothing happens without God's knowledge and leave; because there is justice and wisdom according to His great universal plan. The duty of every true believer is to do his or her utmost to achieve good things and to prevent evil; whether you succeed or fail is up to God. This is one of the reasons why I rarely feel frustrated or depressed. I accept what God gives me wholeheartedly, even when it is in the form of some calamity, because it might be a blessing in disguise. Only God knows what is best for us.

If, after you have finished reading my book, you find there is nothing special and nothing important in it, nothing that evokes cries of adoration or admiration, you are right to feel this way. I am an average man and I am happy the way I am. So, dear readers, do not be disappointed because my story is the story of most men, the man in the street. Very few people excel and God destined that I belong to the millions of common men.

Thank you for your patience and understanding.

Appendix: Important Documents in the Life of the Republic

There are, of course, hundreds, maybe thousands of documents considered important to the Indonesian Republic, but what I am going to outline below are basic documents that affect directly the life and existence of the Republic. Everybody will agree, that the document containing the proclamation of independence is the most important.

Document no. 1

Below is the text of the proclamation, written on the 17th of August 1945. It says :

We, the people of Indonesia, hereby proclaim the independence of Indonesia. Matters concerning the transfer of power and other considerations will be executed in an orderly manner and in the shortest possible time.

On behalf of the Indonesian people
Soekarno and Hatta

Document no. 2

Another very prominent document is the 1945 Constitution, promulgated on the 18th of August, just one day after the proclamation. The preamble of the Constitution is very important, because it states that the Indonesians are going to participate in maintaining a world order based on freedom, everlasting peace and social justice. Indonesia is not isolationist, but wants to take part in shaping a better world

The second part of the preamble runs as follows: " ... the

structure of national independence shall be formulated in the Constitution of the Indonesian state, which shall contain the structural state form of a Republic of Indonesia with sovereignty vested in the people and which shall be based upon the following: belief in the one supreme God, a just and civilised humanity, the unity of Indonesia, and a democracy that is guided by the wisdom and unanimity resulting from deliberation among the representatives, creating conditions of social justice for the whole people of Indonesia."

We also state that freedom is the right of every nation and thus colonisation must be eradicated, because it is not in conformity with basic human rights and justice.

Due to political developments the 1945 Constitution, based on unitarian principles, was changed into an RIS (Republik Indonesia Serikat) constitution, or federal constitution. This federal republic did not last very long, because in 1950 the population demanded to go back to the original unitarian state structure. But a constitution cannot be created or changed overnight. So the government created a Constituent Assembly, with the task of drafting a new constitution.

It took the Republic nine long years to go back to the original 1945 Constitution. The forces in the Constituent Assembly favouring the 1945 Constitution were not strong enough to muster a two-thirds majority, as required by law. The return to the 1945 Constitution was made possible by a Presidential Decree on the 5th of July 1959. This decree ended nine years of uncertainty.

The 1945 Constitution is rather short. It contains 16 chapters, and only 37 articles. There are, however, four transitional articles. The most important features are that the president and vice-president are elected for a five-year terms, and after that can be reelected. Ministers are assistants to the president and as such are not responsible to the parliament. The highest body is the People's Council, which elect the president and vice-president and outline the five year course of the Republic. Normally the People's Council would convene once every five years.

Document no. 3

Next I will outline the state philosophy, called the *Pancasila* or the five pillars, which was mentioned in the preamble of every constitution.

This modern *Pancasila* is the brainchild of President Soekarno, who explained his ideas for the first time on the 1st of June 1945, the day we call the birth of *Pancasila*.

Those five pillars are:

1. Belief in one supreme God.
2. Belief in a just and civilised humanity.
3. Maintenance of the unity of Indonesia.
4. Democracy based on the deliberations and wisdom of the elected representatives.
5. Social justice for all Indonesians.

The *Pancasila* is, according to some scholars, not a new term, because this same word was already known in the 14th century in a book called *Nagarakertagama,* written by Prapanca, and in another book called *Sutasoma,* by Empu Tantular. The wording is different, but the idea is more or less the same. In the life of the Republic *Pancasila* is very important, because it is not only a way of life, a *Weltanschaung,* but is also considered to be the legal foundation of the country. As the foundation of our Republic, it automatically forms the primary source of law.

Pancasila is acceptable to Muslims and Christians alike. Mgr. Sugiyopranoto, a prominent Catholic, said that *Pancasila* is in accordance with the ten commandments of God. Dr. Leimena, a prominent Protestant and national politician, said: "We Christians can accept *Pancasila* as a state philosophy provided we know and are aware of its limits, and provided we fill each *sila* (principle) with Christian spirit."

Hamka, a famous and well-known Muslim scholar said: "There is no need for a religious person, or a person who believes in the one Supreme God, to discuss *Pancasila* at length, because the four other *silas* of the Pancasila are but consequences of the first *sila*, i.e., belief in the one Supreme God." In a Lebaran sermon in the Merdeka Palace grounds, he said that *Pancasila* is like the number 10,000:

243

because the number one precedes the four zeros, it becomes the most important and defining number; if there was no number one in front, there would just be four zeros, or nothing. The same principle applies to *Pancasila*; because of the first *sila*, the whole thing becomes important and meaningful.

On the Indonesian coat-of-arms, the *Pancasila* is represented by the following symbols:

A star – for belief in one supreme God.

A chain – for a just and civilised humanity.

A banyan tree – for Indonesian unity.

A Bull's head – for democracy.

Cotton and rice – for social justice.

Document no. 4

The 11th of March 1966 Presidential order.

This is the most important decree from President Soekarno, apart from the one ordering a return to the 1945 Constitution. This 11th of March decree, or popularly known as SUPERSEMAR, heralded the death of the Old Order, the ORBA (ORde BAru), and the birth of what we called the New Order, the ORLA (ORde LAma). It changed the course of the Republic; we changed from a politically emotional nation, to a pragmatic and realistic state. Due to the importance of this document a translation is offered.

President of the Republic of Indonesia
Order

I. Considering

  1. etc., etc.

  2. etc., etc.

II. In view of

  1. etc., etc.

  2. etc., etc.

III. Has resolved to order Lieutenant-General Soeharto, Minister/ Commander in Chief of the Army, on behalf of the President/ Supreme Commander/Great Leader of the Revolution:

  1. To take all necessary steps to guarantee security, calm and

stability for the running of the government and the continuous course of the Revolution, while securing the personal safety and authority of the Great Leader of the Revolution for the sake of the integrity of the Republic of Indonesia, and execute all the teachings of the Great Leader of the Revolution.

2. To coordinate and implement this order with the commanders in chief of other services as best as possible.

3. To report everything connected with this task and responsibility.

President/Supreme Commander/Great Leader of the Revolution/ Mandatory of the Provisional People's Council (MPRS).

Signed, Soekarno

Document no. 5
Presidential Decree no. 1/3/1966.

It did not take long for General Soeharto to grab this golden opportunity and on the 12th of March he signed on behalf of the President the decree that dissolved the Indonesian Communist Party and declared it an outlawed organization throughout the territory of the Republic of Indonesia.

Document no 6
This decree, no. IX/MPRS/1966, dated 21st of June 1966 from the Provisional Consultative People's Congress, raised the status of the order from President Soekarno as laid down in the SUPERSEMAR, to the status of a decree by the Provisional People's Council. By raising the status of the Presidential order of the 11th of March, it meant that President Soekarno could not cancel this order, because it had been taken over by the highest body of the state. The cancellation would need another decree of the MPRS. With this step the people safeguarded the life of the President's order of the 11th of March, popularly called SUPERSEMAR.

Document no. 7
President Soekarno announced on the 20th of February 1967, that as from this day he transfers the power of government to the

245

executor of the MPRS Decision no. IX/MPRS/1966, chief of the TNI, General Soeharto, in accordance with the spirit of the MPRS decision no. XV/MPR5/1966, without diminishing the meaning and the spirit of the 1945 Constitution. The MPRS decision no. XV states in article 2 that in the case of the President's inability to hold office, the holder of the SUPERSEMAR order will take his place.

Document no. 8

Decree no. XXXIII of the MPRS dated 12th of March 1967 contained the revocation of government power from President Soekarno. President Soekarno is further prohibited from conducting political activities till the general election, and the MPRS mandate is taken from President Soekarno, plus all powers of government as stipulated in the 1945 Constitution. This decree appoints General Soeharto as acting president based on article 8 of the 1945 Constitution, until the election of a new president by the MPRS.

Document no. 9

During President Soekarno's tenure, the MPRS has honoured the President with the title of the Great Leader of the Revolution. By decree no. XXXV/MPRS/1967 this title was revoked. At a session of the MPRS in 1963, President Soekarno was made president for life by virtue of the Decree no. III/MPRS/1963. This title was in contradiction with the 1945 Constitution. So, through decree no. XVIII/MPRS/1966 this title was revoked.

Document no. 10

The next document is MPRS Decree no. XLIV/MPRS/1968.

This decree stated that having heard the deliberations of the Fifth General Session of the MPRS and in view of the following –

1. The 1945 Constitution, especially Part III.
2. The 1945 Constitution, clause 2, article 1.
3. MPRS decree no. IX/MPRS/1966.
4. MPRS decree no. X/MPRS/1966 article 1.
5. MPRS decree no. XIII/MPRS/1966.
6. MPRS decree no. XX/MPRS/1966.

7. MPRS decree no. XXXIII/MPRS/1967.

it was resolved to appoint the bearer of MPRS decree no. IX/MPRS/1966 as president of the Republic. Now General Soeharto, whether he likes it or not, is the lawful President of the Republic of Indonesia and this ends the so called dual leadership in the country.

Document no. 11
From 14th of July till 2nd of August 1969, Indonesia held a referendum in West Irian, called the Act of Free Choice. On the 19th of November 1969 the United Nations General Assembly endorsed the result of the Act of Free Choice. At last the whole family was united again. Now we could say that everything from Sabang to Merauke was ours. Long live the Republic.